W9-CQH-430

Psalm 23

Discovery House Publishers

Books, music, and videos that feed the soul with the Word of God

Box 3566 Grand Rapids, MI 49501

The Song of a Passionate Heart

Psalm 23

Hope & Rest from the Shepherd

DAVID ROPER

Psalm 23: The Song of a Passionate Heart
© 1994 by David Roper. All rights reserved.

Discovery House Publishers is affiliated with RBC Ministries,
Grand Rapids, Michigan 49512

Discovery House books are distributed to the trade exclusively
by Barbour Publishing, Inc., Uhrichsville, Ohio 44683

Unless otherwise indicated, Scripture is taken from the
HOLY BIBLE, NEW INTERNATIONAL VERSION.
Copyright © 1973, 1978, 1984 International Bible Society.
Used by permission of Zondervan Bible Publishers.

Library of Congress Cataloging-in-Publication Data

Roper, David, 1933–
    Psalm 23 : the song of a passionate heart : hope and rest
from the shepherd /
    David Roper.
        p.   cm.
    ISBN 1-57293-012-8
    1. Bible. O.T. Psalm XXIII—Meditations. I. Title
    BS1450 23rd.R66   1994
    223'.206—dc20   94-9196
                                                        CIP

Printed in the United States of America

99 01 02 00
CHG
7 9 10 8

Contents

DEDICATION

In fond memory of my mentor and dear friend

Ray Stedman

Who never sold the truth to serve the hour,
Nor haggled with eternal God for power.

THE SLOPE THROUGH DARKNESS

The great world's altar stairs,
That slope through darkness up to God.

—**ALFRED TENNYSON**

I CAME HOME FROM WORK ONE EVENING a few years ago and realized that I had gone flat. Just a blue Monday, I thought, or a bad case of the blahs. Surely a good night's sleep would set things right. But I was wrong.

During the days that followed I descended into a very dark place. I woke up morning after morning in the grip of melancholy, struggling to pull myself out of my gloom. I felt as if I were clinging to the side of a bottomless pit, my hand-holds precarious, afraid to move for fear I would plunge into a dark abyss.

Work became painful duty, a desperate effort. People with problems were a bother; friends with sunny, cheerful dispositions were a special trial. I wanted to get away from everything and every-one—take early retirement, build a cabin in the woods, or get a permanent job in a lighthouse. I cared for nothing. I enjoyed nothing. I had nothing to live for, and I could think of nothing for which I was willing to die.

Oh, there were flashes of delight—occasions that led me to think that I might be out of the dol-drums, but then I would slip again into the old groove of my misery. Each time I moved closer to despair. I could deal with the dreariness; it was the hope that was hardest to bear.

Friends suggested that my joyless state was the result of stresses, losses, or that I was getting a little long in the tooth—but so what? What could I do? I sought good counsel. I read good books. But like Al Capp's Joe Bfstx, I couldn't get out from under my cloud. Nothing displaced the darkness. Every day was a new shade of blue.

Then one morning something triggered the memory of an old poem—the Twenty-third Psalm—and the lyrics of that work became my safety line. I awakened morning by morning and seized on its words. I stuck to them like a limpet, reciting the words, reflecting on them, proclaiming them to myself. The Twenty-third Psalm became my creed.

One spring morning, not long ago, I woke up; the clouds had dispersed and the sun was beginning to shine. I don't know what brought me out of the darkness, but one thing I do know: My melancholy wasn't wasted. It was part of the good that God had determined to do for me. In the end, I could begin to say with Job, "My ears had heard of you but now my eyes have seen you" (Job 42:5).

What follows are some of the glimpses of God that came my way—a stream of thoughts emanating from the journal I kept during my Dark Age and my subsequent memories and musings. I share them with you in the hope that they will lead you to take another look at this old poem and at that Great Shepherd of the Sheep—the only good shepherd worthy of the name.

A PSALM OF DAVID

*I found in myself, and still find, an instinct toward
a higher, or as it is named "spiritual" life, as do
most men, and another toward a primitive, rank
and savage one, and I revere them both.*

—HENRY DAVID THOREAU

MICHELANGELO'S MARBLE STATUE OF DAVID stands
today in the Galleria dell' Accademia in Florence,
Italy—eighteen feet tall.

Michelangelo was right to sculpt David with
such immensity: He was a giant of a man, combining

in himself the military genius of Alexander the Great, the political savvy of Abraham Lincoln, the musical talent of Beethoven, the literary skill of Shakespeare, the hand-eye coordination of Joe Montana.

But the real measure of David's magnitude was his obsession with God: "One thing I ask of the LORD," he wrote. "This is what I seek: that I may dwell in the house of the LORD all the days of my life, to gaze upon the beauty of the LORD and to seek him in his temple" (Psalm 27:4). He was a man who was preoccupied with the love of God.

Yet, there was that other obsession: David was often consumed by pride, ambition, and lust. Capable of any sin and culpable of many, he frequently gave in to sudden, careless passion and that more deadly device—deliberate and determined evil.

That was David—eaten by lust and by the love of God. His dual obsessions make him familiar to me. He's my kind of man! More importantly, he was God's kind of man as well: "A man after his own heart" is the way God put it (1 Samuel 13:14). Ah, the fools God chooses!

Michelangelo took almost four years to finish his statue of David. The task was difficult because he was working with a piece of flawed marble. The block had been damaged when it was removed from the quarry.

So it was with David. He was flawed in his origins, abused as a child, left all alone, and nearly ruined. The world never met his needs.

But God did. He saw that lonely, ragged, love-starved boy as no one else did and set out to shape him into the man He envisioned David to be. It was hard work because David was deeply flawed, but God never gave up until the deed was done. Out of that labor, David's Twenty-third Psalm was born.

Some say the psalm was one of David's first efforts, composed while he was still a youth. But I disagree. Though the poem enshrines the memories and metaphors of David's early years, it is the thoughts of someone nearer the end of life than the beginning. Only a mature mind can sort out the complexities of life and fix on the things that matter. Only an old soul knows that very few things are necessary—actually only one.

"Wanting"

Most of the time,
I'm half-way content.

—BOB DYLAN

IN THE MOTION PICTURE *CITY SLICKERS,* three New York men head for the Old West hoping to find that one thing that satisfies.

The main character is Mitch Robbins, a wisecracking, thirty-nine-year-old advertising salesman who had "lost his smile." Mitch had a lot going for him—a charming wife, two handsome children, a spacious apartment on Roosevelt Island, two good buddies, and a quirky sense of humor. But the joy had gone out of his life. His birthdays, which used to bring him such happiness, now filled him only with sadness, each one reminding him that he still had not found out what life was for.

Mitch's two friends, Ed and Phil, shared his malaise and dreamed up the idea of joining a cattle drive from New Mexico to Colorado. (The year before they had run with the bulls in Pamplona, Spain.) The Old West seemed just the right place to shake off their unhappiness.

When the three men got to the ranch they were greeted by the last of the Marlboro Men, a leathery old cowboy named Curly, whom Robbins characterized as "a saddle bag with eyes." Under Curly's stern tutoring, Robbins and his friends learned to ride and rope before joining the sweaty brotherhood of drovers.

In Robbins' eyes, Curly was a kind of elemental male—a gruff, earthy man who rarely spoke, wore a perpetual smile, and was fearless, invulnerable, and all-knowing. While trailing the herd, Robbins asked Curly the secret of his assurance.

Curly replied, "You've got to find that one thing."

The trouble was, Mitch had no idea what that one thing was and Curly wasn't talking. Then the old buckaroo died before anyone could uncover the secret of his poise.

The moral of the movie, if there is one, is that each of us must find the "one thing" that will turn us into satisfied, self-assured versions of ourselves. The only problem is, when the house lights go up we're still in the dark: We have no idea what that one thing is.

That elusive "one thing"

Something keeps calling to us: something familiar and yet far away, something we cannot name. It fills us with a vague sense of discontent, a "wanting" for something we cannot identify. "You don't know what it is you want," mused Mark Twain, "but it just fairly makes your heart ache, you want it so much."

The wanting draws us on, promising us that satisfaction and happiness lie just ahead, filling us with restlessness, and keeping us on the move. Yet when we arrive we cannot rest. That's why we enjoy the quest, but not the conquest; the hunt, but not the kill; and that's why finishing can be almost unbearable.

Blaise Pascal, a seventeenth-century philosopher, had this to say:

> When I have set myself now and then to consider the various distractions of men, the toils and dangers to which they expose themselves in the court or in the camp, whence arise so many quarrels and passions, such daring and often such evil exploits, etc., I have discovered that all these misfortunes of men arise from one thing only, that they are unable to stay quietly in their own chamber. . . . Hence it comes that play, the society of women, war and offices of State are sought after. . . . Hence it comes that men so love noise and movement.

I'm always in a hurry to get things done;
I rush and rush until life's no fun.
All I really gotta do is live and die,
but I'm in a hurry and I don't know why.

—ALABAMA

The world intensifies our restlessness. Advertisements entice us to buy this, spend that, and to borrow against tomorrow so we can have what we want today. Generous incentives, rebates, markdowns, sales packages, and good deals urge us on, creating desires that we never knew we had.

The more we have, the more we want. Like a child who has opened a dozen gifts, we think more about what we didn't get than about what we did.

"Is this all there is?" we ask. "Isn't there something more?" It's not that we're greedy; it's just that something has been promised that we've not yet received.

Sex is not the solution, no matter what we're told.

You may recall Mr. Natural, Robert Crum's combination guru and dirty old man whose social comments enlivened the pages of campus newspapers in the 1960s. In one segment Mr. Natural and his student sidekick watch a miniskirted woman walk by. "Is sex the answer, Mr. Natural?" asks the young man. "No, my boy," Mr. Natural replies, "Sex is the question."

Indeed it is. Despite the information glut and all the propaganda in its favor, sex remains a great mystery. Our relentless pursuit of happiness through "good sex" verifies the Rolling Stones' old maxim: "I can't get no satisfaction." What sensual enjoyment remains is little more than a momentary refuge from misery.

It's ironic: the act which, more than any other, ought to assuage loneliness only intensifies it. Where is this great sex that is everywhere advertised but nowhere delivered? Where is the romance and intimacy for which we long? Tina Turner belts out her poignant creed: "What's love got to do with it?" Eventually we too learn to get along without the complications of love.

Friendships don't satisfy. At least they don't touch the deeper currents of life and love for which we long. "Even with the loved around me, still my heart says I am lonely," sighs some forgotten poet. Where is the human tenderness we seek—the readiness to love and accept? When we ask our friends to take away our loneliness we force on them a burden too heavy for anyone to bear. They let us down or go away and we go looking for someone else to curse with our demands. We are very difficult people. All we want is boundless love.

Parents never come through—especially fathers. For some the term *father* brings only blighted memories. To them it means all they've longed for and missed out on in life. Even those of us who had good fathers often felt they weren't what we wanted or needed them to be. We grew up trying to win their approval yet never receiving the validation we sought. "There is never enough father," Robert Bly laments.

As I stood beside my father's casket a few years ago, my wife, Carolyn, speaking in her quiet wisdom, said to me, "It's too late, isn't it?"

Exactly. Too late to gain his approval. A line from one of Len Deighton's books came to mind: "Do we never shed the tyranny of our father's love?"

Education yields only fragmentary results. We do time in various institutions, taking soundings here and there, but we never get to the bottom of things. There's so much labor in learning, so much to know that we cannot know. "I tasted wisdom," said one philosopher, "but it was far from me." That's the silent conclusion of everyone who matriculates. Perhaps that's why there's so much melancholy on campuses.

> *Myself when young did eagerly frequent*
> *Doctor and saint and heard great argument*
> *About it and about, but evermore*
> *Came out by the same door wherein I went.*
>
> —OMAR KHAYYAM

15

Success is never final. The long climb from the bottom to the top is exhilarating. We play all the petty games. We endure the privation, the competition, the demands, the drudgery, the long commutes. There's always one more deal to make, one more sale to push through, one more rung to climb, one more achievement to reach before we'll feel OK. We put in the time, we pay the price, and if we're lucky one transaction puts us over the top. But what then? The top is never the pinnacle we thought it would be.

Success is counted sweetest by those who ne'er succeed.
—EMILY DICKINSON

In an interview with Barbara Walters, Ted Turner confessed that "success is an empty bag." Money talks, but mostly it lies. It deceives us into believing that good fortune will bring satisfaction and security. But having enough is never enough. Having more is the goad that drives us. We pity the disillusioned, lonely, old tycoon with his money fixation, but we don't learn the lesson: "Whoever loves money never has money enough; whoever loves wealth is never satisfied with his income" (Ecclesiastes 5:10).

"Fame is fleeting" may be among the t͏͏ words ever spoken. We may do something or say something that turns heads and causes people to stare at us for a few days, but soon we're forgotten. Emerson was right, "Every hero becomes a bore at last." (And there's nothing quite so heartrending as a has-been trying to make a comeback.)

Marriage is not what it's cracked up to be. Despite the assurance of countless fairy tales, there's no direct relationship between getting married and living happily forever after. Couples start out well but fail because the emptiness and the ache of loneliness are so deep no one can touch them. And then for some desperate souls there are affairs (to use the lighthearted term that we apply to such disastrous ordeals), and then the crude finalities: divorces, bitter custody fights, the demolition of once-happy families, and the estrangement of little ones who are left behind.

Children are a delight. They offer us great happiness but also cause us terribly hard work and at times great suffering.

And then they leave home, as they should, and for some parents the empty nest is more than they can endure. Children are not the final achievement that we seek.

For many, retirement is the chief end. They spend all their adult years trying to make enough money to retire. Then, having reached their goal, they find it empty. Thoreau called it "destination sickness." There they are: exhausted from years of playing the game, well aware that time is running out. All the years spent worrying, scheming, and maneuvering are now meaningless. We see retirees everywhere with that dead look in their eyes. Having "arrived" they find nothing left for which to live.

> *Since I have retired from life's competition*
>   *Each day is filled with complete repetition.*
> *I get up each morning and dust off my wits,*
>   *Go pick up the paper and read the obits.*
>
> *If my name isn't there, I know I'm not dead,*
>   *I get a good breakfast and go back to bed.*
>   —UNKNOWN

Then there is old age, with its failing pride and fading power—and regret. We're "hung by our history," as they say. We look back and see the past strewn with the debris of our sin. Yet there's nothing we can do about it. All history, including our own, is unrepeatable.

Let me disclose the gifts reserved for age
To set a crown upon your lifetime's effort.
First, the cold friction of expiring sense
Without enchantment, offering no promise
But bitter tastelessness of shadow fruit
As body and soul begin to fall asunder.
Second, the conscious impotence of rage
At human folly, and the laceration
Of laughter at what ceases to amuse.
And last the rending pain of reenactment
Of all that you have done, and been; the shame
of motives late revealed, and the awareness
Of things ill done and done to others' harm
Which once you took for virtue.
The fools' approval stings and honour stains.

—T. S. ELIOT

And finally, there is the Big Chill. "Time is no healer," as some have said. "The patient dies." Death stalks us relentlessly. There's no escape. "The statistics are very impressive," George Bernard Shaw grumbled, "One out of every one person dies."

It boggles the mind to think of all the money, time, and energy we spend trying to stave off death —the medical profession, the defense budget, the cosmetics industry. But despite all the schemes we devise to stay alive, or at least look alive as long as possible, we only delay the inevitable. Ashes to ashes; dust to dust. Everybody, no matter how enduring, descends to decay and there's nothing anyone can do about it.

> Like a hen before a cobra, we find ourselves incapable of doing anything at all in the presence of the very thing that seems to call for the most drastic and decisive action. The disquieting thought, that stares at us like a face with a freezing grin, is that there is, in fact, nothing we can do. Say what we will, dance how we will, we will soon enough be a heap of ruined feathers and bones, indistinguishable from the rest of the ruins that lie about. It will not appear to matter in the slightest whether we met the enemy with equanimity, shrieks, or a trumped-up gaiety, there we will be.
>
> —TOM HOWARD

In our fear of dying we try to trivialize it, shrink it, cut it down to size, but let's not kid ourselves: dying matters. Human emotions are governed by stock reactions, and the stock reaction to death is bitter: Why do we have to leave everything behind that we've worked for, made, and loved? It's appalling to think that the world will go on without us as though we had never been born.

That's why most of life is one long effort not to think about dying, but it does no good. Just about the time we've forgotten about it, some friend or acquaintance goes and we have to attend the funeral. The thought of our own death confronts us again, and we know that we too will end up under the ground. Suddenly life seems utterly senseless. "Why go on," we say "when every beat of our heart, like a muffled drum, is marching us closer to the grave?"

"Imagine," Blaise Pascal wrote, "a number of prisoners under sentence of death; if some of them were executed every day in the sight of others, the remainder would behold their fate in that of their companions and look at one another with anguish and despair, expecting their turn to come." This, he concludes, "represents the condition of mankind." Like the monks who stared at the skulls in their cells, we behold our own fate: *Summus Moribundus* (We are destined to die).

This is our condition, and this is our frustration—the frustration of our greatest "want" of all—to live forever. We want to achieve immortality, but dying is what we do. "Where will it all end, Mr. Natural?" "In the grave, my boy," the old sage replies. "In the grave."

Oh, to be sure, there are those who imagine themselves to be happy by not thinking about the futility of life nor the certainty of death and who try to suppress their disquietude by going for all the gusto. But pleasure only shelves our dissatisfaction; it doesn't remove it. When the fun's over it's over, and the old questions return: What's it all about? Why should we eat, drink, work, play, raise money and children, and fight a never-ending sequence of frustrations. What happiness can there be in a world where everyone is born to die? Where has all the hustling, striving, lusting, and spending brought us? Why do we feel so empty and guilty and sad?

> *Faces along the bar*
> *Cling to their average day.*
> *The lights must never go out,*
> *The music must always play*
> *Lest we know where we are,*
> *Lost in a haunted wood,*
> *Children afraid of the dark*
> *Who have never been happy or good.*

—W. H. AUDEN

And so it comes to this: There is no e[...]
faction. Marriage, family, achievement, mo[...]
rity, enlightenment, travel, collections, artistic creation,
flamboyance, excess—nothing completes our joy.
There is always that elusive something more. No lesson
is more comprehensively taught in this world.

Oh, there are serendipitous occasions along
the way—capricious moments when we experience
pure delight—but those moments are fleeting, and
we can neither capture the sensation nor repeat it.
The feeling is gone and we just can't get it back.

> *Enjoyed no sooner but despised straight,*
> *Past reason hunted, and no sooner had*
> *Past reason hated as a swallowed bait*
> *On purpose laid to make the taker mad;*
> *Mad in pursuit and in possession so;*
> *Had, having, and in quest to have, extreme;*
> *A bliss in proof, and proved a very woe,*
> *Before, a joy proposed; behind a dream.*
>
> *All this world knows; yet none knows well*
> *To shun the heaven that leads men to this hell.*
>
> —WILLIAM SHAKESPEARE

It is indeed strange that we go on "mad in
pursuit," making the same mistake every day, trust-

ing that life will someday reveal its long-concealed and exquisite plan, even though experience has taught us that no matter what we achieve or acquire, it does not contain the contentment we seek.

Why do we keep on seeking?

Simply put: because we *have* to. Our seeking is a stirring of absolute need, one that must be satisfied—our eternal need for God. Every desire, every aspiration, every hunger and thirst, every longing of our nature is nothing less than desire for God. As G. K. Chesterton said, even when men knock on the door of a brothel they are looking for God. We were born for His love and we cannot live without it. He is that "one thing" for which we have been looking all our lives. All that we desire is there, and infinitely more.

> *Ah, fondest, blindest, weakest;*
> *I am He whom thou seekest.*
>
> —FRANCIS THOMPSON

It may surprise you to know that your desire is nothing more than desire for God, especially those of you who may not be accustomed to church. But there are moments when you know it's true—when something awakens within you, "a longing on Saturday for something that would have repelled me on Sunday," as a friend of mine once said. Once aroused, that longing is never stilled.

We should listen to our wants. They are meant to draw us to the place where we shall never want. What stupendous simplicity: "The LORD is my shepherd; I shall not be in want."

> *When God first made man,*
> *Having a glass of blessings standing by,*
> *"Let us" (said he) "pour on him all we can;*
> *Let the world's riches, which dispersed lie,*
> *   Contract into a span."*
>
> *So strength first made a way;*
> *Then beauty flow'd, then wisdom, honour,*
> *   pleasure.*
> *When almost all was out, God made a stay,*
> *Perceiving that alone of all his treasure*
> *   Rest in the bottom lay.*
>
> *"For if I should" (said he)*
> *"Bestow this jewel also on my creature,*
> *He would adore my gifts instead of me,*
> *And rest in Nature, not the God of Nature;*
> *   So both should losers be.*

"Yet let him keep the rest,
But keep them with repining restlessness;
Let him be rich and weary, that at least,
If goodness lead him not, yet weariness
    May toss him to my breast."

—GEORGE HERBERT

The Lord is my shepherd, I shall not be in want

Come, let us bow down in worship,
*   let us kneel before the LORD our Maker;*
for he is our God
*   and we are the people of his pasture,*
*   the flock under his care.*

—PSALM 95:6–7

The problem with most of us is that we have no clear picture of the God we long to worship. Our image of Him is clouded by the memory of cold cathedrals and bitter religions, by pastors or priests who put the fear of God into us, or by all that we suffered as children from fathers who were absent, emotionally detached, brutal, or weak. All of us have inexact notions of God.

So the question is God Himself: Who is He? This is the question to which all others lead—the question that God Himself put into our hearts (and if He put it into our hearts there must be an answer in His heart waiting to be revealed).

David gives us a comforting and compelling answer: "The LORD is my *shepherd*."

"*Yahweh* is my shepherd" is the word David actually wrote, using the name that God gave Himself. An older generation of scholars referred to the name as the Ineffable Tetragrammaton—the unutterable four-letter word. God's name (written without vowels as YHWH) was rarely pronounced by the Jews for fear of arousing God's wrath. Instead they substituted some lesser word like *Adonai* (my Lord) or *Elohim* (a generic name for God).

The term *Yahweh*, sometimes shortened to *Yah* in the Old Testament, comes from a form of the Hebrew verb *to be* and suggests a self-sufficient God. But that explanation is cold comfort to me. I prefer David's description: Yahweh is my *shepherd*.

Shepherd is a modest metaphor, yet one that is freighted with meaning. Part of the comparison is the portrayal of a shepherd and his sheep; the other is David's experience and ours. David paints a picture and puts us into it. This is the genius of the psalm: It belongs to us; we can use David's words as our own.

David's opening statement, "The LORD is my shepherd," introduces the controlling image that appears throughout the poem. Each line elaborates the symbol, filling out the picture, showing us how our Shepherd-God leads us to that place where we shall no longer want.

The meaning of the metaphor

David himself was a shepherd. He spent much of his youth tending his "few sheep in the desert" (1 Samuel 17:28). The desert is one of the best places in the world to learn. There are few distractions, and there is little that can be used. In such a place we're more inclined to think about the meaning of things rather than about what those things provide.

One day as David was watching his sheep the idea came to him that God is like a shepherd. He thought of the incessant care that sheep require— their helplessness and defenselessness. He recalled their foolish straying from safe paths, their constant need for a guide. He thought of the time and the patience it took for them to trust him before they would follow. He remembered the times when he led them through danger and they huddled close at his heels. He pondered the fact that he must think for his sheep, fight for them, guard them, and find their pasture and quiet pools. He remembered their bruises and scratches that he bound up, and he marveled at how frequently he had to rescue them from harm. Yet not one of his sheep was aware of how well it was watched. Yes, he mused, God is very much like a good shepherd.

Ancient shepherds knew their sheep by name. They were acquainted with all their ways—their peculiarities, their characteristic marks, their tendencies, their idiosyncrasies.

Back then, shepherds didn't drive their sheep, they led them. At the shepherd's morning call—a distinctive guttural sound—each flock would rise and follow its master to the feeding grounds. Even if two shepherds called their flocks at the same time and the sheep were intermingled, they never followed the wrong shepherd. All day long the sheep followed their own shepherd as he searched the wilderness looking for grassy meadows and sheltered pools where his flock could feed and drink in peace.

At certain times of the year it became necessary to move the flocks deeper into the wilderness, a desolate wasteland where predators lurked. But the sheep were always well guarded. Shepherds carried a "rod" (a heavy club) on their belts and a staff in their hands. The shepherd's staff had a crook that was used to remove the sheep from perilous places or to restrain them from wandering away; the club was a weapon to ward off beasts. David said, "When a lion or a bear came and carried off a sheep from the flock, I went after it, . . . and rescued the sheep from its mouth" (1 Samuel 17:34–35).

Throughout the day each shepherd stayed close to his sheep, watching them carefully and protecting them from the slightest harm. When one sheep strayed the shepherd searched for it until it was found. Then he laid it across his shoulders and brought it back home. At the end of the day, each shepherd led his flock to the safety of the fold and slept across the gate to protect them.

A good shepherd *never* left his sheep alone. They would have been lost without him. His presence was their assurance.

It's this good shepherd that David envisioned as he composed each line of his song.

Jacob . . .

The patriarch Jacob was a shepherd and the first person in the Bible to make use of the shepherd metaphor for God. As he lay dying, he looked back over his life and summed it up with these words: "God . . . has been my shepherd all my life" (Genesis 48:15).

Jacob was born with a difficult disposition. Gripping his twin brother's heel at birth, he continued throughout his life to try to trip him up and get ahead of him. In fact, Jacob's whole life was characterized by wheeling, double-dealing, grasping, grabbing, and jerking people around to gain selfish advantage. Yet God was not ashamed to be called "the God of Jacob" and to be his shepherd every day of his life.

Jacob is reminiscent of those who come into life with a pervasive tendency to go wrong: who inhabit inherited hells—saddled from birth with insecurities, insanities, and sinful predilections; who are addicted to food, sex, alcohol, drugs, spending, gambling, or working; who have dis-

turbed and difficult personalities; who have, as
C. S. Lewis said, a "hard machine to drive."

God knows our tiresome stories. He understands the latent forces and all the sources and possibilities of evil in our natures. He sees the hurt and
the heartbreak that others cannot see and which
cannot be explained—even to our closest friends.
He's aware of the reasons for our moodiness, our
temper tantrums, our selfish indulgences. Others
may be put off by our dispositions, but God never
turns away. He sees beyond the prickliness to the
broken heart. His understanding is infinite.

How damaged we are or how far wrong we've
gone are matters of indifference to Him. Our vile-
ness does not alter His character. He is *eternal*
love—the same yesterday, today, forever. We are
not what He wants us to be, but we are not unwant-
ed. If we will have Him, He will be our shepherd.

Frederick Buechner marvels at the folly of God
to welcome "lamebrains and misfits and nit-pickers
and holier than thous and stuffed shirts and odd
ducks and egomaniacs and milquetoasts and closet
sensualists," but that's the way He is. Whatever we
are, wherever we are, His heart is open to us. As
George MacDonald says, "Love surrounds us, seeking
the smallest crack by which it may rush in."

Isn't it odd
That a being like God
Who sees the facade
Still loves the clod
He made out of sod?
Now isn't that odd?

—UNKNOWN

Isaiah . . .

Isaiah envisions a stellar Shepherd who each night calls out His star-flock by name:

Lift your eyes and look to the heavens:
  Who created all these?
He who brings out the starry host one by one,
  and calls them each by name.
Because of his great power and mighty strength,
  not one of them is missing.

—ISAIAH 40:26

It's not by chance that the stars have their assigned orbits and places in the universe. They do not rise at random, nor do they wander haphazardly through space. They rise at God's beck and call: He brings out the starry host one by one and calls them each by name. Not one is forgotten; not one is overlooked; not one is left behind.

It's a terrible thing to be unknown. We live in fear that we will never be known enough—that others will never know who we really are, what our dreams are and where our thoughts are taking us. Yet we have nothing to fear. God knows every one of His sheep by name.

He's aware of each personality and peculiarity: There are the little ones that have to be carried, the cripples that can't keep up, the nursing ewes that won't be hurried, the old sheep that can barely get along. There are the bellwethers that always want to be out front, the bullies that butt and push to get their way, the timid ones (the sheepish) that are afraid to follow, the black sheep that are always the exception. There are those who graze their way into lostness and there are others more deliberately on the lam. The Good Shepherd knows us all.

> The Sovereign LORD comes with power,
>   and his arm rules for him. . . .
> He tends his flock like a shepherd:
>   He gathers his lambs in his arms
> and carries them close to his heart;
>   he gently leads those that have young.
>
> —ISAIAH 40:10–11

God knows our pace. He knows when grief, pain, and loneliness overwhelm us; when the full realization of our limitations comes home to us; when we're shamed and broken and unable to go on. God does not drive His sheep; He gently leads them. He allows for hesitation and trepidation. He gives credit for decisions and resolutions that are strenuously tested; He understands courage that falters in the face of terrible odds; He can accommodate a faith that flames out under stress. He takes into account the hidden reasons for failure; He feels the full weight of our disasters. He knows our pain as no one else knows it. Our bleating reaches His ears; He hears even our inarticulate cries.

When we lag behind He does not scold us. Rather He gathers us up, encircles us with His strong arm, and carries us next to His heart. The essence, the central core of God's character, lies here: He has the heart of a tender shepherd. "Great is the gentleness of our Lord," says German scholar Johann Bengel.

Jeremiah . . .

The prophet Jeremiah saw a flock of ruined sheep.

My people have been lost [ruined] sheep;
  their shepherds have led them astray
  and caused them to roam on the mountains.
They wandered over mountain and hill
  and forgot their own resting place. . . .
But I will bring Israel back to his own pasture.

—JEREMIAH 50:6, 19

We readily forget God, our "resting place," and wander away. Yet He pursues us wherever we go with no complaint of the darkness, the cold wind, the heavy burden, the steep hill, or the thorny path over which He must pass to rescue one lost sheep. His love does not count time, energy, suffering, or even life itself.

> *"Lord what are those blood drops all the way*
> *That mark out the mountain's track?"*
> *"They were shed for one who had gone astray*
> *Ere the Shepherd could bring him back."*
> *"Lord, why are your hands so rent and torn?"*
> *"They are pierced tonight by many a thorn*
> *They are pierced tonight by many a thorn."*

—ELIZABETH CLEPHANE

His pursuit is not a reward for our goodness, but the result of His decision to love. He is driven by love, not by our beauty. He is drawn to us when we have done nothing right and when we have done everything wrong (especially when we have done everything wrong).

"What do you think?" said Jesus, "If a man owns a hundred sheep, and one of them wanders away, will he not leave the ninety-nine on the hills and go to look for the one that wandered off? And if he finds it, I tell you the truth, he is happier about that one sheep than about the ninety-nine that did not wander off. In the same way your Father in heaven is not willing that any of these little ones should be lost" (Matthew 18:12–14).

Lost sheep are not doomed, they're the ones He came to find. "The ambitious, the vain, the highly sexed," said C. H. Sisson, are His "natural prey."

Ezekiel . . .

Ezekiel announced the birth of the Good Shepherd long before He was born. He said that when He came He would tend God's flock with tender, loving care.

> My sheep wandered over all the mountains and on every high hill. They were scattered over the whole earth, and no one searched

or looked for them. . . . For this is what the Sovereign LORD says: I myself will search for my sheep and look after them. As a shepherd looks after his scattered flock when he is with them, so will I look after my sheep. I will rescue them from all the places where they were scattered on a day of clouds and darkness. . . . I will tend them in a good pasture. . . . There they will lie down in good grazing land, and there they will feed in a rich pasture. . . . I myself will tend my sheep and have them lie down, declares the Sovereign LORD. I will search for the lost and bring back the strays. I will bind up the injured and strengthen the weak.

—EZEKIEL 34:6, 11–12, 14–16

It was Ezekiel's task to care for scattered exiles far from home. He described them as sheep that were scattered "because there was no shepherd, . . . and no one searched or looked for them."

Israel's disbanding was their own fault, the result of years of indifference and resistance to God. They had looked to their idols, shed blood, defiled their neighbors' wives, and done other abominable things (Ezekiel 33:26). That's why they were estranged. Yet, God says, "I will search for the lost and bring back the strays." Good shepherds don't look down on lost sheep; they look *for* them.

Sheep don't have to go looking for their shepherd. It's the other way around: He's out looking for them. Even if the sheep aren't thinking about the shepherd, He pursues them to the ends of the earth:

> He follows them into their own long, dark journey; there, where they thought finally to escape him, they run straight into his arms.
>
> SIMON TUGWELL

There is, in fact, no way to escape Him *except* by running into His arms. Though we are stiff-necked and stubborn, He is equally stiff-necked and stubborn: He will never give up His pursuit. He cannot get us off of His mind.

Furthermore, Ezekiel says, when the Good Shepherd finds His sheep He looks after them: "As a shepherd looks after his scattered sheep when he is with them, so will I look after my sheep."

"Look after" suggests careful examination of each animal. Our Shepherd-God is a good shepherd;

He knows well the condition of His flock; He sees the marks of sorrow on each face. He knows every cut and bruise, every ache and pain. He recognizes the signs of hounding, misuse, and abuse—the wounds that others have given us and the residue of our own resistance.

He promises to do what other shepherds cannot or will not do: "I will bind up the injured and strengthen the weak." He has compassion on the afflicted and the handicapped, on those wounded by their own sin. He understands sorrow, misfortune, broken homes, shattered ambition. He heals the brokenhearted and binds up their wounds (Psalm 147:3). He applies the balm that makes the wounded whole. That's the comfort of God to our beleaguered hearts.

But there is more. Another Good Shepherd was on the way, one who would be one with the Father in pastoral compassion:

> I will place over them one [unique] shepherd, my servant David, and he will tend them; he will tend them and be their shepherd. I the LORD will be their God and my servant David will be a prince among them. I the LORD have spoken.

> EZEKIEL 34:23–24

Another Good Shepherd: David's long-awaited Son, our Lord Jesus, that Great Shepherd who lays down His life for the sheep (John 10:11).

That Great Shepherd of the sheep

Some six hundred years later Jesus stood near the place where David composed his Shepherd Song and said with quiet assurance,

> I [myself] am the good shepherd. The good shepherd lays down his life for the sheep. The hired hand is not the shepherd who owns the sheep. So when he sees the wolf coming, he abandons the sheep and runs away. Then the wolf attacks the flock and scatters it. The man runs away because he is a hired hand and cares nothing for the sheep.
>
> I am the good shepherd; I know my sheep and my sheep know me—just as the Father knows me and I know the Father—and I lay down my life for the sheep.
>
> —JOHN 10:11–15

This is our Lord Jesus, "that Great Shepherd of the sheep" (Hebrews 13:20).

He was one with the Father. He too saw us as "sheep without a shepherd." He "came to seek and to save what was lost" (Luke 19:10). He's the one who left the "ninety-nine on the hills" and went "to look for the one [sheep] that wandered away," forever establishing the value of one person and the Father's desire that not one of them should be lost (Matthew 18:12–14).

> He has a shepherd's *heart,* beating with pure and generous love that counted not His own life-blood too dear a price to pay down as our ransom. He has a shepherd's *eye,* that takes in the whole flock and misses not even the poor sheep wandering away on the mountains cold. He has a shepherd's *faithfulness,* which will never fail or forsake, leave us comfortless, nor flee when He sees the wolf coming. He has a shepherd's *strength,* so that He is well able to deliver us from the jaw of the lion or the paw of the bear. He has a shepherd's *tenderness*; no lamb so tiny that He will not carry it; no saint so weak that He will not gently lead; no soul so faint that He will not give it rest. . . . His gentleness makes great.

> —F. B. MEYER

But there's more: The Good Shepherd laid down His life for the sheep. The Father issued the decree: "Awake, O sword, against my shepherd, against the man who is close to me! . . . Strike the shepherd" (Zechariah 13:7). And the Shepherd was slain.

Since the beginning of time religions have decreed that a lamb should give up its life for the shepherd. The shepherd would bring his lamb to the sanctuary, lean with all his weight on the lamb's head, and confess his sin. The lamb would be slain and its blood would flow out—a life for a life.

What irony: Now the Shepherd gives up His life for His lamb. "He was pierced for *our* transgressions, he was crushed for *our* iniquities; the punishment that brought us peace was upon him, and by his wounds we are healed. We all, like sheep, have gone astray, each of us has turned to his own way; and the LORD has laid on him the iniquity of us all" (Isaiah 53:5–6).

> *We may not know; we cannot tell*
> *What pains he had to bear,*
> *But we believe it was for us*
> *He hung and suffered there.*
>
> —CECIL F. ALEXANDER

44

The story is about the death of God. "He himself bore our sins in his body on the tree, so that we might die to sins and live for righteousness; by his wounds you have been healed" (1 Peter 2:24). He died for *all* sin—the obvious sins of murder, adultery, and theft, as well as for the secret sins of selfishness and pride. He *Himself* bore our sins in His body on the cross. This was sin's final cure.

The normal way of looking at the Cross is to say that man was so bad and God was so mad that someone had to pay. But it was not anger that led Christ to be crucified; it was love. The Crucifixion is the point of the story: God loves us so much that He *Himself* took on our guilt. He internalized *all* our sin and healed it. When it was over He said, "It is finished!" There is nothing left for us to do but to enter into forgiving acceptance—and for those of us who have already entered it, to enter into more of it.

The Shepherd calls to us and listens for the slightest sounds of life. He hears the faintest cry. If He hears nothing at all, He will not give up or go away. He lets us wander away, hoping that weariness and despair will turn us around.

For all
who knew the shelter of The Fold,
its warmth and safety
and The Shepherd's care,
and bolted;
choosing instead to fare
out in the cold,
the night;
revolted
by guardianship,
by Light;
lured
by the unknown;
eager to be out
and on their own;
freed
to water where they may,
feed where they can,
live as they will:
till
they are cured,
let them be cold,
ill;
let them know terror;
feed
them with thistle,
weed,
and thorn;
who chose

the company of wolves,
let them taste
the companionship wolves give
to helpless strays;
but, oh! let them live—
wiser though torn!
And wherever
however far away
they roam,
follow
and
watch
and
keep
Your stupid, wayward, stubborn sheep,
and someday
bring them Home!

—RUTH BELL GRAHAM

Our discomfort is God's doing: He hounds us; He hems us in; He thwarts our dreams; He foils our best-laid plans; He frustrates our hopes; He waits until we know that nothing will ease our pain, nothing will make life worth living except His presence. And when we turn to Him, He is there to greet us. He has been there all along. "The LORD is near to all who call on him" (Psalm 145:18).

But you say, Why would He want me? He knows my sin, my wandering, my long habits of yielding. I'm not good enough. I'm not sorry enough for my sin. I'm unable not to sin.

Our waywardness doesn't have to be explained to God. He's never surprised by anything we do. He sees everything at a single glance—what is, what could have been, what would have been apart from our sinful choices. He sees into the dark corners and crannies of our hearts and knows everything about us there is to know. But what He sees only draws out His love. There is no deeper motivation in God than love. It is His nature to love; He can do no other. "God is love" (1 John 4:8).

Do you have some nameless grief? Some vague, sad pain? Some inexplicable ache in your heart? Come to Him who made your heart. Jesus said, "Come to me, all you who are weary and burdened, and I will give you rest. Take my yoke upon you and learn from me, for I am gentle and humble in heart, and you will find rest for your souls. For my yoke is easy and my burden is light" (Matthew 11:28–30).

To know that God is like this, and to know this God, is rest. There is no more profound lesson than this: He is the one thing that we need.

The King of Love my Shepherd is,
Whose goodness faileth never;
I nothing lack if I am His,
And He is mine forever.

—HENRY W. BAKER

The LORD is my shepherd . . .

Shepherd—the word carries with it thoughts of tenderness, security, and provision, yet it means nothing as long as I cannot say, "The Lord is *my* shepherd."

What a difference that monosyllable makes— all the difference in the world. It means that I can have all of God's attention, all of the time, just as though I'm the only one. I may be part of a flock, but I'm one of a kind.

It's one thing to say, "The Lord is a shepherd"; it's another to say, "The Lord is *my* shepherd." Martin Luther observed that faith is a matter of personal pronouns: *My* Lord and *my* God. This is the faith that saves.

Every morning the Shepherd "calls his own sheep by name and leads them out. When he has brought out all his own, he goes on ahead of them, and his sheep follow him because they know his voice" (John 10:3–4).

This morning as you awakened, His eyes swept over you, He called you by name and said, "Come, follow Me." It's a once-for-all thing; it's an everyday thing.

> *Let not conscience make you linger,*
> *Nor of fitness fondly dream,*
> *All the fitness he requireth,*
> *Is to feel your need of him.*

> —JOSEPH HART

He makes me lie down in green pastures, He leads me beside quiet waters

O happy field wherein
This fodder grew
Whose taste doth us
from beasts to
men renew.

—ROBERT SOUTHWELL

Left to ourselves we would have nothing more than restlessness, driven by the realization that there is something more to know and love. But God will not leave us to ourselves. He *makes* us lie down in green pastures. He *leads* us by quiet waters.

The verbs suggest gentle persuasion—a shepherd patiently, persistently encouraging his sheep to the place where their hungers and thirsts will be assuaged.

In David's day "green pastures" were oases, verdant places in the desert toward which shepherds led their thirsty flocks. Left to themselves sheep would wander off into the wilderness and die. Experienced shepherds knew the terrain and urged their flocks toward familiar grasslands and streams where they could forage and feed, lie down and rest.

The picture here is not of sheep grazing and drinking, but of sheep at rest, lying down—literally, "stretched out." The verb *leads* suggests a slow and leisurely pace. The scene is one of tranquility, satisfaction, and rest.

The common practice of shepherds was to graze their flocks in rough pasture early in the morning, leading them to better grasses as the morning progressed, and then coming to a cool and shaded oasis for noontime rest.

The image of placid waters emphasizes the concept of rest—the condition of having all our passions satisfied. Augustine cried out, "What will *make* me take my rest in you . . . so I can forget my restlessness and take hold of you, the one good thing in my life?"

The compulsion begins with God. "*He* makes me [*causes* me to] lie down in green pastures, *He* leads me beside still waters." "He calls his own sheep by name and leads them out. When he has brought out all his own, he goes on ahead of them, and the sheep follow him because they know his voice" (John 10:3–4).

God makes the first move; He takes the initiative—calling us, leading us to a place of rest.

It's not that we're seeking God; He is seeking us. "There is a property in God of thirst and longing . . ." says Dame Julian of Norwich, "he hath longing to have us."

God's cry to wayward Adam and Eve, "Where are you?" (Genesis 3:9) suggests the loneliness He feels when separated from those He loves. G. K. Chesterton suggests that the whole Bible is about the "loneliness of God." I like the thought that in some inexplicable way God misses me, that He can't bear to be separated from me, that I'm always on His mind, that He patiently, insistently calls me, seeks me, not for my own sake alone, but for His. He cries, "Where are you?"

Deep within us is a place for God. We were made for God and without His love we ache in loneliness and emptiness. He calls from deep space to our depths: "Deep calls to deep" (Psalm 42:7).

David put it this way, "My heart says of you, 'Seek his face!' Your face, LORD, I will seek" (Psalm 27:8). God spoke to the depths of David's heart, uttering His heart's desire: "Seek my face." And David responded with alacrity, "I will seek your face, Lord."

And so it is: God calls us—seeking us to seek Him—and our hearts resonate with longing for Him.

That understanding has radically changed the way I look at my relationship to God. It is now neither duty nor discipline—a regimen I impose on myself like a hundred sit-ups and fifty push-ups each day—but a response, an answer, to one who has been calling me all my life.

> *I sought the Lord, and afterward I knew*
> *He moved my soul to seek Him, seeking me;*
> *It was not I that found, O Savior true,*
> *No, I was found of Thee.*
>
> —GEORGE MACDONALD

Taking God in

But what are those green pastures and quiet waters to which He leads us? And where are they? What is the reality behind these metaphors?

The real thing is God Himself. *He is* our true pasture (Jeremiah 50:7) and our pool of quiet water. He is our true nourishment, our living water. If we do not take Him in we will starve.

There is a hunger in the human heart that nothing but God can satisfy. There is a thirst that no one but He can quench. "Fiercely we dig the fountain, to know the water true," but there's no satisfaction until we come to Him. "Do not work for food that spoils," Jesus said, "but for food that endures to eternal life, which the Son of Man will give you. . . . I am the bread of life. He who comes to me will *never* go hungry, and he who believes in me will *never* be thirsty" (John 6:27, 35).

Malcolm Muggeridge's confession is a striking expression of this thought:

> I may, I suppose, regard myself as being a relatively successful man. People occasionally look at me on the street. That's fame. I can fairly easily earn enough to qualify for the highest slopes of inland revenue. That's success. Furnished with money and a little fame, even the elderly, if they care to, can partake of trendy diversions. That's pleasure. It might happen once in a while that

something I said or wrote was sufficiently heeded to persuade myself that it represented a serious impact on our time. That's fulfillment. Yet I say to you, and I beg of you to believe me, multiply these tiny triumphs by a million, add them all together, and they are nothing, less than nothing, a positive impediment, measured against one draught of that living water that is offered to the spiritually hungry.

Grazing on God; drinking Him in . . .

But how do we graze on God? How do we drink Him in? Once more we're confronted with symbolism. What do the metaphors mean?

The process begins, as all relationships do, with a meeting. As David said:

> As the deer pants for streams of water,
> so my soul pants for you, O God.
> My soul thirsts . . . for the living God.
> When can I go and meet with God?
>
> —PSALM 42:1–2

God is a real person. He is not a human invention, a concept, a theory, or a projection of ourselves. He is overwhelmingly alive—real beyond our wildest dreams. He can be "met," to translate David's commonplace word.

A. W. Tozer wrote,

> God is a Person and as such can be culti-vated as any person can. God is a Person and in the depths of his mighty nature he thinks, wills, enjoys, feels, loves, desires and suffers as any other person may. God is a Person and can be known in increasing degrees of intimacy as we prepare our hearts for the wonder of it.

There's the reality, but there's also the rub: Are we willing to prepare ourselves to meet Him? He responds to the slightest approach, but we're only as close as we want to be. "If . . . you seek the LORD your God, you will find him," Moses promised, then added this proviso: "if you look for him with all your heart and with all your soul" (Deuteronomy 4:29).

We don't have to look very hard or very long for God. He's only as far away as our hearts (Romans 10:8–9), but He will not intrude. He calls us but then waits for our answer. Our progress toward Him is determined by our desire to engage Him in a personal way—to *know* Him.

We say, "Something's wrong with me; I'm not happy; there must be something more," but we do nothing about our discontent. It's this mood of resignation that keeps us from joy. Our first task is to get honest with ourselves. Do we want God or not? If we do, we must be willing to make the effort to respond to Him. "Come near to God," says James "and he will come near to you" (James 4:8). It's a matter of desire. "O God, you are my God, *earnestly* I seek you," the psalmist says (Psalm 63:1).

Solitude

"Begin small and start promptly," is an old Quaker saying. The idea is to keep things simple and to begin now. Simplicity begins with solitude— not mere time alone, but time alone with God.

> Solitude begins with a time and place for God, and him alone. If we really believe not only that God exists, but that he is actively present in our lives—healing, teaching, and guiding—we need to set aside a time and space to give him our undivided attention.
>
> —HENRI NOUWEN

But where can we find that solitude? Where can we find a quiet place in the midst of the din and demands of this world? "In a crowd it's difficult to see God," Augustine said, "This vision craves secret retirement." "Go into your room," Jesus said, "close your door and pray to your Father, who is unseen" (Matthew 6:6).

There is a meeting place—a time and place where we can meet with God and hear His thoughts and He can hear ours, a time for the two of us where He can have our full attention and we can have His.

Solitude is where we are least alone and where our deepest loneliness can be relieved. It's a healing place where God can repair the damage done by the noise and pressure of the world. "The more you visit it," Thomas á Kempis said, "the more you will want to return."

> *You have to get up arly,*
> *Ef you want to take in God . . .*
>
> —JAMES RUSSELL LOWELL

"I will awaken the dawn," says David (Psalm 57:8). There's something to be said for meeting God before our busy days begin and our schedules begin to tyrannize us, though we must not understand this in some legalistic way to mean we have to get up before the sun to merit a meeting with God. For many, morning is the most opportune time; for others, it's more of an opportunity for the devil. There are times when it not only *seems* easier to meet with God, it *is* easier. It's something you have to work out with your body. The main thing is eagerness to meet Him. The advantage of doing so early is that we hear His thoughts before other thoughts invade our minds.

The first step is to find a Bible, a quiet place, and an uninterrupted period of time. Sit quietly and remind yourself that you're in the presence of God. He is there with you, eager to meet with you. "Stay in that secret place," A. W. Tozer said, "till the surrounding noises begin to fade out of your heart, till a sense of God's presence has enveloped you. Listen for His inward voice till you learn to recognize it."

Until we take time to be quiet we'll not hear God. God cannot be heard in noise and restlessness, only in silence. He will speak to us if we will give Him a chance, if we will listen, if we will be quiet. "Be still," the psalmist sings, "and know that I am God" (Psalm 46:10).

"*Listen, listen* to me," God pleads, "and eat what is good, and your soul will delight in the richest of fare. Give ear and come to me; hear me, that your soul may live" (Isaiah 55:2–3).

Listen to Him. There's no other way to take Him in. "When your words came, I ate them" said Jeremiah (Jeremiah 15:16). Sit at His feet and let Him feed you. That's the place to be (Luke 10:38–42).

> *Better than thrill a listening crowd*
> *Sit at a wise man's feet.*
>
> —GEORGE MACDONALD

The problem with many of us is that, though we read God's Word, we're not feeding on God. We're more intent on mastering the text—finding out its precise meaning, gathering theories and theologies—so we can talk more intelligently about God. The main purpose of reading the Bible, however, is not to accumulate data about Him, but to come to Him, to encounter Him as our living God.

> *You are not here to verify,*
> *instruct yourself, or inform curiosity,*
> *Or carry report. You are here to kneel.*
>
> —T. S. ELIOT

Jesus said to the best-read Bible students of His day, "You diligently study the Scriptures because you think that by them you possess eternal life. These are the Scriptures that testify about me" (John 5:39).

The scholars read the Bible, but they didn't listen to God; they never heard His voice. We should do more than read words; we should seek "the Word exposed in the words," as Karl Barth said. We want to move beyond information to seeing God and being informed and shaped by His truth. There's a passing exhilaration—the joy of discovery—in acquiring knowledge about the Bible, but there's no life in it. The Bible is not an end in itself, but a stimulus to our interaction with God.

Start with a conscious desire to engage Him in a personal way. Select a portion of Scripture— a verse, a paragraph, a chapter—and read it over and over. Think of Him as present and speaking to you, disclosing His mind and emotions and will. God is articulate. He speaks to us through His Word. Meditate on His words until His thoughts begin to take shape in your mind.

Thoughts is exactly the right word because that's precisely what the Bible is—the *mind* of the Lord" (see 1 Corinthians 2:6–16). When we read His Word we are reading His mind—what He knows, what He feels, what He wants, what He enjoys, what He desires, what He loves, what He hates.

Take time to reflect on what He is saying. Think about each word. Give yourself time for prayerful contemplation until God's heart is revealed and your heart is exposed.

> Read quietly, slowly, word for word to enter into the subject more with the heart than with the mind. From time to time make short pauses to allow these truths time to flow through all the recesses of the soul.
>
> —JEAN-PIERRE DE CAUSSADE

Listen carefully to the words that touch your emotions, and meditate on His goodness. Feed on His faithfulness (Psalm 37:3). Think about His kindness and those glimpses of His unfailing love that motivate you to love Him more (Psalm 48:9). Savor His words. "*Taste* and see that the LORD is good" (Psalm 34:8).

> Spend one hour a day in adoration of the Lord and you'll be all right.
>
> —MOTHER TERESA

Mother Teresa might say something different to you and me. So much depends on our temperament, our family and job demands, the state of our health, our age and level of maturity. At first ten or fifteen minutes may be all we can manage. Then perhaps we will be ready for an hour every day. It's not important how much time we spend at first. The important thing is to make a beginning. God's Spirit will let us know where to go from there.

Our reading should be toward relishing God, delighting in Him, gazing at His beauty, as David said (Psalm 27:4). When we approach God in that way it inclines us to want more of Him. "I have tasted Thee," Augustine said, "and now I hunger for Thee."

There's no need to worry about texts that we don't understand. Some meanings will escape us. Everything difficult indicates something more than our hearts can yet embrace. As Jesus said to His disciples, "I have much more to say to you, more than you can now bear" (John 16:12). There's much that we will never know, but some of the hard questions will be answered when we're ready for them.

God can never be understood through the intellect. Insight arises from purity of heart—from love, humility, and a desire to obey. It's the pure in heart who see God, Jesus said (Matthew 5:8). The more of God's truth we know and want to obey the more we know.

> The words of the Lord are seeds sown in our hearts by the sower. They have to fall into our hearts to grow. Meditation and prayer must water them and obedience keep them in the light. Thus they will bear fruit for the Lord's gathering.
>
> —GEORGE MACDONALD

Nor should we worry about our doubts. How could God possibly reveal Himself in a way that would leave no room for doubt?

Madeleine L'Engle said, "Those who believe they believe in God . . . without anguish of mind, without uncertainty, without doubt, and even at times without despair, believe only in the idea of God, and not in God himself."

Uncertainty is the name of the game. The best thing is to take our questionings and doubts directly to God, as David often did. His psalms are filled with discomfort and disagreement with God's ways. He fills page after page with confusion and disbelief. It's good to do so. God can handle our hesitancy.

Sometimes we're mentally dull or emotionally flat, weary, and tired. On such occasions it's worthless to try to make ourselves think more deeply or respond more intensely. If the value of our times alone with God depend on our emotional state, we will always be troubled. We should never worry about how we feel. Even when our minds are confused or our hearts are cold we can learn from our solitude. Don't try to make your heart love God. Just give it to Him.

If we're having a hard time with God, if we don't yet trust His heart, we should read the Gospels—Matthew, Mark, Luke, and John. There we hear what Jesus said and did and what was said about Him. There we see Him making visible the invisible God. When Philip, Jesus' disciple, asked to see God, Jesus replied, "Don't you know me, Philip, even after I have been among you such a long time? Anyone who has seen me has seen the Father. How can you say, 'Show us the Father'?" (John 14:9). Philip's request

is the profound expression of deep hunger behind the whole religious quest, speaking for saints and mystics, thinkers, moralists and men of faith of every age. "He that hath seen me hath seen the Father,' is Christ's staggering response. That is what the doctrine of Christ's divine Sonship really means, and why it matters. In His words we hear God speaking; in His deeds we see God at work; in His reproach we glimpse God's judgment; in His love we feel God's heart beating. If this be not true, we know nothing of God at all. If it be true—and we know it is—then . . . Jesus is God manifest in the flesh, the unique, incomparable, only begotten Son of the Living God.

—UNKNOWN

The main use of the Gospels is to help us see the character of God made real, personal, and understandable in Jesus. What we see Jesus doing—caring, suffering, weeping, calling, seeking—is what God is doing and has been doing all along. If you can't love God try to see Him in Jesus. There, He's revealed as one who has no limits to His love; one to whom we can come with all our doubts, disappointments, and misjudgments; one "whom we can approach without fear and to whom we can submit ourselves without despair" (Blaise Pascal). In the Gospels we see that God is the only God worth having.

And then to pray . . .

As we listen to God we should answer. This is prayer—our response to the revelation and unfolding of God's heart. "My God, Thy creature answers Thee," said the French poet Mussett. Prayer, understood in that way, is an extension of our visits with God rather than something tacked on.

Our meetings with God are like a polite conversation with a friend. They're not monologues in which one person does all the talking and the other does all the listening, but dialogues in which we listen thoughtfully to one another's self-disclosure and then respond.

One of my colleagues describes the process this way: If we're reading a note from a loved one in which we're praised, loved, appreciated, counseled, corrected, and helped in various ways and that individual is present in the room while we read, it's only right that we should express thanks, reciprocate love, ask questions, and in other ways react to the message. It would be rude to do otherwise. This is prayer.

Around 1370 a book was published with the title *The Cloud of Unknowing*. It's thought that the author was a spiritual director in a monastery, but we don't know his name. Much of what he wrote is hard to understand, but when it comes to prayer he was profoundly simple.

God, he said, can be known, even through "the cloud of unknowing" by responding to Him with "just a little word . . . the shorter it is the better." His book is a textbook of succinct and simple prayer:

> *It is good to think of your kindness, O God*
> > *and to love you and praise you for that.*
> *Yet it is far better to think*
> > *upon your simple being,*
> *and to love you and praise you*
> > *for yourself.*
> *Lord, I covet you and seek you*
> > *and nothing but you.*
>
> *My God,*
> > *you are all I need, and more;*
> *whoever has you needs nothing else*
> > *in this life.*

If you don't know where to start, pray David's psalms. David's life was characterized by prayer—"I am a man of prayer," he said (Psalm 109:4). The translators supply *a man of,* but the text reads simply,

"I am prayer." Prayer was the essence of David's life and his genius, as it is ours. We have this access to God, this intimacy with Him, this opportunity to receive all that the heart of God has stored up for us. It is the means by which we receive God's gifts, the means by which everything is done. David teaches us to pray.

Prayer is worship. Our praying should be full of adoration, affection, and fondness for God—that He is who He is; that He created us in order to have someone on whom He could shower His love; that He stretched out His arms on the cross; that He intends, in the fullest sense, to make whole men and women out of us. In worship, as the old word *worth-ship* implies, we declare what we value the most. It is one of the best ways in the world to love God.

Prayer is the highest expression of our dependence on God. It is asking for what we want. We can ask for anything—even the most difficult things. "Do not be anxious about anything, but in everything, by prayer and petition, with thanksgiving, present your requests to God" (Philippians 4:6). Anything large enough to occupy our minds is large enough to hang a prayer on.

Prayer, however, by its nature is *requesting*. It is not insisting or clamoring. We can make no demands of God and no deals with Him. Furthermore, we're coming to a friend. Friends don't make demands. They ask and then wait. We wait with patience and submission until God gives us what we request—or something more.

David wrote, "I have stilled and quieted my soul; like a weaned child with its mother, like a weaned child is my soul within me" (Psalm 131:2). David was in exile, waiting for God, learning not to worry himself with God's delays and other mysterious ways. No longer restless and craving, he waited for God to answer in His own time and in His own way. He is *able* to do far more than anything we can ask or imagine, but He must do it in His time and in His way. We ask in our time and in our way; God answers in His.

Prayer is asking for understanding. It is the means by which we comprehend what God is saying to us in His Word. The process by which we gain awareness of His mind is not natural, but supernatural; spiritual things are discerned spiritually (1 Corinthians 2:6–16). There is truth that can never be grasped by the human intellect. It cannot be discovered; it must be disclosed. Certainly we can understand the facts in the Bible apart from God's help, but we can never plumb its depths, never fully appreciate "what God has prepared for those who love him" (1 Corinthians 2:9). We must pray and wait for truth to come honestly into our minds.

Prayer moves what we know from our heads to our hearts; it's our hedge against hypocrisy, the way by which we begin to ring true. Our perception of truth is always ahead of our condition. Prayer brings us more into conformity; it bridges the gap between what we know and what we are.

Prayer focuses and unites our fragmented hearts. We have a thousand necessities. It's impossible for us to purify them and simplify them and integrate them into one. David prayed: "Give me an undivided heart" (Psalm 86:11). He wanted to love God with his whole soul, but he couldn't sustain the effort. Other interests and affections pulled him and divided him, so he asked God to guard his heart and unite its affections into one.

Satisfied in the morning . . .

> He wakens me morning by morning,
> > wakens my ear to listen like one being
> > taught.

> The Sovereign LORD has opened my ears,
>   and I have not been rebellious;
>   I have not drawn back.

—ISAIAH 50:4

Centering on God has to be done each morning as though it had never been done before. In that quiet place He comforts us, He instructs us, He listens to us, He prepares our hearts and strengthens us for the day. There we learn to love Him and worship Him again; we esteem His words and defer to Him once more; we get His fresh perspective on the problems and possibilities of our day.

> Satisfy us in the morning with your unfailing love,
>   that we may sing for joy and be glad all our days.

—PSALM 90:14

Then we should take His presence with us all through the day—journeying, pausing, waiting, listening, recalling what He said to us in the morning. He is our teacher, our philosopher, our friend; our gentlest, kindest, most interesting companion.

He is with us wherever we go; He is in the commonplace, whether we know it or not. "Surely the LORD is in this place," Jacob said of a most unlikely location, "and I was not aware of it" (Genesis 28:16). We may not realize that He is close by. We may feel lonely and sad and desolate. Our day may seem bleak and dreary without a visible ray of hope, yet He is present. God has said,

> Never will I leave you
> never will I forsake you.

—HEBREWS 13:5

So we can say with confidence . . .

> The Lord is my helper;
> I will not be afraid.

—HEBREWS 13:6

The clamor of this visible and audible world is so persistent and God's quiet voice sometimes is so faint that we forget that He is near. But do not worry: He cannot forget us.

> *How oft I wake and find I*
> *have been forgetting Thee.*
> *I am never far from Thy mind;*
> *Thou it is that wakest me.*

—GEORGE MACDONALD

In God's presence there is satisfaction: His lush meadows are boundless; His still water runs deep. "There," I say to myself, "[I] will lie down in good grazing land, and there [I] will feed in a rich pasture" (Ezekiel 34:14).

HE RESTORES MY SOUL. HE GUIDES ME IN PATHS OF RIGHTEOUSNESS FOR HIS NAME'S SAKE

Virtuous and vicious every man must be,
Few in the extreme, but all in the degree.

—ALEXANDER POPE

GOD KNOWS WE NEED RESTORATION. In the face of common temptation we fall—voluntarily and repeatedly. The same old flaws and failures pursue us all through life. New vices awaken and dominate us. We stumble again and again into bad judgment.

Now and then we set out to restore our-selves. Perhaps, we say, this is the day I will deal with my jealousy, hate, and lust; I'll find a way around my self-pity, self-defensiveness, self-indulgence, and all the other permutations and hyphenations of self-love that separate us from God and from one another.

Perhaps, perhaps, but probably not. Despite these periodic fits of morality, nothing enduring gets done. Sin remains our sullen master—untamed and intractable.

We blame bad genes, dysfunctional families, or demented ancestors, but no one ever has to push us into wrongdoing; we go all by ourselves.

> *[God] calls thee to cope with enemies; and first*
> *Points out a conflict with thyself—the worst.*
>
> —WILLIAM COWPER

Theologians write about *original sin,* which might suggest that we sin in novel, creative ways. But there are no innovative ways to sin. It's all been done before. No, *original sin* simply means that we're sinful in our *origins*—"sinful from birth, sinful from the time my mother conceived me" (Psalm 51:5). We are thrown into this world like a baseball with a spin on it; in time we break and the curve is always down and away.

Total depravity is the other term theologians use to describe our state. It means that sin affects the totality of our beings. If sin were blue, we'd be some shade of blue all over. In one way or another, small or great, hidden or revealed, we're tinted and tainted by sin. Sin is biologic—inborn and immutable—a painful reality manifested in the things we do. We're sinful in the core of our beings—not misguided or mistreated. There is something in our makeup that is dreadfully wrong; it makes us desire wrong, causes us to do wrong, and when we try not to do it, it makes it impossible for us to not think about doing wrong.

But then, we don't have to be told that we're defective. Who of us can say, "I have been blameless . . . and have kept myself from sin" (Psalm 18:23)? No, we need only to be reminded, not told. We know what we're like, though we dislike exposing what we're like to others. As Shakespeare put it, our best conscience is not so much to leave sin undone as it is to keep it unknown.

God, however, won't let us keep it unknown. He permits us to do the most embarrassing things at the most inopportune times—crass, unprincipled acts that shame us to tears. "God does not leave us until he has broken our hearts and our bones" (the Shepherd of Hermes).

> But to remind us of our, and Adam's curse
> And that to be restored, our sickness must get
> worse.
>
> —T. S. ELIOT

We must get worse, it seems, before we can get better. We must experience the depths of our depravity and see the miserable stuff of which we're made.

"No man is really any good," says G. K. Chesterton's detective, Father Brown, "until he knows how bad he is; till he's realized exactly how much right he has to all this snobbery, and sneering, and talking about 'criminals' as if they were apes in a forest ten thousand miles away; till he's got rid of all the dirty self-deception of talking about low types and deficient skulls; till he's squeezed out of his soul the last drop of the oil of the Pharisees; till his only hope is somehow or other to have captured one criminal, and kept him safe and sane under his own hat."

Sin is an atrocity. We have to realize how monstrous and scandalous it is and how desperately we need God's forgiveness. We cannot appreciate the magnitude of His acceptance until we comprehend the measure of our sins. We understand and hunger for His grace only at the point of deep and depressing failure.

David knew God's ways. Never has anyone been so ruthlessly revealed. You know the story about how he fell for Uriah's pretty, young wife, Bathsheba. One brief spell of passionate indulgence and David was plunged into ruin. Judah's illustrious ruler, the sweet singer of Israel, became David, the seducer, the adulterer—then a monstrous liar, a murderer, and then a mass murderer, utterly pitiless and unmoved by his horrifying evil. There's no end to sin once we begin.

Moral collapse is seldom a blowout. It's more like a slow leak, the result of a thousand small indulgences, the consequences of which are not immediately apparent. We are seduced by sin's attraction and led on by subtle degrees. We transition into failure:

> *Vice is a monster of so frightful mien*
> *As, to be hated, needs but to be seen;*
> *Yet seen too oft, familiar with her face,*
> *We first endure, then pity, then embrace.*
>
> —ALEXANDER POPE

The attraction becomes fantasy. (Fictional sin seems exciting while fictional good seems dull. That's the fundamental deception of our fantasies.) Fantasy softens us, and our convictions erode. We're then in a frame of mind to listen to our passions and having listened we have no will to resist.

Then comes the yielding and with the yielding the rationalizations. We have to justify our behavior to ourselves and to others. Everything but our own wrongdoing becomes our reason. All our actions must be explained and made to look good.

But our hearts know. There are moments when our wills soften and we long to set things right. If we do not then listen to our hearts there is a metallic hardening and then corruption. Our wrongdoing mutates, altering its form and quality, evolving into dark narcissism and horrifying cruelty: We don't care who gets hurt as long as we get what we want.

And ultimately there is disclosure. Sooner or later we face the horrible experience of being found out. At first we vehemently deny any wrongdoing. Then we dissemble. (People in trouble always lie.) But inevitably our dishonor is shouted from the housetops. There's no place to hide from the shame. We experience the force of inexorable law: Sin, no matter what we do, will not prosper.

Eventually the consequences catch up to us and we have to face the facts, or, like David, we have to face someone who digs up the facts. Nathan, an old and trusted friend, trapped the shepherd-king with a story about a rich man who seized another man's pet lamb to serve to a "traveling stranger," Nathan's metaphor for David's transient passion (2 Samuel 12:1–4).

David, weary of warding off his conscience, flamed out his verdict on the man and his terrible deed: "As surely as the LORD lives, the man who did this deserves to die! He must pay for that lamb four times over, because he did such a thing and had no pity" (12:5). Sheep-stealing was not a capital offense in Israel. According to Israelite law a thief was only required to make fourfold restitution to the victim (Exodus 22:1). David was overreacting, expending on another the stern judgment he should have applied to himself.

"You are the man!" Nathan said, pointing his finger at David. "This is what the LORD, the God of Israel, says: 'I anointed you king over Israel, and I delivered you from the hand of Saul. I gave your master's house to you, and your master's wives into your arms. I gave you the house of Israel and Judah. And if all this had been too little I would have given you more. Why did you despise the word of the LORD by doing what is evil in his eyes?" (2 Samuel 12:7–9).

Brought face-to-face with his corruption, David buried his face in his hands. "I have sinned against the Lord," was his only reply. No excuses, no justification, no extenuating circumstances, no special pleading. And Nathan said, "The LORD has taken away your sin. You are not going to die" (12:13).

God lets us fall not to shame us, but to assure us that though we are guilty, vile, and helpless we are deeply loved by God. God's love in the face of our wickedness is what awakens us to humility and contrition.

Humility and contrition are the keys to the heart of God. Those who cry out, "God, have mercy on me, a sinner," go home justified (Luke 18:13–14). God has never yet despised a broken and contrite heart (Psalm 51:17).

At the moment of exposure and brokenness, our shame can be driven underground, or we can be touched at the heart level by God's amazing grace and know that though we are miserable sinners we are fully accepted. God loves us though we are lost in sin and confusion. God isn't looking for a few good people: "He instructs *sinners* in his ways" (Psalm 25:8).

David uttered his confession and was interrupted with an outpouring of his Father's forgiveness and love. There was not a moment's interval between his acknowledgment of sin and Nathan's assurance that all was well. Though David bore the consequences of his sin, God canceled the guilt that was against him. He could lift up his head. He could forgive himself and forget himself because of the healing experience of God's love.

When Nathan had gone, David poured out his heart to God,

> Blessed is the man
> > whose transgressions are forgiven,
> > whose sins are covered.
> Blessed is the man
> > whose sin the LORD does not count against
> > > him
> > and in whose spirit is no deceit. . . .
> I acknowledged my sin to you,
> > and did not cover up my iniquity
> I said, "I will confess my transgression to the
> > > LORD"—
> > and you forgave the guilt of my sin.

—PSALM 32:1–2, 5

It was the story of the lamb—a little, innocent lamb—that broke David's heart, showed him how great a sinner he was, and brought him to repentance (2 Samuel 12:1–13). And "it is nothing more, and nothing less, than the story of the death of a Lamb, God's lamb, the Lamb of God, slain from the foundation of the world, that brings us to repentance, shows us how great our sin is and how much greater is God's forgiveness" (Clarence E. Macartney).

God stays with us despite our ruin; He discerns the possibilities even in our defilement. He uses our sin to awaken our need for His grace. Sin softens us and makes us more susceptible to His shaping. When we fall, we have fallen into His hands.

"Sin is dark, dangerous, damnable," F. B. Meyer wrote, "but it cannot staunch the love of God; it cannot change the fact of a love that is not of yesterday, but dates from eternity itself."

Rather than mourn our humiliation, we must accept God's grace and His offer of forgiveness and then move on. "By sorrow of heart the spirit is broken," says an old proverb (Proverbs 15:13, KJV).

We must not let sorrow and self-pity set us up! It will break us in the end. We must forget "our own paltry self with its well-earned disgrace, and lift up our eyes to the glory which alone will quicken us" (George MacDonald).

Sin may have consequences with which we must live, but sin acknowledged and confessed can only work for good. It is, in fact, one means by which God shapes us into His image.

> I asked the Lord that I may grow
>   in faith and love and every grace,
> Might more of his salvation know,
>   and seek more earnestly his face.
>
> 'Twas He who taught me thus to pray,
>   and He I trust has answered prayer,
> But it has been in such a way
>   as almost drove me to despair.
>
> I thought that in some favored hour,
>   at once He'd answer my request,
> And by His love's transforming power,
>   Subdue my sins and give me rest.
>
> Instead of that He made me feel
>   the hidden evils of my heart,
> And bade the angry powers of hell
>   assault my soul in every part.

Nay, more, with His hand He seemed
  intent to aggravate my woe,
Crossed all the fair designs I schemed,
  blasted my gourds, and laid me low.

"Lord, why this?" I trembling cried.
  "Wilt Thou pursue this worm to death?"
"This is the way," the Lord replied,
  "I answer prayer for grace and faith."

"These inward trials I employ
  from sin and self to set thee free,
And cross thy schemes of earthly joy
  that thou might find thy all in Me."

—JOHN NEWTON

God's love at work . . .

"Even from my sin," said Augustine, "God draws good."

God's love in the face of our sin is what causes us to long for His righteousness. His love softens our hearts, draws us to repentance, and makes us hungry for righteousness. It is the love of God and His goodness to us that draws us to repentance.

Brennan Manning said it well:

When I am in conscious communion with the reality of the wild, passionate, relentless, stubborn, pursuing, tender love of God for me, then it's not that I have to or I got to or I must or I should or I ought; suddenly, I want to change because I know how deeply I'm loved. One of the wonderful results of my consciousness of God's staggering love for me as I am is a freedom not to be who I should be or who others want me to be. I can be who I really am. And who I am is a bundle of paradoxes and contradictions: I believe and I doubt, I trust and I get discouraged, I love and I hate, I feel bad about feeling good, I feel guilty if I don't feel guilty. Aristotle said we are rational animals. I say I am an angel with an incredible capacity for beer. It is the real me that God loves. I don't have to be anyone else. For 20 years I tried to be Brother Teresa. I tried to be Francis of Assisi. I had to be a carbon copy of a great saint rather than the original God intended me to be. The biggest mistake I can make is to say to God, "Lord, if I change, you'll love me, won't you?" The Lord's reply is always, "Wait a minute, you've got it all wrong. You don't have to change so I'll love you; I love you so you'll change." I simply expose myself to the love that is everything and have an immense, unshakable, reckless, raging confidence that God loves me so much he'll change me and fashion me into the child that he always wanted me to be.

"Faith is the courage to accept acceptance," says Paul Tillich. At the heart of real faith is a deep conviction that God knows us and loves us as we are and not as we should be. Furthermore, we can love God and move toward obedience to Him because He first loved us. God's love compels us, says Paul (2 Corinthians 5:14).

He guides me in paths of righteousness . . .

Oh that my baa-ing nature would win hence
Some woolly innocence!

—C. S. LEWIS

"If I don't have the hope of one day being good," a friend once confided in me, "if there is no escape from the evil I keep doing, nothing could reconcile me to life." I share his sentiment.

God does too: He would have us

rid of all discontent, all fear, all grudging, all bitterness in word or thought, all gauging and measuring of ourselves with a different rod from that we would apply to another. He would have no curling of the lip; no indifference in us to the man whose service in any form we use; no desire to excel another, no contentment at gaining by his loss. He would not have us receive the smallest service without gratitude; would not hear from us a tone to jar the heart of another, a word to make it ache, be the ache ever so transient.

—GEORGE MACDONALD

It is God's will that we should be holy (1 Thessalonians 4:3), by which Paul assures us that God's ultimate intent is to make us good. Every day He is leading us along the path toward righteousness.

We're inclined to think of God's will solely in terms of where we will go and what we will do when we get there, and certainly God does have a plan for each moment of our lives. But God's direction primarily has to do with holiness and His determination to change us beyond recognition—to make us as good as He is.

The goodness that comes from God

Some people try too hard; they're upright, but uptight. Goodness, for them, is stern, demanding business. They're chaste, honest, sober, respectable, Bible-toting, church-going, psalm-singing people, but everything seems out of phase. As William James said, "Their faith exists as a 'dull habit.'" They have an appearance of righteousness with their self-imposed worship, obvious humility, and harsh treatment of the body, but they lack the cordial love that springs from contact with God.

Edicts, dictums, creeds, rites, rituals can never modify us; nor do admonishments to read the Bible more, pray more, and go to church more often. There is a life beyond earnestness. "From such silly devotions deliver us, good Lord," prayed St. Francis of Avila.

The problem with rules and regulations is that they have no mechanism for overriding our natural tendencies to go wrong. All they can do is reveal those tendencies and say to us, "You should!" "You shouldn't!" "You haven't!" "You can't!" The rest is up to us.

It takes too much energy to keep the rules. We must never lose control. We must maintain a safe distance from people and resist intimacy. But though the spirit may be willing the flesh is weak. Inevitably we get weary and sick of trying. Then, no matter how hard we try to suppress our instincts, we become unable to sustain the effort. Some unsightly, emotional display, some inappropriate reaction to a relational failure, some other humiliating behavior blows our cover. Our facade cracks and others see behind it. We have that horrible experience of being found out. Others come to know what we have known all along—that much of us is ugly and unacceptable.

No, self-effort doesn't work. It only makes things worse. We must take sin seriously and want with all of our hearts to put it away, but we must not be self-conscious, compulsive, and preoccupied about it. As a plaque on a friend's wall reads, "Today I will not should on myself."

> *Suffer us not to mock ourselves with falsehood*
> *Teach us to care and not to care*
> *Teach us to sit still*

Even among these rocks
Our peace in His will . . .
And let my cry come unto Thee.

—T. S. ELIOT

A job for God . . .

Goodness is a job for God. We must stop horning in on His business and instead ask Him to bring about our change: To those "who are far from righteousness," He says, "I am *bringing* my righteousness near" (Isaiah 46:12–13).

Being godly does require discipline, but that discipline should never be construed as a rigorous technique. Following Christ requires effort, but it is the effort to stay close to Him and listen to His voice. Serious effort is needed if we are to focus on Him and become sensitive to His desires.

As we draw close to Him—walking with Him, talking to Him, listening to His words, relying on Him, asking for His help—His character begins to rub off on us. Quietly and unobtrusively His influence softens our wills, making us thirsty for righteousness, inclining us to do His pleasure, restraining our passions, keeping us from evil, making us ashamed of evil, giving us the courage to choose what is good. In His quiet love He takes all that's unworthy in us and gradually turns it into something worthwhile for Him.

Change is not passive; we must hate evil and love righteousness. To love righteousness is to will it to grow. It's a matter of inclination and desire. It's not what we are, but what we *want* to be that matters. Do we want righteousness? Do we want to do better? "When the fight begins within himself, a man's worth something," Robert Browning said.

Paul puts it this way: "The one who sows to please his sinful nature, from that nature will reap destruction; the one who sows to please the Spirit, from the Spirit will reap eternal life. Let us not become weary in doing good, for at the proper time we will reap a harvest if we do not give up" (Galatians 6:8–9). It's the law: Every time we sow to the flesh—harbor a grudge, nurse a grievance, wallow in self-interest and self-pity—we are sowing seeds of self-destruction. On the other hand, every time we till the soil of the Spirit—long to please God's Spirit and ask for His help—we sow seeds that will endure to eternal life. Every time we make a right choice, God begins to turn us into someone a little different from the person we were before.

We cannot rid ourselves of our sins, "but we can set about sending them away. We can quarrel with them and proceed to turn them out. The Lord is on his way to do his part in their final banishment" (George MacDonald). God is the only source of authentic and lasting change. Whatever conformity to goodness we achieve is the fruit of His doing.

Fruit is exactly the right word, suggesting as it does some hidden element, quietly at work to produce results. Jesus said: "I am the vine; you are the branches. If a man remains in me and I in him, he will bear much fruit; apart from me you can do nothing" (John 15:5). The relationship of a branch to its vine is the relationship we must sustain to our Lord: We must remain, or *abide*, to use the older term. We must set aside everything we normally rely on and cling to Him—closely joined to Him, sustained by His life, waiting for His impulses that will in time produce the fruit of righteousness for which we yearn.

"There is no true virtue without a miracle," Augustine said. God must work His magic on us. Any progress we make toward righteousness is the product of our association with Him. We must come again and again to Him with our desires and lofty ideals and lay them at His feet. We must bring our weakness, our shame, our compulsions, our doubts and fears, our misjudgments, our weariness, and our staleness and ask Him to complete us. He is the only one who can take the vision of all that we have never been and bring it into being.

Waiting . . .

Waiting is a necessary part of the process. There are no shortcuts to maturity. Our personalities resist change, flawed as they are by nature, nurture, and our own indulgence. We've been wounded by others and we've wounded ourselves, yet we can be assured that our healing is going on every day. We are in recovery, gradually being delivered from evil. God is working even now for that distant end. We are becoming today what we will inevitably be. We must

> *Wait for God's silent molding;*
> *Wait for his full unfolding;*
> *Wait for the days to be.*
> —FRANCES HAVERGAL

We must believe that God's processes are adequate to deal with our sin. The key word is

97

process. We must "be comfortable with ourselves in process," as a friend of mine once said. God heals by degrees. We grow slowly from one degree of likeness to the next—inch by inch, here a little, there a little. "We, who with unveiled faces all reflect the Lord's glory, are being trans-formed into his likeness with ever-increasing glory, which comes from the Lord, who is the Spirit" (2 Corinthians 3:18). Gain is gain, however small.

When God wants to change us we will know; we will feel what Danish philosopher Sören Kierkegaard called "the infinite weight of God." The sign of God's convicting is never free-floating guilt and a vague sense of wrong. That's the devil's doing. When God speaks to us there is little ground for doubt or confusion. We are unmistakably convinced of our sin. When that convincing comes we can turn to Him from our sin—*repent,* to use the biblical word—thank Him for His forgiveness, and ask for His enabling. Then we can leave the process to Him and go on.

And going on is all that matters. God doesn't look for perfection, only progress. We're certain of failing, but not overcome with fear. "Nothing will undo us if we keep picking ourselves up each time.

We shall of course be very muddy and tattered children by the time we reach home. . . . The only fatal thing is to lose one's temper and give up" (C. S. Lewis).

As for me, if I've made any progress at all, it's not been by quantum leaps and bounds, but by tentative steps and a number of falls. It's been a creeping thing, better seen in retrospect than in prospect. The path has been chaotic and haphazard, but I have David's confidence: God is leading me in paths of righteousness. Every day He is taking me along the path toward the place He wants me to be.

Everything worthwhile takes time, but time is on our side. We have the rest of our lives to grow. God is wonderfully patient. He will never give up on us until His work is done. What He is making of you and me is not yet complete—we are unfinished—but one day very soon God will finish. "Dear friends, now we are children of God," John assures us, "and what we will be has not yet been made known. But we know that when he appears, we shall be like him" (1 John 3:2).

And that's good enough for me.

EVEN THOUGH I WALK THROUGH THE VALLEY OF THE SHADOW OF DEATH, I WILL FEAR NO EVIL, FOR YOU ARE WITH ME; YOUR ROD AND YOUR STAFF, THEY COMFORT ME

In pastures green? Not always; sometimes He
Who knoweth best, in kindness leadeth me
In weary ways, where heavy shadows be.

—H. H. BARRY

IN THE MIDDLE OF THE MEADOW the path plunges down into the valley of the shadow of death. The words awaken primal memories and stir up ominous images. In all of Scripture there's no place more familiar than this and none more evocative.

I remember the impression I had as a child when I first heard the words, "the valley of the shadow of death." I conjured up a mental picture of a storm-shrouded landscape, a yawning abyss at my feet, broken crags, precipitous cliffs, and a narrow, twisting footpath along narrow ledges, leading inexorably into thickening gloom below. The picture is locked in my mind.

The phrase *shadow of death* is one word in Hebrew, meaning "deep darkness." It's a dreary word, used elsewhere in the Bible to describe the impenetrable darkness before creation (Amos 5:8), the thick darkness of a mine shaft (Job 28:3), and the black hole that is the abode of the dead (Job 10:21; 38:17). It's a word associated with anxiety and unfocused dread.

In *The Pilgrim's Progress* John Bunyan captures something of the terror of the place when he describes it as "dark as pitch," inhabited by "hobgoblins, satyrs, dragons of the pit and fiends." A way "set full of pits, pitfalls, deep holes and shelvings." In the midst of the valley was "the mouth of hell."

As Bunyan's pilgrim and his companion ventured into the valley they saw that "there was on the right hand a very deep ditch. . . . Again, behold on the left hand, there was a very dangerous quag, into which, if even a good man falls, he can find no bottom for his foot to stand on. Into that quag King David did fall, and had no doubt therein been smothered, had not He that is able, plucked him out."

The valley of the shadow of death is usually associated with the end of life, but Bunyan places it in the middle, where it rightly belongs. In fact there is not one valley; there are many, falling between the pastures where we find intermittent rest. There's no way around them. "We *must* go through many hardships to enter the kingdom of God," Paul insists (Acts 14:22). The desolate places are an inevitable and necessary part of the journey.

The valleys bring to mind the day an employer said "clean out your desk"; when a doctor said "your baby will never be normal"; when you found the stash in your son's closet; when your teenage daughter told you she was pregnant; when the doctor said you had cancer; when your spouse said he or she had no energy left to put into the relationship.

Those are the dark days when we lose all perspective, when we say in despair, "It's no use; I can't go on."

The valleys are emblematic of periods of prolonged failure when we're shamed and broken by the full weight of the darkness within us; when we experience the isolation of despair, the exhausted aftermath of self-gratification and spent vice; when we feel unalterably defiled and wonder if we will ever regain our sense of worth.

The valleys symbolize those dreary days of deep loneliness when we say with David, "No one is concerned for me. I have no refuge; no one cares for my life" (Psalm 142:4); when no one seeks us; no one asks about us; there are no cards or letters; the phone doesn't ring; no one seems to care. Even God seems aloof and remote; there's an unaccountable chill in the air. We cry out with David, "My God, my God, why have you forsaken me? Why are you so far from saving me, so far from the words of my groaning? O my God, I cry out by day, but you do not answer" (Psalm 22:1–2).

Oh, yes, there are valleys far worse than death.

Suffering successfully

I used to think that life was mostly green pasture with an occasional dark valley along the way, but now I realize it's the other way around. There are days of surprising joy, but much of life is a vale of tears.

Life is difficult. "The world is painful in any case; but it is quite unbearable if anybody gives us the idea that we are meant to be liking it," Charles Williams said.

When people tell me that life is hard, I reply, "Of course it is." I find that answer more satisfying than anything else I can say. Every year confirms my belief that life is indeed difficult and demanding. Any other view of life is escapist.

The path by which God takes us often seems to lead away from our good, causing us to believe we've missed a turn and taken the wrong road. That's because most of us have been taught to believe that if we're on the right track God's goodness will always translate into earthly good: that He'll heal, deliver, and exempt us from disease and pain; that we'll have money in the bank, kids who turn out well, nice clothes, a comfortable living, and a leisurely retirement. In that version of life everyone turns out to be a winner, nobody loses a business, fails in marriage, or lives in poverty.

But that's a pipe dream far removed from the biblical perspective that God's love often leads us down roads where earthly comforts fail us so He can give us eternal consolation (2 Thessalonians 2:16). "Suffering ripens our souls," said Alexander Solzhenitsyn.

God doesn't cushion the journey; He lets life jolt us. We should keep that idea in mind when the way seems difficult and long. As F. B. Meyer said, if we've been told that we're supposed to be on a bumpy track, every jolt along the way simply confirms the fact that we're still on the right road.

When we come to the end of all valleys we'll understand that every path has been selected, out of all possible options, for our ultimate good. God, in fact, could not have taken us by any other way. No other route would have been as safe and as certain as the one by which we came. And if only we could see the path as God has always seen it, we would select it as well.

He chose this path for me,
Though well he knew that thorns would pierce my feet,
Knew how the brambles would obstruct the way,
Knew all the hidden dangers I would meet,
Knew how my faith would falter day by day;
And still my whisper echoes, "Yes I see
This path is best for me."

He chose this path for me;
Why need I more: this better truth to know,
That all along these strange bewildering ways,

O'er rocky steeps where dark rivers flow,
    His mighty arm will bear me all my days
        A few steps more, and I shall see
        This path is best for me.

You are with me . . .

When Bunyan's pilgrim plunged into the valley he heard the voice of a man going before him, saying, "Even though I walk through the valley of the shadow of death, I will fear no evil, for *you* are with me." He gathered that others were in the valley as well, and that God was with them. "Why not with me?" he gathered, "though by reason of the impediment that attends this place, I cannot perceive it."

That was David's conclusion: "Even though I walk through the valley of the shadow of death, I will fear no evil for *you are with me*. Your rod and your staff, they comfort me." His Shepherd was by his side, armed to the teeth, warding off his enemies and keeping him from wandering off the trail. God was with him in the midst of his fears.

The grammar of this poem shifts significantly at this point. David moves from speaking of God in the third person, he, to the second person, you. He had been speaking *about* God; in the valley he turns and speaks *to* Him. That's a small detail in the text, but it makes a big difference to our hearts to know that God is with us in the valley. His presence was David's comfort.

What God said to Moses is true for all times: "My Presence will go with you, and I will give you rest" (Exodus 33:14). He said to Jacob: "*I am with you* and will watch over you wherever you go" (Genesis 28:15). He said to Joshua: "As I was with Moses, so *I will be with you*; I will never leave you nor forsake you" (Joshua 1:5). He said to Israel: "Do not fear, for *I am with you*; do not be dismayed, for I am your God. I will strengthen you and help you; I will uphold you with my righteous right hand. . . . When you pass through the waters, *I will be with you*; and when you pass through the rivers, they will not sweep over you. When you walk through the fire, you will not be burned; the flames will not set you ablaze" (Isaiah 41:10; 43:2). He says to us: "Surely *I am with you always*, to the very end of the age" (Matthew 28:20).

God is with us, walking everywhere incognito, as C. S. Lewis said. "And the incognito is not always hard to penetrate. The real labor is to remember, to attend. In fact, to come awake. Still more, to remain awake." The main thing to remember is to make ourselves think about His presence; to acknowledge that He is with us, as real as He was in the days of His flesh when He walked with His disciples amid the sorrows and haunts of this world.

Friends fail us, spouses walk out on us, parents disappoint us, therapists refuse to return our calls, but God is with us every moment of every day. When we ford the deep waters, when we pass through the fire, when we walk through the valley of the shadow of death, He is there.

Difficulty and drudgery make us think of ourselves as being all alone, but He has said, "I will never leave you nor forsake you." Of Him alone it can be said, He will never say good-bye.

> *About, above me, evermore*
> *God's gentle presence broods,*
> *He shares with me my silences,*
> *He fills my solitudes.*
>
> *His face and form I cannot see,*
> *No spoken word can hear,*
> *But with some better sense of soul*
> *Do I perceive him near.*

Are not these joys too good to last?
May he not soon depart?
'No, I am with you all the days'
He answers to my heart.

—UNKNOWN

Seeing what cannot be seen . . .

"God becomes a reality," Richard Foster says, "when he becomes a necessity." The dark valleys make God more real to us than ever before. How many times have I heard from those who have endured intense suffering that the experience of their pain has cured them of the idolatries that once robbed them of joy. The father who abandons us, the spouse who leaves us, the financial catastrophe that ruins us, the rude interruption of our plans, the revelation of a horrifying illness, the painful, pro-longed delay—all escalate our love for God. All are His ways of prying our fingers from things that are false and that will not satisfy. They pull us away from lesser loves and enlarge our intimacy with our Shepherd, which is what brings us peace and unimaginable joy.

"One sees the truth more clearly when one is unhappy," wrote Fyodor Dostoevsky from Siberia.

Then he continued:

> And yet God gives me moments of perfect
> peace; in such moments I love and believe
> that I am loved; in such moments I have
> formulated my creed, wherein all is clear
> and holy to me. This creed is extremely
> simple: here it is. I believe that there is
> nothing lovelier, deeper, more sympathetic,
> more rational, more manly and more per-
> fect than the Savior: I say to myself with
> jealous love that not only is there no one
> else like him, but that there could be no
> one.

We're inclined to fix on the valley and its
pain, but God chooses to look forward and antici-
pate its effect. He deals with our divided hearts
through disappointment, grief, and tears, weaning
us from other loves and passions and centering us
on Him. We learn to trust Him in the darkness;
when all that is left is the sound of His voice and
the knowledge that He is near; when all we can do
is slip our hand into His and feel "the familiar clasp
of things divine." These are times that wean us
away from sensuality—that tendency to live by feelings rather than by faith in God's unseen presence.

We become independent of places and moods and content with God alone.

The dark days cause us to enter into a very special relationship with our Lord. As Job said, "My ears had heard of you, but now my eyes have seen you" (Job 42:5). There are glimpses of God that can only be revealed when earthly joy has ceased.

The most perfect human love cannot satisfy us. That's because our human hearts crave for a relationship deeper and more lasting than anything possible in this world. We were made for God's love and without it we sink into loneliness. The darkness, the breakdown of human ties, the limitations and losses of human affection lead to that higher friendship, that larger, more permanent love.

> *God's strong arm*
> *extends to selfish bullies, willful, crude;*
> *endures the self-deceived; ignores the rude;*
> *forbears with murder; incest does not quell—*
> *and when my arm would sweep them all to hell,*
> *He draws them to his heart.*
>
> *God's strong arm*
> *in love applies the rod, employs the lash;*
> *impairs a face; in beauty strikes a gash;*
> *denies the hungry; wounds a mother's breast.*

> *And while I raise my fist, beseech, protest,*
> *He draws me to his heart.*

> —RUTH BELL GRAHAM

David himself understood the adversity that draws us to God's heart. Subjected to neglect by his mother and father and demeaned by the rest of his family, he was deeply scarred. His family would have ruined him if he had not fled to his heavenly Father for refuge. Out of his loneliness and heartache David wrote, "Though my father and mother have forsaken me, the LORD has taken me in" (Psalm 27:10).

And then the work went on . . .

> *Latest born of Jesse's race,*
> > *wonder lights thy bashful face,*
> *While the prophet's gifted oil,*
> > *seals thee for a life of toil.*
> *Heartache, woeful care, distress,*
> > *blighted hope, and loneliness;*
> *Wounds from friend and gifts from foe,*
> > *dizzied faith, and guilt, and woe;*
> *Loftiest aims by earth defiled,*
> > *gleams of wisdom sin-beguiled;*

Sated power's tyrranic mood,
  counsels shared by men of blood;
Sad success, parental tears,
  and a dreary gift of years.

—UNKNOWN

David was hammered and hurt throughout his entire life, every blow converting him, exposing his ambivalence, until he would finally cry, "Surely, I was sinful at birth, sinful from the time my mother conceived me. . . . Create in me a pure [undivided] heart" (Psalm 51:5, 10).

God's work is never done: "Thus always—the rod, the stripes, the chastisements; but amid all, the love of God, carrying out his redemptive purpose, never hasting, never resting, never forgetting, but making all things work together until the evil is eliminated and the soul is purified" (F. B. Meyer).

Then David cried out, "My soul finds rest in God *alone . . .*" (Psalm 62:1). It was through darkness, suffering, and pain that all David's passions were integrated into one.

And so, all of life is consummated in loving God. That's what we were made for; that's where ultimate satisfaction lies. If that's true, and I firmly believe it is, then although it is often hard to do, we should welcome any valley that leads us to Him.

There will be an end . . .

One thing more: No valley goes on forever. We walk *through* the valley of the shadow of death. God knows what we can endure. He will not let us be tempted or tested beyond what we can bear (1 Corinthians 10:13). The deliverance we seek may be subject to delay, but we must never doubt that our day will come. "Weeping may remain for a night, but rejoicing comes in the morning" (Psalm 30:5). Sorrow has its time to be, but God will mitigate the tears when their work is done. Those who mourn will be comforted. There will be an end.

YOU PREPARE A TABLE BEFORE ME IN THE PRESENCE OF MY ENEMIES. YOU ANOINT MY HEAD WITH OIL; MY CUP OVERFLOWS

*"Hush! What if this friend
happens to be—God!"*

—ELIZABETH BARRETT BROWNING

SOME SAY THAT DAVID DROPPED THE SHEPHERD FIGURE at this point and shifted to another metaphor, but I see no need to cut the poem in two. The scene is still pastoral: The first four verses portray the shepherd with his sheep in the pasture; the final two verses place him in his tent providing sanctuary, serving as a gracious host, spreading a lavish meal, overwhelming his guests with hospitality.

The ancient shepherd's tent was a safe house where "every wanderer, whatever his character, or his past might be, was received as a 'guest of God'—such is the beautiful name they still give him—furnished with food, and kept inviolable, his host becoming responsible for his safety" (George Adam Smith).

It was this custom that David had in mind when he composed this line.

We are God's guests! He seats us at His table; He welcomes all comers. It's not as though He doesn't know what we're like. We're uninteresting, exasperating, and otherwise unattractive company, but there's no censure or condescension, only eternal affirmation and supply. He welcomes us warmly and overwhelms us with His lavish love.

> *Love bade me welcome; yet my soul drew back*
> *Guilty of dust and sin.*
> *But quick-eyed Love, observing me grow slack*
> *From my first entrance in,*
> *Drew nearer to me, sweetly questioning*
> *If I lacked anything.*
> *"A guest," I answered, "worthy to be here."*
> *Love said, "You shall be he."*

"I the kind, the ungrateful? Ah, my dear,
   I cannot look on thee."
Love took my hand, and smiling did reply,
   "Who made the eyes but I?"
"Truth, Lord, but I have marred them: let my shame
   Go where it doth deserve."
"And know you not," says Love, "who bore the
blame?"
   "My dear, then I will serve."
"You must sit down," says Love, "and taste my
meat,"
   So I did sit and eat.

—GEORGE HERBERT

It is God's nature to humble Himself and
serve. Think of the occasion when Jesus gathered
His disciples in the upper room.

> Jesus knew that the time had come for him
> to leave this world and go to the Father.
> Having loved his own who were in the
> world, he now showed them the full extent
> of his love. . . . He got up from the meal,
> took off his outer clothing, and wrapped a
> towel around his waist. After that, he
> poured water into a basin and began to

wash his disciples' feet, drying them with
the towel that was wrapped around him.

—JOHN 13:1, 4–5

Footwashing was an essential act of hospitality
in those days. Normally servants performed that
unbecoming task, but there were no servants in the
apostolic band and no one volunteered for the job.
So our Lord took on the duty. Girding Himself as a
servant, He stooped and washed His disciples' feet,
one by one.

We never think much about the humility of
God. Theologians remark on His other attributes
but rarely on that virtue. Imagine: the Incarnate God
of the universe, garbed as a servant, girded with a
towel, on hands and knees washing rank and filthy
feet, moving steadily downward in submission and
service to those in need—even to Judas who was
about to betray Him. What incredible modesty!

There was also the time when our Lord fed
His disciples beside the Sea of Galilee. They had
been fishing all night but had caught nothing. They
were tired, dispirited, gloomy. "When they landed,
they saw a fire of burning coals there with fish on
it, and some bread. . . . Jesus said to them, 'Come
and have breakfast' " (John 21:9, 12).

120

John says the disciples *knew* it was the Lord. They recognized Him by that propensity to cater to others; always, there was His inclination to serve. He came not to be ministered to, but to minister— to us.

To such a one we come. He delights to serve. His giving supplies the nourishment our spirits crave. At His table there is "wine that gladdens the heart of man, oil to make his face shine, and bread that sustains his heart" (Psalm 104:15). He gives full measure, pressed down, running over. His grace is more than sufficient; His goodness over-flows; we have all and abound!

"You anoint my head with oil," David says. Anointing the head with oil was a token of esteem in ancient times. Love was manifest by the costliness of the oils. Myrrh, aloes, cassia, and other exotic fra-grances were mixed together in precise measure and permanently sealed in alabaster vases. When the time came for anointing one's guests, the bottles were broken at the neck and the oil inside was poured lavishly onto the heads of the guests until it ran down onto the person's robes, leaving a lingering fragrance. It was called the "oil of joy" (Psalm 45:7).

"My cup overflows," David continues. He sees God hovering over him, waiting for the moment of slightest need, filling and refilling his cup with wine. David has more than enough. "Abundance and redundance are his," as one old saint said.

> Does David not mean us to infer that life is a feast, in which we are guests and God is the host? And does he not also mean to teach that God greets us in love and welcome?—He is not niggardly or churlish, but glad to see us glad and to make us happy; conferring on us luxuries as well as necessities; and taking pains at great cost to Himself, to show us that he is well pleased to accept us and show us grace in the Beloved.
>
> —F. B. MEYER

God's table is a metaphor for His gracious, ongoing provision. "Can God spread a table in the desert?" we ask (Psalm 78:19). Can He meet our needs in the midst of our dearth? You bet your life He can! God is able to supply *all* our needs; He is equal to all our emergencies and essential needs.

God wants to give. Ask and receive, Jesus said. That's the utter simplicity of faith. For all our desire He gives all of Himself. All that He is, is ours.

When we understand the fullness of His heart and His desire to give we can ask anything. That vision of God "makes life a continuous prayer," said Bishop Walcott.

We should understand that God's resources are granted neither for shows of strength nor for selfish ambition. God has a greater thing in mind for us: Most of His giving is to make us good.

Jesus put it this way: "I am the vine; you are the branches. If a man remains in me and I in him, he will bear much fruit; apart from me you can do nothing. . . . *If you remain in me and my words remain in you, ask whatever you wish, and it will be given you.* This is to my Father's glory, that you bear much fruit, showing yourselves to be my disciples" (John 15:5, 7–8). His unequivocal promise: "Ask whatever you wish and it will be given you," is conditioned by the context and controlled by the concept of fruit. The "fruit" is the fruit of the Spirit: "love, joy, peace, patience, kindness, goodness, faithfulness, gentleness and self-control" (Galatians 5:22).

We can ask anything that involves acquiring the characteristics of God. When we ask for His character He begins to give it, working through time and circumstance to conform us more closely to His will. This is the use to which He puts His power.

When we've come to the end of our resources, when we've run out of all that's essential—that's when God comes through.

"Heaven helps those that help themselves," is supposed to be ancient wisdom, but it's not something you'd ever hear God say. It sounds more like good advice from the devil. God insists that heaven helps those who are helpless. King Uzziah of Judah was "greatly helped *until* he became powerful" according to the prophet (2 Chronicles 26:15). Uzziah's strength was his failing; it tied God's hands. When the king got too powerful God couldn't help him any more.

"I yam what I yam," Popeye says. By the grace of God, we are what we are, and what we are is inadequate. Inadequacy is a fact of life, a hard truth that makes life much easier when we accept it. "We're all ordinary people," G. K. Chesterton said, "and it's the *extra*ordinary people who know it."

The problem with us is that we're much too well equipped and much too adept at what we do. We believe too much in ourselves—in our experience, our education, our appearance, our humor, our personality. But our essential humanity is useless. "The flesh [human effort] counts for nothing" (John 6:63).

"Blessed are the poor," Jesus said. By *poor* He meant "poverty-stricken," a word commonly used in the Gospels for beggars who sat on the streets in rags and in utter need, holding out their hands, appealing to others for aid. These are the people who catch God's eye. "This is the one I esteem: he who is humble [poor] and contrite in spirit, and trembles at my word" (Isaiah 66:2).

Human limitation is a fact of life. It's foolish to believe that we're strong. It doesn't take much to bring us down: a tiny virus can devastate us physically, a slight miscalculation can ruin us financially, a small miscue can undo us socially. Life cannot be controlled and contained; there are just too many contingencies. We don't have what it takes.

Howard Butt, in an article entitled "The Art of Being the Big Shot," said this:

> It is my pride that makes me think I call my own shots. That feeling is my basic dishonesty. I can't go it alone. I can't rely on myself. I am dependent on God for my very next breath. It is dishonest of me to pretend that I am anything but a man, small, weak, limited. So living independent of God is self-delusion. It is not just a matter

of pride being an unfortunate little trait and humility being an attractive little virtue. It is my inner psychological integrity that is at stake. When I am self-dependent, I am lying to myself about what I am. I am pretending to be God and not man. My independence is the idolatrous worship of myself, the national religion of hell.

Some people asked Jesus once what good work God required. Jesus' answer caught them completely by surprise: "The work of God is this: to *believe* in the one he has sent" (John 6:28–29). How audacious of anyone to think that mere human beings can do God's work. If anything is to be done at all He must do it.

Whatever we have to do—putting down the smallest rising thought of anger and wrong or self-ishness in our souls, giving up our hard-earned leisure time to serve someone in need, showing quiet, unnoticed compassion to another—it must be done by faith. Those who work the works of God are those who realize their unfitness and utter inadequacy and rely on Him for His strength.

We are flimsy and frail—"thinking reeds," Pascal said. Easily crushed and bruised. The world overwhelms us. We wear out; we become weary and worn thin. The tragedies and ambiguities of life sap our strength and bring us to our knees. "Even youths grow tired and weary, and the young men stumble and fall" (Isaiah 40:30). We are limited, dependent beings, but therein lies our strength. When we are weak, says Paul, then we are strong (2 Corinthians 12:10).

> *Crushed!—it filled with patience,*
> *Wounded!—it beamed with love,*
> *Wearied!—it mounted upward,*
> *Up to a great life above.*
>
> *Weak!—it grew with greatness,*
> *Feeble!—it rose with strength,*
> *Fitful!—it heaved majestic,*
> *Heaved to calm peace at length.*
>
> *This is the constitution,*
> *Opposites always combined,*
> *Of body, soul, and spirit,*
> *Limited—undefined.*
>
> **—OSWALD CHAMBERS**

Isaiah insists that those who hope in the Lord will exchange their strength for God's. "They will soar on wings like eagles; they will run and not grow weary, they will walk and not faint" (Isaiah 40:31).

Our limits are limitless, but He has no limits. No demand is too difficult, no dilemma too hard, no complication too complicated. He never wears out, gets weary, or grows tired. When we acknowledge our boundaries and ask for His help, He replaces our "strength" with His.

Some days we outdo the eagles and rise above our circumstances, unconfined and unencumbered; we soar and see things from God's point of view. (Enjoy such moments!)

There are other days when, as the White Queen said to Alice, "it takes all the running you can to keep in the same place," or in the words of a plaque that used to hang over my mother's desk, the "hurrier you go the behinder you get." Those are the days we can maintain the pace with poise and persistence, sustained by God's inexhaustible strength.

And then there are those ordinary days when the desk is piled with dreary duties or the sink is full of dirty dishes and the routine is tedious and dull; when, as Ruth Bell Graham recalled, there's only "nothingness, inertia, skies gray and windless, no sun, no rain, no stab of pain, no strong regret, no reaching after, no tears, no laughter, no black despair, no bliss."

God delivers us through this. We can walk when the novelty has worn off, when the glory has faded, when the strength of youth is gone. This is the strength of God.

God's boundless, uninterrupted strength freely exchanged for our merely human effort? God's greatness flowing through our basic incompetence? This is grace!

> *When we have exhausted our store of endurance,*
> *When our strength has failed ere the day is*
> *half done,*
> *When we reach the end of our hoarded resources,*
> *Our Father's full giving is only begun.*
> *His love has no limit, His grace has no measure*
> *His power no boundary known unto men;*
> *For out of his infinite riches in Jesus*
> *He giveth and giveth and giveth again.*
>
> —ANNIE JOHNSON FLINT

There's something winsome and wonderfully compelling about those whom God is making strong. They're easier to get along with, easier to work with and live with, more gentle and genial. Their goodness is like old wine—mellow and fragrant. They have a profound and bewildering effect upon others. Their actions keep reminding people of . . . well, of God.

That sort of influence cannot be conjured up or contrived. It's not a matter of feminine force or male machismo; it's not a function of self-assertiveness, intellect, charisma, charm, or chutzpah. It *happens*—the fruit of our association with God.

Self-conscious influence is pretentious and puts people off. It looks like what it is: *self*-righteousness, and it annoys others to no end. When we try to be influential we become aggressive and intrusive. We crowd people and push them away from the truth. (When we do so, we're sure of just one ally—the devil.) But those whom God is making good are powerfully persuasive. They have a fragrance like a subtle perfume. Wherever they go, they leave behind the unforgettable aroma of their Lord (2 Corinthians 2:14–17).

God is never done. His work of nourishing us and strengthening us goes on all through our lives. Paul writes, "We do not lose heart. Though outwardly we are wasting away, yet inwardly we are being renewed day by day (2 Corinthians 4:16).

As age breaks down our natural energy and strength we're more inclined than ever before to depend on God's provision. We have more time for contemplation and prayer. His nearness keeps rubbing off on us. We reflect more of His goodness. Youthful knowledge and zeal, tempered by worship and God-awareness, become the wisdom that time alone can yield. What once we did with youthful strength we now can do with greater sensitivity and humbler hearts. Wisdom softens our faces.

Then our influence has a peculiar power. Tested character and ripened experience has a spiritual vitality and vision that a busier age cannot have. Those at the beginning of life acquire knowledge, but those more near its end gain gentle wisdom. It has to do with character and people skills and kinder, gentler ways of getting things done. That wisdom is "pure; then peace-loving, considerate, submissive, full of mercy and good fruit, impartial and sincere" (James 3:17).

We grow to ceilings in every other realm of life, but there are no ceilings to growth in grace. No one yet has ever outgrown God's willingness to give. As our days, so shall our strength be.

> *Give me strength for my day, Lord,*
> *That wheresoe'er I go,*

There shall no danger daunt me
And I shall fear no foe;
So shall no task o'ercome me,
So shall no trial fret,
So shall I walk unwearied
The path where my feet are set;
So shall I find no burden
Greater than I can bear,
So shall I have a courage
Equal to all my care;
So shall no grief o'erwhelm me,
So shall no wave o'erflow;
Give me Thy strength for my day, Lord,
Cover my weakness so.

—ANNIE JOHNSON FLINT

SURELY GOODNESS AND LOVE WILL FOLLOW ME ALL THE DAYS OF MY LIFE, AND I WILL DWELL IN THE HOUSE OF THE LORD FOREVER.

Abashed the devil stood and felt how awful goodness is.

—JOHN MILTON

"SURELY GOODNESS AND LOVE WILL FOLLOW ME all the days of my life," David declares. "Surely," denotes a fact as certain as it is comforting. Too good to be true? No, God is much too good not to be true.

He is *good*—as good as we're capable of imagining Him to be—the only good person in the world. As Jesus said with such utter finality, "*No one* is good—except God" (Luke 18:19).

He is *love*—as loving as we need Him to be. Everything is about love—or the lack of it, as reductionists say. It's a simple human fact that we cannot long survive without tenderness, caring, and someone who is willing to accept us as we are.

The psalms are filled with affirmations of God's love for us: "I trust in your unfailing *love*" (13:5), David writes. "I . . . rejoice in your *love*" (31:7). "You are forgiving and good, O Lord, abounding in *love* to all who call to you" (86:5). "The LORD is good and his *love* endures forever" (100:5). "Give thanks to the LORD, for he is good; his *love* endures forever" (106—2 times). "Give thanks to the LORD, for he is good; his *love* endures forever" (Psalm 118—5 times). "Give thanks to the LORD, for he is good; his *love* endures forever" (Psalm 136—26 times).

David's word for God's tender affection is a term used in the ancient world to mean love that flows out of deep emotion rather than duty. It's a kind and gentle love. That quaint, old word *lovingkindness* may still be the best translation of all.

It's the way God thinks of Himself: "The LORD, the LORD, the compassionate and gracious God, slow to anger, abounding in [*lovingkindness*] and faithfulness" (Exodus 34:6). David took that revelation to heart, twice quoting God's exact words: "But you, O Lord, are a compassionate and gracious God, slow to anger, abounding in [*lovingkindness*] and faithfulness (Psalms 86:15; see 103:8).

David often linked God's goodness and lovingkindness together. In his mind they were inseparable components of God's gracious care. Here in his shepherd poem he personifies these two attributes as God Himself. In these tender manifestations He follows us, shadowing us, attending us, assuring us that no matter what transpires today, tomorrow, or the next day—it cannot separate us from God's goodness and love.

"Who shall separate us from the love of Christ?" says Paul.

> Shall trouble or hardship or persecution or famine or nakedness or danger or sword? As it is written: "For your sake we face death all day long; we are considered as sheep to be slaughtered." No, in all these things we are more than conquerors through him who loved us. For I am convinced that neither death nor life, neither angels nor demons, neither the present nor the future, nor any powers, neither height nor depth, nor any-

thing else in all creation, will be able to separate us from the love of God that is in Christ Jesus our Lord.

—ROMANS 8:35–37

I may fall flat on my face; I may fail until I feel old and beaten and done in. Yet your goodness and love is changeless. All the music may go out of my life, my private world may shatter to dust. Even so, you hold me in the palm of your steady hand. No turn in the affairs of my fractured life can baffle you. Satan with all his braggadocio cannot distract you. Nothing can separate me from your measureless love—pain can't, disappointment can't, anguish can't. Yesterday, today, tomorrow can't. The loss of my dearest love can't. Death can't, life can't. Riots, wars, insanity, non-identity, hunger, neurosis, disease—none of these things, nor all of them heaped together can budge the fact that I am dearly loved, completely forgiven and forever free through Jesus Christ, your beloved son.

—RUTH CALKINS

It occurred to me one day that everything the devil does is designed for one purpose only: to draw us away from God's love. He does so not because he hates us, but because he hates God and will do anything to break His heart, and nothing breaks God's heart more than being separated from those He loves.

According to John Milton, the devil is the prowling Wolf,

> *Whom hunger drives to seek new haunt for prey,*
> *Watching where Shepherds pen their flocks at eve*
> *So climbs this grand thief into God's fold.*

The Bible gives us a vivid picture of this enemy behind all enmity. Jesus described him as a *liar* and a *murderer* (John 8:44). His strategy is to deceive; his objective is to destroy. He is the source of all our doubts about God's goodness. He is the one behind the deceit that buffets us all day long—the messages that encourage us to find ourselves in something or someone more trustworthy than God; the subtle seductions to meet our needs our way rather than trust our Shepherd's wise provision. The devil fills us with guilt over the past, denying God's unfailing forgiveness. He makes us anxious about the present, insinuating that God cannot provide. He exacerbates the final terror of death, ignoring our Lord's conquest over the tomb.

The marks of Satan's presence are anxiety, guilt, and fear—all based on the lie that God either will not or cannot do anything about our condition; that our sin, our suffering, our inadequacy, our destiny—all are beyond His control or beyond His care. Satan's subtle craft is to make us suspicious of God: "He is holding out on you," he whispers in our ears. That's the devil's fundamental deception.

He's behind the bitterness of some of our questions: Why must little children become drug-dependent in utero? Why are women battered, abused, and then abandoned—discarded like pieces of waste? What of the homosexual's lonely despair? Does it occur to God that it is hard for us to live with only His invisible presence; that sometimes we long for human arms to give us a hug? Is He aware that His silence deafens us to His Word; that it's hard to believe He's still speaking to us today? Can He possibly comprehend the awful pain of our loneliness?

Satan plagues us with these questions and uses them to push us away from God.

We ask, "If God is so loving and kind, why is this?"

Any view of justice seems to demand that life ought to be better than it is, especially for those of us who want God and who are responsive to His love. God should go soft on us and give us the good life. Things should get easier as we get along in years, grow closer to Him, and get more in touch with His heart. For some that certainty is an article of faith, but God doesn't back up that creed.

We suffer. Painful, frustrating, discouraging, depressing, and costly things keep happening to us. Sorrow upon sorrow is often our lot, and sometimes the hardest parts of the journey are yet further along. All of this may convince us that the world is a very unfair place and leave us with serious doubt as to whether or not God is good.

But one thing we have to say about God: At least He took His own medicine. He subjected Himself to all the indignities and indecencies the world inflicts on us.

> Whatever the game he is playing with his creation, he has kept his own rules. He can exact nothing from man that he has not exacted from himself. He has himself gone through the whole of human experience, from the trivial irritations of family life and

the cramping restrictions of hard work and lack of money to the worst horrors of pain and humiliation, defeat, despair, and death. When He was a man, He played the man. He was born in poverty and died in disgrace and thought it well worthwhile.

—DOROTHY SAYERS

We look at our Lord's life and death here on earth and listen to His words and we say, "Here is one who understands what I'm going through!" He has experienced all of life's bitterness and heartache. He knows how difficult it is to burn the bridges we're called to destroy; He understands our inertia and our soul's resistance to change. He understands the power of sensual attraction. He has felt the disdain of others; He has seen their smirks and amused smiles; He has experienced coldness and the inability of others to understand. He knows. He understands. We can approach Him "with confidence [boldness], so that we may receive mercy and find grace to help us in our time of need" (Hebrews 4:16).

Doubts come and go, but we need not be dismayed by them. Doubt is not at first a sign that our faith has failed but that it's being assailed. When doubts come we should counter by reminding ourselves of their source and that what the devil says about God is not true—Satan is a liar. Then we can renew our minds and strengthen our hearts with the truth that God is the God "who does not lie" (Titus 1:2). He is Eternal Good, and He is working for our good.

For our good . . .

Paul writes: "We know that in all things God works for the good of those who love him, who have been called according to his purpose. For those God foreknew he also predestined to be conformed to the likeness of his Son, that he might be the first-born among many brothers" (Romans 8:28–29).

Life is "a tale told by an idiot, full of sound and fury, signifying nothing," wrote William Shakespeare in *Macbeth*. God, however, says that every circumstance has purpose. All things are working together for good.

Of course, not everything that comes our way is good. There is nothing good about cancer, aging, or permanent disability. Life is often hard, but God inspires the harshest events, transforming them into advantage, exploiting them for good. The hard occurrences crack our facades and reveal the neediness inside. They loosen our grip on the outside world as we see that its goodness is but an illusion, and then they draw our hearts inward to God's love. They center us on Him and conform us to His gracious will, for we have entered into this world for this purpose: "I have come to do your will, O God" (Hebrews 10:7). God uses every difficulty and complication to draw us to Himself and to conform us to His will. When it comes to that "good," any old circumstance will do.

> *When God wants to drill a man*
> > *And thrill a man*
> > *And skill a man*
> *When God wants to mold a man*
> > *To play the noblest part;*
> *When he yearns with all his heart*
> > *To create a being so bold*
> *That all the world will be amazed,*
> > *watch his methods, watch his ways!*
> *How he relentlessly perfects*
> > *Whom he royally elects!*
> *How we're hammered and hurt*
> > *And with mighty blows converted*

Into trial shapes of clay
    Which only God understands;
While our tortured heart is crying
    And we lift beseeching hands!
How God bends, but never breaks
    When his good he undertakes;
How he uses whom he chooses
    And with every purpose fuses us;
    By every act induces us
To try his splendor out—
    God knows what he's about!

—UNKNOWN

The severity of God is kinder than the kindness of man. As David put it, "Let us fall into the hands of the LORD, for his mercy is great; but do not let me fall into the hands of men" (2 Samuel 24:14). There is a love deeper than the love of those who seek only ease for those they love.

The nearness of God is our good . . .

One of David's fellow poets struggled valiantly with the goodness of God. "God is good to Israel, to those who are pure in heart," said Asaph rather lamely (Psalm 73:1). But the truth did not ring true. There was too much wrong with his world. He struggled intensely with his own pain and that of his neighbors. He couldn't understand why those who were pure in heart should have to suffer at all.

He was about to lose his grip on God: "But as for me, my feet had almost slipped; I had nearly lost my foothold. For I envied the arrogant when I saw the prosperity of the wicked" (73:2–3).

The "arrogant" are those who make no room in their lives for God. They give themselves all the credit; they never say thanks! They have a mindset like Toad Tarkington, one of writer Stephen Koontz's characters, who boasts, "Humble is for those who can't. I *can*."

The poet Asaph warmed to his task:

They [the arrogant] have no struggles;
    their bodies are healthy and strong.
They are free from the burdens common
    to man;
    they are not plagued by human ills.
Therefore pride is their necklace;
    they clothe themselves with violence.
From their callous hearts comes iniquity;
    the evil conceits of their minds know
      no limits.

They scoff, and speak with malice;
    in their arrogance they threaten
        oppression.
Their mouths lay claim to heaven,
    and their tongues take possession of
        the earth.
Therefore their [Hebrew: "his," i.e., God's]
        people turn to them
    and drink up waters in abundance.
They say, "How can God know?
    Does the Most High have knowledge?"
    [Does He know or care?]
This is what the wicked are like—
    always carefree, they increase in wealth.

—PSALM 73:4–12

The phrase "They have no struggles" might be translated "There are no pains in their death"—they die peacefully and painlessly. In contrast to the psalmist, who is plagued all day long (73:14), they are not plagued by human ills. They wear their pride boldly. Others observe their prosperity and "drink up waters in abundance." Using our idiom, they "drink it in," and it prejudices them against God.

Yet God, as the psalmist observed, continues to put up with human arrogance. He not only endures pride, He continues to provide the proud with good. "The rain rains on the just and on the unjust, but chiefly it rains on the just because the unjust steals his umbrella," laments an old adage.

The psalmist was dismayed: "Surely in vain have I kept my heart pure; in vain have I washed my hands in innocence," he lamented. "All day long I have been plagued; I have been punished every morning" (73:13–14).

The poet faced the full rigor of the problem: There's no payoff for knowing God. Why bother?

But then came a moment of truth: Asaph went into the place of revelation to hear what God had to say. There God disclosed an unknown or forgotten fact: This isn't all there is. There is more to life than the here and now. "When I tried to understand all this, it was oppressive to me till I entered the sanctuary of God; then I understood their final destiny [Hebrew: their *after*]" (Psalm 73:16–17). To use the poet's precise word, there is something *after*.

Although Asaph had little earthly good, he had God—forever! "I am always with you; you hold me by my right hand. You guide me with your counsel, and afterward you will take me into glory" (73:23–24).

This is the answer to all of Satan's lies: We may not have the good life—struggle, pain, disappointment, vexation, opposition, and loss may be our lot—but we have God, and God Himself is our good. "Happiness is neither outside nor inside us," Pascal said, "it is in God, both outside and inside us. . . . Our only true blessing is to be in him, and our sole ill to be cut off from him."

Life's disappointments show us how empty life is. Then, when the world's attractiveness begins to fade, we begin to move toward God as our good. As we come to Him again and again—listening to His Word, meditating on His thoughts, following Him in obedience, tasting of His goodness—He makes Himself increasingly known. We enter into intimacy with Him and come to love Him for Himself.

"The most fundamental need, duty, honor, and happiness of men is . . . adoration," said Friedrich von Hügel. In adoration we enjoy God for Himself. We long for the Giver rather than for His gifts. We ask nothing more than to be near Him and to be like Him. We want nothing but the hunger to give ourselves to Him. In adoration we learn why every other chase has left us breathless and restless, worn out and wanting for more.

And so, though it is hard to accept, we need nothing more than God's presence. Our toys and lesser joys can never satisfy; they are small delights. God *alone* is the answer to our deepest longings.

Once more we're confronted with unexpected simplicity: "The LORD is my shepherd, I shall not be in want." In this world or in the next, He is all we need.

So when I hear what God has to say I know the only thing left for me to do is to turn my energies toward Him, giving Him my full attention and my heart's devotion, asking Him every day to bring me to the place where I find Him more interesting than anyone I know, anything I do, any place I go, or anything I possess. It's a matter of centering myself on God. "Not consecration, but concentration," as Oswald Chambers said. Beyond salvation, beyond sanctification, beyond glorification lies the greatest joy of all: the joy of knowing God! (see Romans 5:1–11). It's what I was made for. If I do not *know* Him, my life is a failure.

> *Be thou my Vision, O Lord of my heart;*
> *Naught be all else to me, save that Thou art;*
> *Thou my best thought, by day or by night;*
> *Waking or sleeping, Thy presence my light.*
>
> **—ELEANOR H. HULL, TRANSLATOR**

All the days of my life . . .

God's goodness and love follow after us, cleaning up the messes we've left behind, undoing our wrongdoing (to the extent that it can be undone in this world), treating us as if it had never happened.

He follows us into our present, going behind and before, guiding us, leading us to pasture and still water, protecting us with His rod and staff, calling to the dispersed and gathering them in, carrying His lambs in His arms, leading us inexorably toward home.

Life is full of uncertainties, complexities, and complications. We have little power to change it or to mold it to our way. Every single day we face unknown, uncharted territory. There are no signs, landmarks, or milestones. We're left with Yogi Berra's ambiguity, "When you come to a fork in the road, take it."

What we need is a guide—someone who can give us wise counsel and bring discernment to our decisions.

Typically lost, we're always being escorted in the right direction; often perplexed, we're always on track. A. W. Tozer said boldly, "The man or woman who is wholly and joyously surrendered to

Christ cannot make a wrong choice." He means, of course, that our eternal destiny is not riding on our next decision. No choice that we make is final or ultimately fatal. We may take the oddest path through the wilderness, but we can be assured of this fact: Every day, whether we know it or not, we're being led along the path that leads us *home*.

We're inclined to think of God's help in terms of big decisions—where we will go to school, what career we will choose, where we will locate geo-graphically, whom we will marry—when in fact life's biggest decision may be which way we turn when we leave our garage. Someone at the next intersection could run a red light and end or radi-cally change our lives.

Life is hazardous—not merely a maze but a minefield! Who knows what eventualities lurk at the next crossroad? That uncertainty brings us to the place where all we can do is entrust ourselves to God and count on His goodness and love. "I am still confident of this," David said, "I will see the goodness of the LORD in the land of the living" (27:13). That confidence enables us to move brave-ly and optimistically into every day—as long as we know we are moving in the right direction.

"Which way do I want to go?" Alice asks the Cheshire Cat, "Would you tell me, please, which way I ought to go from here?" "That depends a good deal on where you want to get to," said the Cat. "I don't much care where—" says Alice. "Then it doesn't matter which way you go," replied the Cat.

—LEWIS CARROLL

Someone once pointed out to me that in terms of God there are only two options: we either say, "My will be done" or "Thy will be done." "Herein lies the healing of our confusion," Frank Buchman says, "make God the final authority! Not merely to say that with our lips, but with the discipline of the heart." Humility and docile acceptance of God's will are the essentials. We must give our wills to Him so He can make them His.

Those who do not want His way will miss it, but the one who is "firmly settled upon this, 'Whatever God wants, God helping me I will do it,' will not be left in doubt as to what God does wish him to do" (Alexander McLaren).

Jesus said, "The eye is the lamp of the body. If your eyes are good [focused on God], your whole body will be full of light. But if your eyes are bad [unfocused or trying to focus on more than one object], your whole body will be full of darkness. If then the light within you is darkness, how great is that darkness! (Matthew 6:22–23). If we want God and any other god we will always be in the dark, but if we fix our eyes on our Lord He will shed light on our way.

The wise man says, "Trust in the LORD with all your heart and lean not on your own understanding; in all your ways acknowledge him, and he will direct your paths (Proverbs 3:5–6). The question is always this: Do we want God's way? If so, He will direct our paths. The main thing is to want Him in all that we do and to entrust ourselves to His goodness every day—present ourselves before His face in humble submission—and leave the consequences to Him.

God's Word . . .

God has given His Word as our guide. As we read it He whispers His secrets into our ears; He "confides in those who fear him" (Psalm 25:14).

As we fill our minds with His thoughts we learn to discern good and evil; we learn to distinguish between the worthless and the worthwhile, the admirable and the ignoble. His Word enables us to make our way through life and to avoid the land mines. It gives us practical wisdom, it makes us street smart. We do well to saturate our minds with this erudition.

> We need minds so soaked with the content of Scripture, so imbued with biblical outlooks and principles, so sensitive to the Holy Spirit's prompting that we will know instinctively the upright step to take in any circumstances, small or great. Therefore the most important use of Scripture in relation to guidance is that through the study of it you may become acquainted with the ways and thoughts of God.
>
> —JOHN WHITE

Once, when Jesus was on His way to Jerusalem, His disciples took exception to His course: "Don't you know," they said, "they're planning to kill you there?" Their implication was that Jesus' judgment was flawed.

Jesus answered them with a question: "Are there not twelve hours of daylight? A man who walks by day will not stumble, for he sees by this world's light. It is when he walks by night that he stumbles, for he has no light" (John 11:9). His point was simply this: If God's Word is a lamp to our feet we will not wander too far from His way. We know in part and will surely err from time to time, but we will not make any ruinous mistakes—nothing that will impair the ultimate good of knowing God and enjoying Him.

The small stuff . . .

But what of the morally neutral decisions, the so-called small stuff of life: what we will eat or drink and what we will wear? We have little ground for uneasiness here. Unknown to us, God's compelling hand is behind every decision we make and everything we do. He cares about the bits and pieces of our days, and He arranged everything to suit Himself.

Our path is His business not ours. Our business is to trust Him with all our hearts and to refuse to rely on our own understanding. Certainly we must plan and prepare, but we must hold our schemes and dreams loosely, giving God the right to revise them or replace them without our approval or knowledge, permitting Him to advise us, correct us, inspire us, and prompt us, knowing that His compelling hand is directing everything we do.

Trusting Him to lead us means that we'll often be over our heads and out of control, living with uncertainty, giving up the security of our own plans, existing in a world where our confidence in God's goodness and love is the only sure thing.

Henri Nouwen writes, "The movement from illusion [the illusion that we are in control] to dependence is hard to make since it leads us from false certainties to true uncertainties, from an easy support system to a risky surrender, and from many 'safe' gods to the God whose love has no limits."

How true this is! To depend solely on God takes a special kind of humility on our part that admits that we cannot control the circumstances of our lives, that we do not have the answers to the hard questions of our existence, and that we are powerless to effect any eternal results. All we can do is trust our Shepherd's wisdom and love, and follow Him wherever He leads. But if we follow Him He will quietly, unobtrusively, direct our paths.

But we say, "How will I know what to do?"

I cannot tell you how. All I know is that when the time comes to know, we know. "He will help you," George MacDonald assures us, "Do not fear the 'how.' "

If we're uncertain, we should not hurry to decide what to do. We should rather wait—wait before God in silence and faith. He will speak; He is more willing to speak than we are to listen. He is, in fact, already speaking. It's only necessary to listen.

And so, as we make our way through life, we pray, as David prayed, "Show me your ways, O LORD, teach me your paths; guide me in your truth and teach me, for you are God my Savior, and my hope is in you all day long" (Psalm 25:4–5).

> *He's helping now—this moment,*
> > *Though I may not see it or hear,*
> *Perhaps by a friend far distant,*
> > *Perhaps by a stranger near,*
> *Perhaps by a spoken message,*
> > *Perhaps by the printed word;*
> *In ways that I know and know not*
> > *I have the help of the Lord.*
>
> *He's keeping me now—this moment,*
> > *However I need it most,*
> *Perhaps by a single angel,*
> > *Perhaps by a mighty host,*

Perhaps by the chain that frets me,
  Or the walls that shut me in;
In ways that I know or know not
He keeps me from harm and sin.

He's guiding me now—this moment,
  In pathways easy or hard,
Perhaps by a door wide open,
  Perhaps by a door fast barred,
Perhaps by a joy withholden,
  Perhaps by a gladness given;
In ways that I know and know not,
  He's leading me up to heaven.

He's using me now—this moment,
  And whether I go or stand,
Perhaps by a plan accomplished,
  Perhaps when he stays my hand,
Perhaps by a word in season,
  Perhaps by a silent prayer;
In ways that I know and know not,
  His labor of love I share.

—ANNIE JOHNSON FLINT

I will dwell in the house of the LORD forever . . .

Is any promise sweeter in all our Father's Word?
"I will dwell forever in the house of the Lord."

—ANNIE JOHNSON FLINT

There's a natural watershed in our lives. We reach the top, stand for a moment, and then we're over the hill. Everything is downhill from that moment on. But no matter; we're headed for home.

> *Home from those wayward wanderings,*
> *Home from that cold foreign clime,*
> *Home, to the arms of "Our Father,"*
> *Where I am all His and He's mine.*
>
> **—OSWALD CHAMBERS**

Home—that's where my heart is.

"I have come home at last!" shouted C. S. Lewis's heaven-struck unicorn as he stamped his right fore-hoof on the ground. "I have come home at last! This is my real country! I belong here. This is the land I have been looking for all my life, though I never knew it till now. The reason why we loved the old Narnia is that it sometimes looked a little like this."

It's not that heaven is somewhat like home. It *is* home. Our earthly homes are mere signs or reflections—primitive symbols of warmth, love, togetherness, and familiarity. The ultimate reality is our Father's house—where there is a father who never dies, who makes a home for the lonely, who treats us like family; where real love awaits us; where we're included—"taken in."

We hear about Odysseus, the Flying Dutchman, Frodo, and E.T., and we too want to go home—to that place where everything is impervious to change, where God will wipe every tear from our eyes, where we can cease "to break our wings against the faultiness of things," where everyone has a friend, where love will never end, where everything finally works out for good.

Everything goes wrong here; nothing will go wrong there. Nothing will be lost; nothing will be missing; nothing will fall apart or go down the drain. Heaven is God's answer to Murphy's Law.

Not all our hurts can be healed in this life. There are wounds we will bear all our lives, but, as a friend once said to me, "If you hold your wounds up to the sunlight of God's love they will never fester and in heaven they will be healed." Some harm awaits heaven's cure. That's where that "great bleeding wound from which all of us suffer will be eternally healed" (C. S. Lewis).

In this life we're delivered from shame, guilt, and fear by God's forgiving love; there is substantial improvement, but there's no complete healing. We were born with broken hearts, and some sense of that brokenness will be with us throughout our days on earth. We'll never quite be whole. There will always be some measure of inner pain that will coexist with our joy and peace, some vague longing—homesickness—that will linger until we get home. We are satisfied here, but never quite content.

One of these days we'll go home and then everything will be complete. Think of a place where there is no sin, no sorrow, no quarrels, no threats, no abandonment, no insecurity, no struggling with sagging self-worth. Heaven is where everything that makes us sad will be banished. We will be delivered from everything that has defiled or disrupted our lives.

It's disturbing to look ahead and see the same impossible road stretching out in front of us, going on indefinitely. We're driven to despair or rebellion when we think there's no point to our misery and no end to it. That's why we find comfort in the realization that it will *not* go on forever. One day, everything that God has been doing will be done. He will come for us and we will go home.

It may surprise you to know that David knew that much about heaven. Most folks who read the Old Testament never think to look for heaven there, but it occurs—in symbol and song, in metaphor and type. Ancient people took to analogy much better than we. They drew pictures: green pastures, Elysian fields, light. One of the most convincing images is that of God Himself taking us in.

The thought occurs in the story of Enoch, who walked with God for three hundred years and "then he was no more, because God took him away" (Genesis 5:24). Enoch and God took a walk one day and got too far from home. The old patriarch was too weary to walk all the way back so God took him.

One of Israel's singers saw himself and others as "destined for the grave," but as he goes on to say, "God will redeem my life from the grave; he will surely take me to himself" (Psalm 49:14–15).

And then there's the poet who learned God's presence from his peril: "I am always with you," he concluded. For now, "you hold me by my right hand. You guide me with your counsel, and afterward you will take me into glory" (Psalm 73:23–24).

Taken in. I like that way of looking at my death. It reminds me of something Jesus said: "I am going . . . to prepare a place for you. And if I go and prepare a place for you, I will come back and take you to be with me that you also may be where I am" (John 14:2–3).

That's the fundamental revelation of heaven in both Testaments: being taken in, welcomed, received, embraced, included. Death for God's children is not bitter frustration, but mere transition into a larger and permanent love—a love undisturbed by time, unmenaced by evil, unbroken by fear, unclouded by doubt.

All God's idylls end favorably; all God's children live happily forever after. That's the most cherished article of my creed.

> Never again will they hunger;
>   never again will they thirst.
> The sun will not beat upon them,
>   nor any scorching heat.
> For the Lamb at the center of the throne
>   will be their shepherd;
>   he will lead them to springs of living water.
> And God will wipe away
>   every tear from their eyes.

—REVELATION 7:16–17

NOTE TO THE READER

The publisher invites you to share your response to the message of this book by writing Discovery House Publishers, Box 3566, Grand Rapids, MI 49501, USA. For information about other Discovery House books, music, or videos, contact us at the same address or call 1-800-653-8333. Find us on the Internet at http://www.dhp.org/ or send e-mail to books@dhp.org.

"WHAT *THE EXORCIST* WAS TO CATHOLICISM *THE TRIBE* IS TO JUDAISM. THIS TERRIFYING TALE OF CABALISTIC MYSTICISM AND MAGIC WILL HOLD YOU SHIVERINGLY SPELLBOUND.

"The writing is clear and compelling, the dialogue is dramatic, the characters are captivating and the plot is suspenseful. What is the mysterious link between the Belzec concentration camp Jewish captives miraculously found alive and well-fed in their powdery gray clay coated barracks and the five teenagers who, 35 years later, after murdering a Rabbi's son, are found hideously murdered in a powdery gray clay-coated clubhouse? The author will have you furiously flipping pages to find the fascinating and frightening answer. . . .

"This story has all the excitement of a murder mystery and all of the terror of a tale of horror. The author, whose previous bestsellers include *The Killing Gift* and *Twins,* has written another successful supernatural saga—and secured her place among suspense storytellers."

—*Los Angeles Herald Examiner*

THE TRIBE

A complex, shocking novel of compelling suspense and unspeakable horror!

Recommended Reading from SIGNET

☐ **THE KILLING GIFT by Bari Wood.** (#E9885—$3.50)
☐ **TWINS by Bari Wood & Jack Greasland.** (#E9886—$3.50)
☐ **A GARDEN OF SAND by Earl Thompson.** (#E9374—$2.95)
☐ **TATTOO by Earl Thompson.** (#E8989—$2.95)
☐ **CALDO LARGO by Earl Thompson.** (#E7737—$2.25)
☐ **THE WORLD FROM ROUGH STONES by Malcolm Macdonald.**
(#E9639—$2.95)
☐ **THE RICH ARE WITH YOU ALWAYS by Malcolm Macdonald.**
(#E7682—$2.25)
☐ **SONS OF FORTUNE by Malcolm Macdonald.**
(#E8595—$2.75)*
☐ **THE EBONY TOWER by John Fowles.** (#E9653—$2.95)
☐ **DANIEL MARTIN by John Fowles.** (#E8249—$2.95)
☐ **COMA by Robin Cook.** (#E9756—$2.75)
☐ **THE CRAZY LADIES by Joyce Elbert.** (#E8923—$2.75)
☐ **THE FINAL FIRE by Dennis Smith.** (#J7141—$1.95)
☐ **SOME KIND OF HERO by James Kirkwood.** (#E9850—$2.75)
☐ **KINFLICKS by Lisa Alther.** (#E9474—$2.95)

*Price slightly higher in Canada

Buy them at your local bookstore or use this convenient coupon for ordering.

THE NEW AMERICAN LIBRARY, INC.,
P.O. Box 999, Bergenfield, New Jersey 07621

Please send me the books I have checked above. I am enclosing $_____
(please add $1.00 to this order to cover postage and handling). Send check
or money order—no cash or C.O.D.'s. Prices and numbers are subject to change
without notice.

Name_____

Address_____

City _____ State _____ Zip Code _____
Allow 4-6 weeks for delivery.
This offer is subject to withdrawal without notice.

THE TRIBE

BARI WOOD

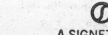

A SIGNET BOOK

NEW AMERICAN LIBRARY

TIMES MIRROR

NAL BOOKS ARE AVAILABLE AT QUANTITY DISCOUNTS
WHEN USED TO PROMOTE PRODUCTS OR SERVICES. FOR
INFORMATION PLEASE WRITE TO PREMIUM MARKETING DIVISION,
THE NEW AMERICAN LIBRARY, INC., 1633 BROADWAY,
NEW YORK, NEW YORK 10019.

Copyright © 1981 by Bari Wood

All rights reserved. A hardcover edition of *The Tribe* was
published by The New American Library, Inc., and simultaneously
in Canada by The New American Library of Canada Limited.

SIGNET TRADEMARK REG. U.S. PAT. OFF. AND FOREIGN COUNTRIES
REGISTERED TRADEMARK—MARCA REGISTRADA
HECHO EN CHICAGO, U.S.A.

SIGNET, SIGNET CLASSICS, MENTOR, PLUME, MERIDIAN AND NAL
BOOKS are published by The New American Library, Inc.,
1633 Broadway, New York, New York 10019

First Signet Printing, November, 1981

1   2   3   4   5   6   7   8   9

PRINTED IN THE UNITED STATES OF AMERICA

PUBLISHER'S NOTE

This novel is a work of fiction. Names, characters, places, and incidents are either the product of the author's imagination or are used fictitiously, and any resemblance to actual persons, living or dead, events, or locales is entirely coincidental.

To Israel and Gertrude,
my father and mother

I want to thank four people:

Geraldine Hawkins who died in 1977,
Samy Gay of the Brooklyn Police Department,
Ned Leavitt, and Louis Sica.
I couldn't have written this book without their help.

Black Striga
        black on black
who eats black blood
        and drinks it
like an ox she billows
like a bear she growls
like a wolf she crushes.

—Charm against Lilith
(14th Century)

THE
TRIBE

"WHY ARE you here?" Abrams asked.

"General Pearce ordered me to see you, I'm seeing you," Bianco said. He peeled tinfoil off the insides of a cigarette pack.

"Major, Major," Abrams scolded softly, "I meant why are you in Nuremberg?"

"Because I'm in the Army," Bianco said. He concentrated on rolling the tinfoil into a ball.

"You can be in the Army at Bragg, Jeffersonville, Tacoma ... why Nuremberg?"

He turned in his chair and looked out of the open window. The breeze that came in was hot and full of stone dust from the rubble that still covered the city. A mansion had stood on the lot next door; wrought-iron gates showed through dust and broken columns.

"You were supposed to go home in January, Lou," Abrams said. "It's July. That's seven months in this hole that you didn't have to spend."

Bianco rolled that last of the tinfoil and held up the ball.

"For the war effort," he said.

"The war's over," Abrams said.

"So it is." Bianco pitched the ball into the wastebasket.

3

"Then why are you still here?"

"Pearce told you, didn't he?"

"Pearce says you're waiting for them to capture Johann Speiser," Abrams said.

"With his permission," Bianco said.

"He thought you meant a couple of weeks, not seven months."

Bianco didn't say anything.

"What did you do here for seven months?" Abrams asked.

Bianco shrugged. "Memorized *Gone with the Wind*, screwed whores, went to the movies."

"And to the trials?"

"At first," Bianco said.

Abrams leaned across the desk. "How'd you feel?"

It wasn't a trick question, Bianco realized, Abrams really wanted to know.

"I felt sorry for them," Bianco said.

"Me too," Abrams said softly. "They were just shaky men whose clothes didn't fit . . ." He trailed off, and lit a cigarette. After a moment he said, "You opened Belzec, didn't you?"

"It's in the file, Doctor."

Shouts came through the open window; they heard glass breaking somewhere.

Abrams said, "Speiser was commandant of Belzec, right?" No answer from Bianco. "That's why you're waiting for him, isn't it, Major. For what he did at Belzec." His voice got very gentle. "Look, Lou," he said, "if we capture Speiser, we'll hang him. If no one gets him, he spends the rest of his life rotting in a Brazilian jungle. What can you do to him that'll be worse than that?"

"I don't want to do anything to him. I want to ask him a question."

4

"You waited seven months to ask a question?"

"I guess I did," Bianco said.

"What question?"

Bianco didn't answer. The office was quiet in the heat; the breeze stopped and the stone dust in the air settled, leaving another layer of powder over everything. Bianco lit a cigarette. The smoke didn't move and he looked at Abrams through it.

"What question?" Abrams asked again.

"You're a psychiatrist, right?"

Abrams nodded.

"So Pearce can't order you to tell him what I say."

"He can, but I don't have to obey."

"Will you?" Bianco asked.

"Not if you don't want me to."

Bianco sat back. "I don't."

Then he said, "Okay, I'll tell you. I want to tell someone. But it's not what you think. It's not because of the lime pits and ovens. As bad as that was, we were used to it by the time we got to Belzec. No, not used . . . I'm still not used to it. But that's not why I'm here. It's something else. A feeling I got there . . ."

"I'm supposed to be able to deal with feelings," Abrams said.

"Sure, sure." Bianco paused, then said, "I don't know how to start . . ."

Abrams leaned over and opened a metal cabinet next to his big carved-oak desk and took out a bottle of whisky and two paper cups.

"A little schnaps'll make talking easier," he said, and he poured two stiff shots and gave one to Bianco. Bianco sipped. It was good stuff and went down smoothly—the spoils of war, he thought. He took another sip, then drank it down at once and waited for it to settle the

5

shaky feeling he had most of the time. The wind came up again, riffled papers on Abrams's desk, then died, and everything was quiet.

"We got to Belzec in April," Bianco said quietly. "April ninth, just as the snow was melting." He held out the cup, and Abrams refilled it. "The weather was crazy then. It would rain, then the sun would come out, then it would rain again. Little squalls like that all day long. It was warm for April, but there was still a crust of ice on the ground, and our boots broke it and sank in the mud, so we had to go slowly, staggering from barracks to barracks, following the food trucks and medics. There was an English squad with us and their major was an aristocrat of some kind. Named Reynolds. One of those thin-nosed Englishmen who looks like everything smells bad. Only there it did. Awful. And Reynolds had this silver flask with him and he'd take a sip, then hand it to me, and when we finished it, he'd send his sergeant back to the truck to fill it up again. I can see that flask clearer than I can see Reynolds's face. It was silver, and it had vines and flowers carved on it; and the guy's initials, and some kind of crest . . ." Bianco stopped, then smiled. The skin around his narrow light brown eyes was dark, and he was too thin, but the smile was attractive and made him look younger. "I'm not here to describe English heirloom silver, am I?" he said.

"No," Abrams said gently.

"The point is, I looked at the flask so I wouldn't look at what was all around us. We drank, and checked lists to keep from looking at it. Ah, the lists . . ." Bianco finished his third whisky, and Abrams poured another.

"The Krauts kept lists of everything. Who the prisoners were, where they came from, when they died. Lists of kapos, and the Jews who wouldn't be kapos. Lists of the supplies that came in and of the stuff that went out.

6

... That was some list, that was." He leaned forward, holding his cup. "Clothes, money, jewels, gold by the ounce, from their teeth, Captain. But you know that. They cut the women's hair, weighed it, put it on a list, and sent it home to stuff mattresses ..."

Bianco's voice had gotten shaky, and he stopped. Abrams was quiet, and after a moment, Bianco went on.

"By noon, we'd checked the dead and dying in Barracks 552, and went on to 554 ... pretty drunk by then. Staggering in the mud with the wind blowing rain off the pine needles. I remember I had to keep wiping my glasses. We stopped in front of 554, swigged some more, then pushed open the door. It was pretty dark at first, so I couldn't see who was there and who wasn't. Then the sun came out, lit the place up, and two little boys ran to us ... *ran* ... and yelled 'Welcome, Americans!' in English. I realized then that the place didn't smell. I mean it did, but only of mud and wet wood. So I thought they were long dead and gone, except for the kids. Then I saw them. Thirty-five of them standing next to their bunks in a line, like soldiers at inspection. We all stared at each other for a long time. They had hair, and teeth. Oh, they were thin, but not starving. And pale, but winter pale, not the color of starvation.

"Then one little man left the lineup and came up the aisle. He had dark hair, with a beard, and a little cap on his head. Tears ran down his face and he held out his hand to me, and said, 'My name is Jacob Levy. Thank you for coming,' in English. I didn't want to touch him; the prisoners were covered with lice and there'd been typhus in the camp. But I took his hand. I couldn't help it—something about the man—and I started to say something, I don't know what; 'you're welcome' maybe. But all at once *I* started crying. Then Reynolds shook hands with him, and he cried. Christ, what a scene. They all

7

came toward us then, all in tears, but all smiling; and me and Reynolds and the little guy stood at the door like hostesses at a wedding, and shook hands with those ghostly-looking men as they went out into the open air. They hugged the little guy, and he was the last one to leave. Just before he did, he looked back at the place, and I watched his face. But it was blank, except for the tears. I couldn't tell what he was thinking. Then he followed the others outside as one of the transport vans pulled in through the mud.

"I know I was drunk. But even so, I knew it was nuts for thirty-five men, all from one village . . . they were, you know . . . one village . . . to be alive, and well. So I stayed there to look around. I didn't expect to find anything but I looked anyway. I walked down the aisle between the bunks with the sun going and coming, and at the back wall, behind the bunks, I found this pile of sealed cartons. I ripped one open, and found the answer."

Bianco paused, and Abrams leaned forward.

"They were full of cans of food," Bianco said. "Cans and cans. Beans and figs, fish, and some kind of meat paste. *Meat*, Doctor. In Belzec in 1945. They were from Poland, Germany, Latvia, and I picked them up and looked at them like I'd never seen a can before. I tore open the other cartons and found more food, enough to feed a platoon. I sat there on my haunches, a little dazed and trying to figure where they got the stuff. Who they murdered or bribed. Then I saw some gray stuff on the wall in front of me; and I stood up to look closer at it. It was faint, but there all right, and I touched it gingerly because it could have been any kind of crap. It was powdery, and it came off on my fingers. I looked around and saw that it was everywhere. You just had to look for it. It was under the windows, embedded in the wood grain of the wall and floor. Everywhere. The sun had stayed out, the barracks was getting hot, and I started to sweat. But not just from booze and sun. There was something about the place all of a sudden. About those cans of food, and that gray stuff all over. I didn't like having it on me for some reason, so I bent down and ran my fingers against the floor to get it off. But more got on me from the floorboards, and I was really getting spooked. Then I heard something behind me and I pulled my gun. I don't know what I thought I'd see, but there was this hazy figure in a dusty beam of sunlight, and I was so shaky I almost fired at it; but it was the little Jew. He stepped out of the sun and looked at me, then at the torn-open boxes.

"I said, 'I found this food.' And he nodded and said something in German. I don't know what. Then I said, 'Where'd it come from?' and he smiled at me—the sweetest, gentlest smile I've ever seen—and he said in broken English that it came from God.

"I wanted to tell him that I couldn't believe that. God wasn't at Belzec that I could see, and I wanted to ask him about the gray stuff on the walls and bunk sides, but he shook his head, and, like a magician doing a trick, he stepped back into the sunlight. I yelled at him to stop, but he didn't answer. Then I ran after him, but the place was empty. I just stood there for a second, all alone with the cans of food, and that dried mud or whatever it was. I meant to go back and make one more list of what I'd found. I even turned around to do it; but I couldn't. I couldn't. Don't ask me why, that's part of what I have to ask Speiser. Something in there scared the shit out of me, and after a minute or two, sweating and shaking, I gave up and left the place.

"The van was gone by then, but I wasn't worried. They were taking the healthy ones to DP camps, and I thought they'd be there for days yet and I could question

9

them in the morning. But Resistance Jews had started hijacking the trucks and helping the refugees get to Palestine; or as close to Palestine as they could. And they got that truck and all the men on it."

Bianco put the paper cup down, "I don't know where they are now. Or if they're anywhere."

Abrams stared at Bianco for a moment without saying anything, then he asked, "Is that it?"

Bianco nodded.

"Cans of food," Abrams said, "and gray dust on a wall? That's what you want to ask Speiser about?"

"Yes," Bianco said.

"You waited seven months in Nuremberg, away from your wife, kids, home, to ask about shit like that? And a spooky feeling that grabbed you after you'd had a couple of flasks of whisky?"

"I know it sounds lame."

"Lame isn't the word. Speiser probably won't even know what you're talking about."

"He will though. He requisitioned that food . . . he forged the papers to get it, and we thought it was for him and his brass. But all we found in their mess was moldy potatoes."

Abrams opened Bianco's file and started writing. "I'm asking Pearce to send you home, Major."

Bianco jumped up. "You can't do that. If you send me home now, I'll never find out. . . ."

Abrams went on writing.

Bianco said, "Listen to me, for Christ's sake; just listen." He pulled a folded piece of paper out of his pocket and shoved it in front of Abrams. It was a list of names arranged in alphabetical order:

ALLDMANN, DABROWA, POLAND
DWORKIN, DABROWA, POLAND

FELDSHER, DABROWA, POLAND
FINEMAN, DABROWA, POLAND
GERSHON, DABROWA, POLAND

The list went on down the page.

"Thirty-five of them," Bianco said, "all from that one village. Some were old, two were little kids. All transported in 1941, and all alive. Why? And not just alive. Fed! That was a death camp, Captain. They were killing them day and night at the end. Thousands of 'em. But not these men. These men they fed when they were starving themselves. Thirty-five Jews ate applesauce and canned fish while the SS ate garbage. Why?"

General Pearce closed Bianco's folder. "Captain Abrams says I should send you home, Major. I'm sending you home."

"I thought we had an agreement," Bianco said.

"We did," Pearce said. "I'm breaking it."

"Why now . . . sir?" Bianco asked.

"You are, according to Abrams, 'at serious risk emotionally'; he recommends you go home to get treatment."

"Do you think I need treatment, General?"

Pearce didn't answer; he concentrated on folding the orders. When Bianco first saw him, he'd had a pink, tight, midwestern-looking face and the beginnings of a belly. Now his face was gray and slack, like Bianco's, and his uniform was too big. Pearce put the orders in an envelope.

"Kind of sudden, isn't it?" Bianco asked without the sir.

Pearce looked up. "There's a truck convoy leaving for Frankfurt tonight from Dürer House at nineteen hundred. Don't be late. From Frankfurt you have a lift to Kirkwall. . . ."

Bianco loved night flying, looking down at the black North Sea flecked with white foam. At Kirkwall there'd be strong tea waiting for him, oatmeal in the morning, and a view of Scapa Flow.

"From Kirkwall you catch a morning flight to Mitchell."

Mitchell was fifty miles from home. Bianco had planted hemlocks the spring he left, and juniper to edge the driveway. That was four years ago.

Pearce held the envelope out to Bianco. Bianco didn't move.

"I've been waiting for Speiser for seven months, and all I got for that were some drunken questions at the Easter dance. Now all of a sudden, I get an hour with the busiest psychiatrist in the world and orders to leave *tonight*. Why?"

Pearce said, "Take the envelope, Major."

Bianco hesitated, then took it. "You're going home, Major," Pearce said softly. "Good luck." He swiveled his chair to the side and picked up the phone. Bianco saluted and left the office carrying the envelope.

He was going home. The thought was so sudden, so full of emotion, that he had to stop and lean against the hall wall. Men passing looked curiously at him, and he pushed himself away from the wall and went into the men's room. Like everything else in Nuremberg, the toilet belonged in a palace. The commode was raised on a marble pedestal, the sink was chipped marble, shaped like a shell. He ran water and looked at himself in the gilt-framed mirror over the sink. He looked sick and old, nothing like he had the last time he saw his wife, and he wondered how she'd react to this face.

He was smoothing water through his black and gray hair when it hit him that they weren't sending him home because he'd waited longer than was sane for a man who'd never be found. They were sending him home now . . . tonight . . . because they'd caught Speiser at last, and they were afraid he'd find him and kill him before the Tribunal could hang him.

Abrams was half-drunk when Bianco tracked him to the club. They were showing *Grapes of Wrath* for the third time and a bunch of officers sat in the club lobby, drinking and waiting for the movie to start.

Abrams sat alone, threading his fingers through his beard, drinking. He looked away when he saw Bianco, but Bianco came to the table and sat down.

"They got Speiser, didn't they?"

Abrams closed his eyes. "How'd you know?"

"Just figured it out."

Abrams said thickly, "They found him in a basement, in Munich. *Munich.* You'd think he'd have gotten farther in all this time. Still, he's lucky it was us, not the Russians."

"Why?" Bianco asked. "They'd hang him higher?"

Abrams finished his drink without answering.

"Did you believe what I told you today?" Bianco asked.

"I guess so," Abrams said. "Yes, I did. Yes."

Bianco grabbed Abrams's hand; officers at nearby tables noticed and looked away, embarrassed.

"Let me see him," Bianco said, trying to keep the pleading out of his voice. "It means everything to me. If you believed me, you know I won't hurt him. Let me see him."

They looked into each other's eyes. Abrams looked away first.

"I can't . . ." he said.

Bianco squeezed his hand. "I won't have a second's peace if you don't. Not for the rest of my life." Bianco

13

was whispering, but the pleading in his voice was raw. He felt Abrams's hand go limp in his.

"You swear you won't hurt him?" he asked.

"I swear," Bianco said.

Then Abrams said, "I want to hear what he says. What those men did."

"Okay," Bianco said.

Abrams thought another minute, but Bianco knew he had him. Then Abrams said, "It's my ass if they find out."

"Do you care?"

"No," Abrams said, "I don't."

They stood up together; Abrams bought a half-pint of vodka, and they opened the bottle and drank from it as they walked through the empty ruined streets to the Tribunal. Nearby, everything was quiet, but they heard yells in the distance, and the echo of someone running in another block. It was almost nine, but still light. The long northern twilight had just started and their shadows blended with the shadows of broken walls. At the Tribunal entrance, Abrams capped the bottle and put it in his pocket. A WAC with high, pointy breasts pushing her khaki jacket sat in the hot marble reception area. She nodded at Abrams and barely looked at Bianco, and together the two men went up the curving marble staircase to the second floor.

At the top of the stairs, MPs guarded double carved-oak doors. Abrams asked if the prisoner had been fed; one of the men said he had, but hadn't eaten much. Abrams asked if the Judge Advocate's man had been there yet. He had, said the MP, and they were coming back at ten to move the prisoner. Then the MP opened the door and closed it after them.

Bianco thought the room was empty until a tall man came out of the shadows next to the windows and stood in the middle of the room looking at them. Abrams and Bianco saluted, and the man returned the salute. He looked like Bianco thought he would: thin and blond with wide-set blue eyes and white lashes. His hair was combed back from his high forehead, and a protuberant ridge in his skull made a line from his hair to his eyebrows. His nose was thin, so were his lips, but they were well formed, with a deep bow. He would have been handsome except that his skin was yellowish-white, and Bianco remembered that he'd been in hiding for six months. In a basement without sun or fresh air.

The room they'd put him in was typical Nuremberg; except for the scarred oak-paneled walls, everything in it was red—carpet, drapes, torn plush chairs. It was a deep red, almost maroon, and where the fabrics were worn, the nap was pink. The color of the room trapped the heat. Bianco's shirt stuck to his back in a second and Speiser's face shone with sweat.

"Ah, the Jewish doctor." Speiser's English was good. "I didn't expect to see you again. But I welcome visitors. This room isn't restful."

Abrams said, "This is Major Bianco."

Speiser smiled at Bianco and Bianco saw that his gums were swollen and gray, and his teeth looked loose. If he had scurvy, the Army would give him fresh oranges and massive doses of vitamin C before they hanged him. Bianco smiled back.

"And who is Major Bianco?" Speiser asked.

Abrams answered, "He commanded the American squad that opened Belzec and he has some questions to ask you."

"I'm not required . . ."

Bianco interrupted, "I'm not from the Tribunal. In fact I'm going back to the United States tonight. This is a . . . personal question."

"You don't have to answer any questions, Commandant," Abrams said quickly. "You have the same right as any prisoner in a democratic . . ."

Speiser waved at Abrams to be quiet, and he looked closely at Bianco. "Bianco's an Italian name, isn't it? Are you Italian?" he asked.

"My grandfather was," Bianco answered.

"Ah . . . so it's the grandfather who comes from that country of yellow scum that sold out the noblest army in history. . . ." He was full of life for a second; Bianco could imagine him in the gray uniform with the lightning on the lapels. Then the man sagged and lowered himself shakily into the worn plush armchair. "You hear the creaking of a corpse," he said. "I don't care where you or your grandfather came from." He turned to Abrams. "Before the major asks his question, could I have some tea, and maybe a small piece of cake? They gave me meat to eat, but I couldn't get it down. Still, I'm very hungry."

Abrams almost ran to the door. "Of course," he said. "Of course . . . in a second . . ."

He left them alone, and Bianco offered the commandant a cigarette, then lit it for him. Speiser inhaled deeply, then said, "The question is about Belzec."

"It is."

Speiser grinned, showing those ghostly gums. "I would have thought everything you found there was clear."

Staggering rage overcame Bianco. He wanted to hit Speiser in the face, to smash the cigarette against his mouth. He took a deep breath, and said as steadily as he could, "It was clear."

Abrams came back with the tea and a plate of cupcakes. They poured the tea, held their cups, and drank. Speiser put four cubes of sugar in his cup, and ate three of the cupcakes, then licked his fingers, poured another cup of tea, and sat back and said to Abrams, "Leave us alone, Captain." It was an order. Abrams looked at Bianco and Speiser said, "He won't hurt me, but I don't care if he does. Neither should you."

"But I—"

"Leave us alone, Captain."

Abrams gave up and left them.

"It's hard to discuss Belzec in the presence of a Jew," said Speiser. A fog had come up and was drifting in through the open windows. The dampness settled on their skin, made them feel itchy, and the air took on a misty look that softened the red color of the drapes and carpet. Bianco wondered if Speiser was as uncomfortable as he was. He wiped his face, and handed Speiser his list of names, looking again as he did.

LEVY, DABROWA, POLAND
LIPPMANN, DABROWA, POLAND
LURIA, DABROWA, POLAND

"Do you remember those men?" Bianco asked.

Speiser glanced at the list, started to hand it back. "There were thousands in the camp. I don't remember their names. . . ."

"These were special," Bianco said softly. "They were all in Barracks 554."

Speiser's hand held the list in midair stretched toward Bianco. Sweat rolled down the side of his face and his pale skin got whiter. After a moment, he drew the list back and looked at the names again. "Are they alive?" he asked softly.

"They were when we opened the camp. Alive and well, alive and fed in a death camp—old men, children—with the gas and ovens going day and night . . . but they all survived . . ."

"Not all," Speiser said mildly. "Three of them died in 1941."

Bianco sat back. "You remember."

"Of course," Speiser said, then he laughed. "Don't look so tense, Major. I remember, and I'm going to tell you all about how those men stayed alive." Here Speiser's smile changed; his eyes shone and Bianco had a sudden impulse to follow Abrams out the door. Speiser leaned forward so his face was close to Bianco's. Bianco looked down at his hands, then folded them like a little girl at communion, and waited. Nothing happened and he looked up again. Speiser was still smiling. He deliberately reached out and put one of his hands over Bianco's with a gentle touch such as he might give a woman.

"But I'm warning you, Major, you don't want to hear it. Go after the Jew; get drunk together, find a woman, go home. Do anything but stay here and listen to me."

"I want to hear," Bianco said. He sounded stubborn and silly to himself, like a child. He looked up at Speiser, and Speiser patted his hand.

"Good," Speiser said. "Very good, because I want so much to tell you. But I did warn you, didn't I? So my conscience is clear."

Bianco laughed at that before he could stop himself. Speiser laughed, too, then he stopped and drank down the rest of his tea. Bianco leaned forward and Speiser put the cup down.

"You're very anxious, Major."

"I've been waiting a long time," Bianco said.

"The waiting's over," Speiser said quietly, then in the same soft voice he started to tell Bianco what had happened in Barracks 554. It was a long story, he told it well, and after a while, Bianco forgot to smoke, forgot to give Speiser cigarettes, forgot everything but what the other

18

man was telling him. They laughed again later, crazy, joyless laughter that they couldn't control, and Speiser grabbed Bianco's arm, and Bianco tried to break free and he saw their wrestling shadows on the oak paneling, which made him laugh harder. Still later, Speiser spilled his tea, which they let run across the scarred table and drip on the red rug.

When Speiser stopped talking, Bianco stayed in a listening posture with his head to the side for a few minutes, then without a word he stood up, put the pack of cigarettes on the table, and went to the door.

"Aren't you going to thank me?" Speiser asked from his chair.

Bianco opened the door and the MPs stationed on either side came to attention. Behind him Speiser called, "Don't forget I warned you. Don't forget they'll live for years. . . ." Bianco slammed the door and took the stairs two at a time. But no matter how fast he ran away from that room, he thought he could hear Speiser's voice coming from behind the heavy carved doors, "Alive somewhere . . . Palestine . . . America . . . somewhere . . ."

Abrams was in the lobby with the bottle, and right there, surrounded by inlays of green and rose marble, with the big-busted blond WAC frowning at them from behind the receptionist's desk, he opened it and handed it to Bianco.

"What'd he say?" he asked Bianco. Bianco took a swallow, handed the bottle back, and walked out onto the street. Abrams followed.

"What'd he say?" he asked again. "Why did he feed them?"

"He doesn't know why he did anything," Bianco answered. "He's crazy."

He left Abrams and hurried up the street toward

Dürer House. He had six minutes to make the convoy. Abrams stood uncertainly on the Tribunal steps, then, clutching the bottle, he ran after Bianco. He caught up at the corner, but Bianco didn't stop. The city was fogging up from the heat, the stone felt warm under their feet.

"He's not crazy." Abrams was out of breath. "Sick, scared, but not crazy." Bianco ignored him and kept going. Abrams got a pain in his side and had to stop for a second, then he ran on, but by the time he caught up again, they were at the convoy. The headlights of the thirty or so trucks coming through the fog blinded Abrams and he thought he'd lost Bianco; then he saw him handing his orders to the convoy leader. Abrams wasn't usually persistent, and even though he was drunk, he felt shy about asking Bianco again. But when Bianco got his orders back from the captain and started down the line of trucks, Abrams grabbed the other man's arm. Bianco pulled away and swung up on his seat next to the driver.

"I know he's not irrational," Abrams shouted, but just then the motors started up. The roar was deafening, and Bianco shook his head to show that he couldn't hear over the noise.

Four months later, the day after his first Thanksgiving home, Bianco and his brother David decorated their variety store for Christmas. They packed away the cardboard turkeys and plastic souvenir whales; they wrapped silver demitasse spoons with "Craig Harbor, L.I." enameled on them, and packed them in a box with sateen gold-fringed flags and pillows that also said Craig Harbor. They took orange and gold paper leaves out of the windows, and put paper holly in their place; they put long-sleeved blouses on the half-forms in the windows, and on the display racks inside the store they hung plaid mufflers, ruffled aprons, and ties that said Merry Christmas. They put ribbon and wrapping and cards in the bins and put away the hunting boots and work shoes. They brought out boxes of costume jewelry and arranged it—pins, rings, bracelets, and earrings—on green velvet.

Before the war, Bianco had enjoyed the decorating, and had done most of it himself. He'd liked the sense of order it gave him, and he'd found that he was even a little fussy. Now it annoyed him. The jewelry seemed too small for his hands to manage. His cuff caught in the gold-filled chains and pulled them off the velvet, and he gave up, left the jewelry arranging to his brother, and went down to the basement to get the toilet water and cologne they'd ordered for the season. He tried to carry too much and he dropped a seven-dollar bottle of Prince Matchabelli's Duchess of York cologne. It smashed on the cement floor and, as the heavy sweet smell of the stuff filled the basement, he had an impulse to smash the rest of the bottles against the furnace.

He cleaned up the mess and they finished the windows and displays, then unwrapped the cellophane Christmas tree they'd been using for years. The transparent needles were limp and torn; the decorations brightened it up some, but it was still a dismal-looking thing. They hung scallops of tarnished tinsel across the ceiling, and he and David stood back to admire the effect.

Bianco thought the place had looked better before they decorated it and that his brother was acting like an old maid. He longed for his clean spare quarters at Camp Lee and the sense of doing things that mattered.

"Let's get out of here," he said to his brother.

They locked the front door and drove home.

A green Packard was parked in front of the garage, the

living room lights were on, and when he opened the door, he heard Captain Abrams's voice. He was telling June that German pastries were wonderful. Bianco closed the door quietly, and stood in the living room entrance to the side so Abrams couldn't see him.

"Puff pastry filled with cream," Abrams was saying, "covered with chocolate and nuts."

"Bullshit," Bianco cried. "There wasn't an ounce of cream left in Germany." Abrams laughed and they shook hands.

"What was I going to talk about?" Abrams said shyly. June said something about dinner and left them alone. He hadn't been Abrams's friend, they barely knew each other, but Bianco was enormously glad to see him. They examined each other, openly, kindly. Bianco realized that Abrams was dressed to go with a Packard, in the new look, with narrow shoulders and lapels and thin-legged trousers. He looked taller than Bianco remembered, much handsomer; and Bianco wished he had something better on than his old hunting jacket and plaid shirt, he wished he was in uniform. During dinner he admitted it to Abrams and Abrams said he'd only been back a week and hadn't had a chance to miss being a captain yet. Over dessert, coffee, and whisky, he told Bianco that Pearce's diverticulitis got so bad they sent him home. He also told him that the trials were more unpopular than ever and they were even having trouble finding judges. Finally, after they took the bottle of whisky into the living room to sit in front of the fire, and June had said good night and gone upstairs, Abrams told Bianco that Speiser had been tried in August, found guilty, and hanged at Spandau two weeks ago.

"That's why I'm here in a way. I saw him the day they hanged him; he asked me if I would ever see you again and I said I might, and he said, 'Tell the major not to forget that the men from 554 were still alive.' "

As soon as Abrams said that, Bianco felt a grim, perverse satisfaction. The store, the Christmas tree, the decorations were a lot of fussy shit; the peace and sense of belonging they were supposed to give was specious. Somehow, and for all time, Bianco thought, Speiser had had the last word.

Roger Hawkins

Chapter
1

ADAM LEVY stopped at the top of the subway stairs. It was dark, the street was empty, and Adam was a little scared. He'd been in Minnesota for four years, teaching philosophy at a small college on the edge of the northern wilderness, and he had to get used to Brooklyn and the neighborhood all over again.

His father still lived on the next block; his father's shul, where Adam had been bar mitzvahed and married, was still on the corner of Nostrand, but most of the people he'd known were gone, and the ones who'd taken their place spoke Spanish, let their children rove the streets in gangs, and had turned the once neat street into a slummy-looking block with litter in the gutters and ranks of broken-down cars lining the curbs. Still, he told himself as he looked up the long empty block, they belonged here as much as he did.

He clutched his book and briefcase, came out of the shadow of the subway kiosk, and walked up the street.

It was hot for September, and dry. The leaves were falling early and a hot wind came up and blew grit in his face and mouth; paper sailed up out of the gutter and clung to his legs. He pulled it away and kept walking. If he looked up at the nice old graystones instead of down

27

at the mess, the street was still pretty, he thought. He was next to the old Shapiro house when he noticed three boys—sixteen or seventeen—keeping pace with him across the street. They glanced quickly at him, then looked away. He walked faster, they did too; then he slowed down and so did they. He thought he heard one of them giggle, and his heart started racing. He stopped and pretended to study the front of one of the houses, and when he looked again, they had crossed the street and were standing across the sidewalk between him and the lights on Nostrand half a block away.

They came toward him, walking in step; they were grinning, and still clutching his briefcase and book, he turned to run back to the protection of the subway. But there were two more boys behind him, blocking his way. He froze and all five advanced on him and circled him like children playing Hi Ho the Merrio, with Adam as the cheese.

One boy broke the circle and came close to Adam. He had his hand out away from his body and Adam saw he had an open knife in it. He was a handsome boy, with black, wavy hair, blue eyes, and a silky mustache just starting to grow. But he was very thin, and Adam thought desperately, *They're hungry, that's all, just hungry kids.* They'd take his money, about thirty dollars, then they'd run away to buy food with it.

The blue-eyed boy half crouched like a knife fighter in a movie. "Turn 'em out, Jew," he said.

Adam didn't know what he meant, and he didn't move.

"The pockets, Jew. Turn 'em out."

Adam turned his pockets inside out. Change spilled and rolled, but the boys didn't bother with it. His keys fell and his handkerchief fluttered to the sidewalk. One boy stepped closer to Adam and pulled his jacket open. He felt in the inside pocket, then snapped his knife open and, looking into Adam's eyes, he slashed the jacket lining and outside pockets.

"The watch," said blue-eyes.

Adam gave them the watch, and they passed it around. Then one said, "He's got a ring."

His wedding ring. On the verge of tears, Adam tried to pull it off his finger, but it stuck. Blue-eyes waved the knife and Adam said hoarsely, "I'll get it off." He managed to raise enough saliva to wet his finger and pull the ring free. They passed that around too. Then blue-eyes opened the briefcase. He found Adam's bottle of Allerest and pitched it away down the street. Then he turned the case over and the books and papers spilled around them on the sidewalk and into the gutter. The boy bent the top of the case back until the hinges broke and it flopped loose, then he threw it down and picked up the book. It was called *Objectivity: New Essays on Epistemology.* Adam had been going to assign it for a seminar he was leading. Blue-eyes showed it to the other boys, but they didn't react, and he slashed the spine, and tore off the book's covers.

"That it?" he said to Adam.

For some reason, their brutality made Adam calmer; he looked into the boy's eyes, which seemed to glow with hatred.

"Thirty lousy dollars and a two-bit watch. Is that all, Jew?"

"I'm afraid it is," Adam said quietly. He kept looking at the boy, and that must have annoyed him, because he raised his hand and hit Adam in the face, using the knife handle to make the punch harder. The sound was sickening, and Adam was afraid he would throw up. He knew from the blinding pain and dead-space feel of his face that the jaw was broken. He wanted to yell at them to stop—that his best friend was Roger Hawkins, Inspector

29

Roger Hawkins who ran this town. And if anything happened to him, Hawkins himself would come after them and make sure they'd pay. But he couldn't talk, and he knew they wouldn't care anyway. They hated him, and wanted to kill him—he'd never know why—and his only chance was to run. He opened his hurt mouth as wide as he could and gave a fierce, piercing shriek. It startled blue-eyes so much he jumped back, and Adam smashed past him and ran for Nostrand.

His jacket flapped out behind him, the hot wind blew his hair flat, and he thought for a few steps he might make it. The lights weren't far, he was a good runner; but his jaw throbbed with every move and the pain radiated into his ear and eye. It blurred his vision and the lights on Nostrand looked hazy and further away than ever. He was slowing down, they were catching up. He was in shock, and even though he knew that one of them had jumped on his back and stabbed him as he fell, he didn't feel the knife cut, or any pain. It was like a punch, nothing worse. He sank forward, face down, and felt more blows; on his back, shoulders, buttocks. He knew one of them stabbed him in the neck. He also knew that he was dying. He had a sudden vision of his father and wife, in the kitchen a block away, making a kugel to celebrate coming home. He could see their hands and the Pyrex casserole they used. He could see the light golden noodles, and raisins and nuts. He could see the old linoleum on the kitchen floor that he and Hawkins had laid years ago, and the curtains. But he couldn't see anyone's face. He kept his eyes open, trying. The blood was pouring, the weight was off his back, and he heard the boys running. He knew he should pray, but he couldn't remember any prayers; he tried to keep his eyes open, but they closed involuntarily; and just before he lost consciousness for good, he dreamed that he and his wife,

Rachel, were back in Minnesota, in the million-acre wilderness park that stretched across Canada to the edge of the Arctic, to Siberia for all he knew. They'd gone there in the summer, two New York Jews, used to taxis and subways and noise; used to doormen, porters, janitors, handymen. And they'd carried a canoe for three miles through the pine woods. They laughed and complained, they were sore and sweaty, and just when they thought they'd never come to the end, the pines thinned and they stood on the bank of an empty lake that was smooth, dark, and silent, like ink in a well. They set the canoe into the shallow water, dipped their paddles in the still surface, and glided away from the shore. Adam felt free and at ease; Rachel lifted her paddle smoothly out of the water, looked at him over her shoulder, and smiled.

In spite of the windows open to the river, the guests at the mayor's birthday party sweated in the tuxes and long gowns. Roger Hawkins's stiff shirtfront had gone limp; his collar was damp and he longed to unhook it. But he kept smiling and circulating. He stopped at group after group, listening, talking, laughing at the other men's jokes. He had a fine deep laugh, husky and rich. He was well liked and hadn't stood alone yet that evening.

He was black, medium dark, and he had high, wide cheekbones and a long Masai nose with flaring nostrils. He was tall like the Masai, but heavier-boned, massive. Between his size and the aristocratic cut of his features, people would turn to look at him.

Julie Kassin, who owned this house on Beekman Place, was watching him now. He had a glass of champagne with the mayor, another with the commissioner, keeping as far away from her as possible. But she went on staring as she talked to her guests. She stared at his mouth, then into his eyes. She was over forty, but still handsome; her dress was cut deeply at the neckline and he looked at her smooth pale crease of cleavage before he could stop himself. She saw where his eyes went and smiled at him, and without wanting to he saw himself making love to her in front of the mirrored mantel under the elegant Renoir after the guests were gone. But she was white, and rich, and if anyone found out, he'd be done for. He watched her for a second, wondering if she'd talk about it, then knew she would. Maybe to Sally Barnard or even to the mayor's fat little wife. He could almost hear her: *Darling, it was almost rape. And he's enormous . . . but gentle, terribly gentle. There's something about black men, don't you think?* The chief would hear about it, they'd find some way to break him, and in a few months he'd be back in Brooklyn where he'd started. He smiled back at her, and almost imperceptibly he shook his head, then looked around for someone else to talk to.

Joe Alston was standing under a Matisse on the far side of the room, and when Hawkins saw Julie Kassin heading for him, he crossed the room and started talking to Alston. Alston was black too. He was the Democratic party chairman, and he seemed to like Hawkins.

Alston got two more glasses of champagne from the circulating waiter and gave one to Hawkins. "We need to talk," he said, sounding significant.

At the end of the long room, in front of big windows that looked out over the East River, a black woman was singing on a small platform. She was at the piano, without a mike, and her voice came through the room softly, blending with the talk.

> *Saturday night 'n Sunday too . . .*
> *True love on my mi . . . ind.*
> *Monday mornin' good 'n soon,*
> *White man's got me gwine . . .*

Alston smiled. "White man's got me gwine . . ." he said softly.

Hawkins drank and listened to the song. The woman's voice was full and sweet and more guests stopped talking to listen.

> *Blue Jay pulled a four-horse plow . . .*
> *Sparrow, why can't you . . .*
> *'Cause my legs is li'l 'n long*
> *'N they might get broke in two . . .*

Nonsense, Hawkins thought. Some old, tribal song that no one remembered the real words to. But Alston was enchanted; he closed his eyes and swayed to the music. He was much shorter than Hawkins, and thinner. His shirt was still crisp, his tie sharp, and his jacket hung on him the way it was supposed to. Hawkins envied him for a second. His own shirt was wrinkled and starting to come out of his pants; his jacket felt so tight he thought if he moved his arms forward too far, the fabric would split up the back, exposing the vest ties that didn't meet in the back.

"White man got you goin' too, Roger?" Alston asked him.

"Sometimes," Hawkins said.

"Don't let 'em. We've got power in this town."

"Blacks, cops, Democrats? Who, Joe?"

Alston laughed. "All of the above," he said. "A high-echelon cop like you could do some real good. You look good, you're reasonably articulate . . . what college did you go to?"

"None," Hawkins said.

"Really?"

"Well, in some circles that's a disadvantage," Alston said. "In others . . ."

They went to the buffet in the palace-sized dining room. Alston talked while Hawkins made a thick, fold-over sandwich of pâté and French bread.

"College or no college, you've got currency. The mayor likes you; the governor asked me who you were last month at the commissioner's. You could help, I mean you *are* a Democrat. . . ."

The butler interrupted to tell Hawkins he had a phone call and the caller said it was important. He left Alston, and nodded at Julie Kassin in the hall. She shrugged delicately, as if they had an assignation he was delayed in keeping. The butler led him to an empty room where a Degas pastel hung on a paneled wall. The pastel was of a dancer bending to tie her shoe ribbon, and she looked alive enough to straighten up any second and move out of the picture. He wished Jacob were here to see the pastel. Jacob had probably never been in a house like this. The butler left him alone and he finished his sandwich and picked up the phone.

"Roger . . ." It was Mo Ableson from the precinct in Brooklyn. He sounded terrible. "Roger, it's Mo. Rog, sit down."

Hawkins knew his mother was dead; he forced the bread down and braced himself against the phone table. Mo said, "Roger, Adam Levy's dead. . . . He was stabbed. Fifteen, twenty times, Roger. In the gut, the back . . ."

Feelings started to come—he was never going to see Adam or talk to him again, and when he thought that, tears ran out of his eyes and he sobbed. He remembered that there were people in the hall and some might hear him even over the party noises. He pulled out his handkerchief and pushed it against his mouth. "Jacob," he mumbled, but Ableson didn't understand.

He waited a second, took the handkerchief away from

his face, and said as clearly as he could, "Someone's got to tell Jacob."

The chief told him to take the department limousine. It was a gray Cadillac and the chauffeur, Johnny Baer, drove too fast and would do anything to avoid a traffic jam. Tonight he started down Second toward the bridges, but it was tight, so he cut over to the Drive. Hawkins put his head back and tried to think what he was going to say to Jacob Levy. *Jacob. Your son is dead. Adam's dead.*

They passed the Houston Street exit. Years ago, a couple of miles west of here, he'd taken Adam to a bar in the West Village to get laid. They found two pretty white girls, students at the New School. The women took them to a run-down apartment building on Bank Street, almost to the river, and afterward Hawkins and Adam went to a greasy little restaurant on Bleecker. They'd ordered hamburgers and pecan pie. But when the food came, Adam said he felt too guilty to eat. Hawkins had wanted to say something wise to him—that the guilt would pass, that lust and sadness were natural partners—but Adam was twenty-eight then, only two years younger than Hawkins, and he was sure Adam knew all that, so he kept quiet and ate Adam's hamburger and pie. On the way home, though, as they crossed the slick humming grid of the Brooklyn Bridge, Hawkins did say, "I used to feel like you."

"When did you stop?" Adam had asked. His thin, pale face turned to Hawkins in the flashing lights of the other cars.

"When I got married."

"You're married?" Adam sounded upset.

"No . . . no. She walked out." Hawkins had turned and smiled at him. "*Ran* out," he said.

"Why?"

"I was too—slow."

It was a bad explanation, but he couldn't think of anything better, until he remembered Pierre Bezuhov. "Like Count Bezuhov in *War and Peace* . . . you remember him?" Adam nodded.

"That was me," Hawkins said, then added, "*is* me. Big, and slow. No dash."

His wife had found a tall, thin man who made book in Jersey. He wore raw silk suits that hung on him like Alston's did. He had long skinny legs that were always moving, and he wore a heavy ring set with diamonds on one of his long, thin fingers.

Adam had stared earnestly at Hawkins. "She was a fool." Then he added in his soft Israeli accent, "I think you very dashing. . . ."

Adam . . . Adam, Hawkins thought. He started crying again and pressed his damp handkerchief to his eyes. Johnny Baer watched him in the rearview mirror.

"You okay, Inspector?"

"No," Hawkins choked.

"I'm sorry . . . you want me to . . ."

"Just drive, Johnny," Hawkins said gently. "Keep driving."

He closed his eyes and didn't open them again until they'd reached Flatbush. The street was long and crummy, lined with delis, pizza stands, and discount stores. It didn't look like New York anymore, but like the strip in any depressed town. A few bums sat in doorways, kids leaned wearily against cars and store windows.

They left the lit stores behind and swung around Grand Army Plaza and into Nostrand and the neighborhood that had been his beat after he came back from Vietnam.

They turned off Nostrand at Sterling, a dark, tree-lined

street with short stoops leading to once neat two-family houses. But now, Hawkins saw litter in the gutters and on the sidewalk. Red-and-white-labeled cans, brown paper bags, silver foil that caught the street light. In the next block the litter was sparser, and in the block after that it almost disappeared. Baer pulled up in front of Levy's building, and Hawkins got out, his head throbbing as he moved. Someone had scratched initials on the mailboxes; half-washed-out graffiti covered the walls and the elevator was broken. He rang the downstairs bell.

Adam's wife called, "Adam?" and Hawkins stopped on the stairs and untied his bow tie because he felt like he was choking. Then he went up the stairs.

She didn't move when she saw him; he stopped a few steps down from the landing and she raised her hand to her throat.

"Is Adam with you?" she whispered.

"No," he said.

She went on looking at him, hand at her neck. Then in her eyes he saw that dawning intuition that he'd seen other people have at times like this. The hand dropped to her side and she said without hope, "He's dead. . . ."

He nodded and she moaned sickly. He tried to touch her, but she put her arm out straight to keep him off, and she turned back and moaned again. He followed her into the living room where she grabbed the back of the plush easy chair he remembered from the old days. The lace doilies were still on the arms, the place was still too hot, the air too dry. She held the back of the chair and rocked, still moaning. She was six or seven months pregnant, and her legs looked too frail to carry her belly. He thought he could span her ankles with his hand. Her hair was thick, black, and cut short; he could see the point of bone at the back of her neck.

Jacob Levy came in from the dining room holding a steaming casserole in his hands, which were covered with oven mitts.

"The kugel!" Levy cried. He saw Hawkins, not Adam. He saw Hawkins's rumpled tux, and his daughter-in-law bending in anguish over the chair. It was eight-thirty; Adam should have been home at seven, and he was never late. Levy turned very slowly back to the dining room. He carried the hot dish carefully to the table and put it on the mat, then stood there without moving, his back to Hawkins. His head was bowed over the steam that still came up from the casserole and Hawkins realized that Levy's hair was entirely white under his yarmulke. The first time he'd seen Levy it was still black.

He was twenty-four then and new on the beat. It was spring 1965 and Dutch elm disease was everywhere. The elms on Nostrand were dying, and the city was cutting them down. Hawkins had stopped to watch a man sawing at a limb from a metal box raised on a mechanized arm; the branch snapped as a blast of spring wind came up the street and pulled the branch out of the ropes. Hawkins dodged, but he was too slow and the thick part of the branch grazed his head. He didn't think it had hit him with any force at all; but he sat down without knowing he was going to. He saw people coming out of the shops and rushing toward him along the street, and felt his own blood run down the side of his face and into the corner of his mouth. He meant to lean back until the dizziness went away, and all of a sudden he was back in Vietnam—Laos, to be exact—in a tree, his parachute hopelessly tangled in the branches, his arm caught up in the shrouds and broken. The B-52 pilot was dead, he knew the rest of the crew was dead, too, and there was nothing for miles in any direction but the Laotian jungle. He tried to pull free. But the pain made him faint, and when he woke up it was raining. At least he wouldn't die of thirst, and he raised his head, opened his mouth, and let the fungus-tasting rain wash down his throat. Later he slept. When he woke, he reached for one of the frond-like leaves of the tree he hung in; he chewed it, then spat it out. It rained again; the pain radiated from his arm to his groin, to his ankle, then it changed direction and focused in his ear and the back of his head. Then it eased, or he numbed, and he fell asleep again. It rained again, the integument of his skin began to break down, and he could feel insects inside his clothes. He fantasized that there were leeches in his boots, and he thought he would rot before he died, hanging there in the fog and rain. As the rest of his consciousness thinned out, the pain got worse, until he wasn't aware of anything else except that he thought he'd been hanging there for three days. He heard something in the bush; he prayed for a tiger or some wild animal capable of killing him; but from the sounds he knew it was men coming through the jungle and he hoped the VC would kill him quickly, not try to keep him alive as a prize of war. They got closer, and through the fog he saw that they were Americans. They cut him down, laid him back on a stretcher, gave him a shot, and in a few minutes the pain stopped. The end of that pain was the best feeling he'd ever had. It was so good, he risked opening his eyes.

A middle-aged man was kneeling next to him on the sidewalk. His face was very pale against his black hair, and his wide-brimmed black hat threw a shadow over his face which made him look a little unearthly. Good unearthly, like an angel. Sure enough, he smiled, the sweetest smile Hawkins had ever seen, and he said, "*Nu*, you wake up. *Gut*." Then he frowned and asked, "Do you know where you are?"

Hawkins looked past him up the street. "Nostrand Avenue," he said.

The man beamed. "Good, good. Do you know who you are?"

"Yes," Hawkins answered.

"*Nu?*" the man said.

"I'm Roger Hawkins."

The man looked like Hawkins had just said something brilliant. "I'm Jacob Levy," he said. He took Hawkins's hand, and even though he was short and very thin, he helped Hawkins to his feet.

Levy was forty-eight then; he was a rabbi and he owned a small bookstore on the corner of Nostrand and .President. He had books in Hebrew, Yiddish, Polish, Russian, and some in English, and in ten or twelve years, Hawkins read Pushkin, Dostoevski, Goncharov, and Tolstoy. He even read Sholokhov, and Olyesha, whom Levy said had offended the government and had disappeared. He read English and American novels, too: Henry James, Dickens, George Eliot. He even bought a set of Gibbon, thinking that if he could read Sholokhov, he could read anything. But three pages of Gibbon put him to sleep, and he never got past the first chapter. Levy confessed that he never had either, but he believed his English, not Gibbon, was to blame.

Levy was dark and frail-looking and he never raised his voice or lost his temper. If Hawkins wanted to stop reading something Levy thought was good, Levy would spend hours convincing him to go on. They sat at the folding table in the front of the bookstore, drinking tea, with Isaac Luria always there on a raised chair, his long legs bent up, holding an open book. When Levy left

Hawkins alone to take care of a customer, Hawkins would try not to look at Luria. Once he did and caught Luria staring at him. Both men looked away.

Hawkins stopped at the bookstore every morning and when his shift changed, and every afternoon but Saturday. The little shop turned into a refuge. He would see old men and women who'd been bludgeoned, stabbed, robbed, and ten- or twelve-year-old girls who'd been raped, holding bloodstained skirts around them, too frightened and abused to even cry, and he would run to Levy's. He would fight with his wife and slam out of his house, leaving his wife, mother, sister shouting at the kitchen table and his daughter in her high chair with her eyes wide with shock at all the noise, and he would run to Levy's. He started bringing Levy gifts of food he searched the city for. Pickles from Max's on Essex Street, homemade herring from the BG, sturgeon from Zabar's, and blueberry knishes from Delancey Street.

Every June, Levy would go to Israel to see his son and Hawkins dreaded the month. Luria kept the shop open, but Hawkins never went in. He'd walk by and look in the window, and once Luria saw him. The two men stared at each other through the glass and across the rows of books; Luria didn't wave at him to come in, and after a minute, Hawkins turned away and didn't go back until Jacob was there again. July first was the best day of the summer. He'd take the squad car out to Kennedy to wait for the El Al flight that brought Jacob home.

Hawkins had seen pictures of the son, and Levy talked about him, but he stayed shadowy in Hawkins's mind, and there were times—when the plane had finally landed, and Levy was waving up to him from the customs hall—that it almost seemed to Hawkins that he was the son Levy was coming home to.

Hawkins bought his own car and started taking Levy

for drives into the city or out on the Island. Luria came with them, and he brought another man, Abe Dworkin, who was as short as Levy and had soft brown eyes and thick, curly hair.

Levy loved the ocean. He would walk for hours on the beach with Hawkins. People stared at the big black man walking with a little Jew who wore a black skullcap held on his head with a bobby pin, and a white tieless shirt. Levy never rolled up his sleeves, but he would fold over the bottoms of his trousers, take off his shoes, and wade out a few feet into the Sound, looking for shells. Luria and Dworkin stayed behind in whatever shelter was available, and little Dworkin would hold his jacket across his thin chest and complain about the cold. But Luria watched Levy, and if he lost sight of him for a few minutes, he would come after them.

Contact with Levy and constant reading started to pay off. Hawkins passed the detective exam ahead of Ableson, and he made sergeant; then Elaine left and took their daughter. His sister got married and moved to Weehawken and his mother retreated into TV and born-again Christianity. He told Levy how lonely he was and Levy had listened, with an expression of pain in his dark eyes.

Then Hawkins met Alma and, on a hot day in May, when he and Levy were walking on a pebble beach on the Sound side of the Island, he told Levy about her.

Levy stopped walking and sat on a boulder facing the water. "Would you marry this girl Alma?" he asked.

"I don't know," Hawkins said.

"You're lonely," Levy said, "vulnerable. You married wrong once and now should be very careful."

"I'll try."

"Tell me what she's like."

Hawkins wanted to do her justice, but nothing about her seemed worth mentioning. He tried anyway. "She's pretty. She plays pool, dances, loves sex ... she's ... fun ..." he finished lamely.

"Ah ... fun," Levy said. "I, on the other hand, loved a serious woman. ..."

Hawkins saw Luria and Dworkin coming across the beach, holding their hats against the wind.

"Why are they always with us?" Hawkins asked suddenly.

"Because you're an outsider," Levy said, "and they don't trust you."

"The *shvartze*, right?"

Levy smiled. "That makes it worse," he said gently. "But they'd be suspicious of anyone."

"What are they to you?"

"Old friends," Levy said, looking out at the Connecticut shore.

"Just them?" Hawkins asked.

"No. There're more. You know them. Fineman, Walinsky ... the old man, Feldsher."

They were only a few yards away and Hawkins asked, "What do they think I'll do to you?"

Levy leaned over and whispered to Hawkins, "Kill me and eat me. ..."

They laughed so hard Levy fell off the boulder, and Hawkins helped him up. They were still laughing when Luria and Dworkin got to them. Dworkin smiled to keep them company, but Luria stood like a post with his black jacket whipping in the wind. They stopped laughing, Hawkins put his jacket back on, and arm in arm, he and Levy walked back across the beach to the parking lot. Dworkin and Luria followed, and Hawkins could feel Luria watching his back. For the first time he realized that Luria hated him and wanted to get rid of him.

In August, Luria almost succeeded. The Gallo wars were

at their height, and Hawkins and Ableson had found Benny Gonnona, a small-time bookie, kneeling on the floor of his office with his hands tied behind his back and three bullets in his head. His head caught the edge of his old rolltop desk as he fell, and the desk held him there, half upright, so he looked like he was praying with half his head gone. The super found him, and he was still sick by the time Hawkins and Ableson got there; Hawkins had seen more gruesome scenes, but there was something especially awful about the position of the corpse in that dirty little office with its phones, filthy window, bare splintered floor.

He went back to the precinct, showered, and put on a clean shirt, but he still felt soiled by what they'd seen. He had a drink with Ableson; but he needed Levy. He left Ableson, bought a bottle of slivovitz, and took it to the shop.

It was warm, and the street was quiet. Luria was on his stool, Levy was in the back with two young Hasidim. Hawkins caught glimpses of them in the stacks. They wore long black coats and wide-brimmed hats. They were pale and their side curls were damp and clung to their cheeks.

Hawkins poured a drink for Luria, and Luria took the glass and raised it.

"To the return of Adam," Luria said.

"Adam . . ." Hawkins said stupidly.

Luria got down from the stool. His jacket was off, and Hawkins realized that Luria was almost as big as he was. He leaned on the table, massive hands flat, supporting his heavy arms. He'd taken his glasses off and his narrow gray eyes were bright.

"Adam, you *shlemiel*. Jacob's son, the light of our lives. You don't know Jacob has a son Adam?"

"Of course I do," Hawkins said. His voice was tight.

"Of course you do," Luria mimicked. "Well, he's coming home, Sergeant, with a doctorate from the University of Jerusalem. Next month he'll sit where you sit, he'll talk and laugh with his father, and I don't think Jacob will have time for us anymore. Not with such a smart, loving, handsome son to fill his evenings. No, Sergeant, our time together is over. . . ."

"Isaac!" Levy cried sharply from the edge of the stacks.

Hawkins stood up and backed away from Luria. He was dazed; the beloved little shop was suddenly stifling and he went up the steps to the street to get air. Levy called his name, but he kept going. He crossed Nostrand and headed down Sterling, to the end of the street where they'd demolished Ebbets Field to put up a huge apartment complex. He went right into the construction site, which looked like it had been bombed, and he sat down in the dust at the foot of a bare girder. He wasn't sure how long he stayed there before he heard something moving in the rubble. He thought it was a cat, or a rat, and he started to get up when Jacob Levy came out of the shadows and stood over him. From this angle, Jacob looked enormous and the reflection of the moonlight coming off the stone and concrete all around them sunk his eyes into holes and threw the lines and ridges of his skull into relief.

He looked down at Hawkins sitting in the rubble and said, "I need you more than you need me. . . . You're my hope for knowing and understanding what is now, whether I like it or not, my world. And I *do* like it. It's a better world. I wouldn't go back if I could, not in miles or time. You . . . you keep me here, in my mind as well as the ground I stand on. You with your brightness, your life . . . your newness. The others aren't here, but they aren't there either, poor souls. But with your help my son

45

and I will find a home here. Besides," he said shyly, "I . . . care for you."

Then he sat down in the stone dust next to Hawkins and opened the bottle of slivovitz he had brought from the shop. He took a deep swallow, and gave the bottle to Hawkins.

"You think you're jealous of Adam," Levy said, "but you won't be. He's part of me, so you'll love him. You can be his father, too, and his brother."

Levy took the bottle back and looked around the site. "Looks like there's been a war here," he'd said.

Chapter
2

THEY RAISED the cover and Levy looked at Adam's face. The gashes on the side of it were wide and rubbery, slightly green, and Levy gagged, turned away, and almost fell, but Hawkins caught him and held him up.

"It's my son," Levy croaked. "It's my Adam." He held on to Hawkins with one hand, and grabbed the collar of his shirt with the other. "I need a knife."

"No, Jake . . ."

"I need a knife."

Pescado came over to them. "It's for *keriah*," he told Hawkins. "It's a ritual."

"So get him a knife," Hawkins snapped.

All they had was a scalpel.

"Take it," Levy said. Hawkins did. "Now cut my shirt, here."

Hawkins put one arm firmly around Levy, and with the scalpel in his free hand, he caught the point on the fabric of Levy's shirt and pulled. It ripped and Levy moaned.

"Take me home, Roger. Please take me home."

Pescado said softly, "You have to sign, Rabbi."

Levy signed the forms and dropped the pen.

"Now, please," he told Hawkins.

They were almost at the door when a man in a white uniform stopped them. He was holding a needle, tip up, catching the light.

"What's that shit," Hawkins snarled.

"Librium," Pescado said from across the bare room. "I'll put him to sleep."

They rolled up Levy's sleeve, the needle point glittered, and Hawkins looked away. He smelled alcohol and something like old ice, and Levy leaned against him. Then they left them alone, and Levy and Hawkins went slowly and carefully out of the morgue. Like two old drunks, Hawkins thought, just trying to get home.

The elevator was still out, and Hawkins carried Levy up the six flights. He cradled him against his chest, holding his head so his hat wouldn't fall off. Rachel was waiting on the landing, and she held the door open for him while he carried Levy in and down the narrow hall to Adam's old room. Adam had loved horses, and the walls were covered with pictures of ponies photographed against rocks, of Arabians running and big, solid Percherons standing still. The only other picture in the room was a faded black and white of Levy as a young man. In it Levy was wearing a fur-brimmed hat and smiling at a girl who was just as young and almost as beautiful as he was. Hawkins had never seen the picture before, but he knew that this was Leah, Adam's mother, Rachel's mother-in-law. . . .

Rachel was crying silently, but she helped him anyway, and they got Levy onto the bed, got his hat out from under his head and, working together, they rolled him back and forth between them and got his jacket off. Then she undid his belt and took off his shoes, while Hawkins unbuttoned his collar and cuffs. He watched her hands as they moved precisely, gracefully, long fingers at the belt buckle, then shoelaces. He kept looking up at her face and realized that even though she was pale, and her eyes were swollen and red, she looked lovely to him. He didn't know if that was because she was really so beautiful or if there was just something about her face that fascinated him. He'd only seen her a few times before tonight. The first time was the day Adam married her four years ago, just before they left for Minnesota. He remembered thinking that Adam's wife would probably look like Rose Pinchik, who was pleasant-plain with short legs; but when she raised her short veil to kiss Adam, he'd been shocked at how pretty she was, so pretty he couldn't talk to her except to say how happy he was for them. After that he'd jockeyed around people who got in his line of sight so he could watch her.

"Let's get his shirt off," she said, "it's hot in here."

He lifted Levy and she got his arms out of the sleeves. They settled him back and for the first time Hawkins saw the blue numbers tattooed on Levy's arm.

He touched them with his fingertips.

Rachel watched him. "Didn't he tell you?" she asked.

"No. Adam did once. A long time ago." One night at Vinnie's bar. Hawkins was drunk at the time and all at once he was angry. Not at the Nazis, but at Adam for telling him about something so terrible, so alien. Every Jew in Brooklyn had a hard-luck story, he thought . . . the camps, the pogroms, the college quotas. The Irish, too, like Mike Carr and Maguire, always sitting with their backs to a wall, as if someone was going to shoot them from the door, and moaning about their troubles. The blacks were no better. Marsh Robinson got drunk there every Wednesday night, picked fights with whites, and carried on about slavery as if he'd just been impressed from Africa instead of being born and raised in Cleveland.

But tonight, as he looked at Levy's thin white arm

with its line of blue numbers, he remembered that little girls in Belfast made a game of setting fire to their dollies; that when his father was young in North Carolina, he'd ridden the back of the bus, drunk from a special fountain, pissed in a special toilet, and bowed his head in helpless rage and inexplicable guilt when white men called him nigger. And only forty years ago some German with lightning on his collar pulled Jacob Levy off a cattle-car transport from Poland and tattooed these numbers on his arm. . . .

Rachel was watching him. "Do you want a drink?" she asked. He nodded. They put a light blanket over Levy and left him alone with the light on. Hawkins followed her to the dining room. She said, "We've got brandy." She tried to sound normal, but she was getting white. She couldn't bend over to open the cabinet, so he did it for her; he looked up and saw her swallow hard and put her hand to her mouth. She swayed and he jumped up and grabbed her arms.

"I'm going to be sick." Then she said, "No, maybe I'll just faint . . ." Then she started sobbing, with her hands flat on her belly, looking straight at him, her face twisted so it should have been ugly but wasn't. He led her into the living room, which was dark, and hot, and he opened the windows. The phone rang and he answered it. It was Rose Pinchik calling to find out if it was true. Yes, he said, it was true, and she should get here because Jacob was drugged and Rachel . . . then he heard Rachel dry-gasping in the living room, and he hung up. But she was still just sobbing, trying now to catch her breath. The sobs turned to hiccups, and he left the lights out and rubbed her back, between the shoulder blades, firmly, steadily, in rhythm, until the little spasms stopped. The phone rang again. This time it was Golda Cohen asking if it was true. He said it was, then he got the bottle of brandy out of the cabinet and two glasses and went back to the living room. She was sitting now, still crying. He poured the brandy and was going to hand it to her, or feed it to her if she couldn't take it, when the doorbell rang.

Hawkins pushed the downstairs buzzer, and when he opened the door Luria and Dworkin were coming down the hall. Little Dworkin was still out of breath from climbing the stairs. "Is it true?" Dworkin gasped. "Yes," Hawkins said. In the background they heard Rachel crying. Luria raised his hand silently and he grabbed the collar of his shirt and tore it. The ripping sound filled the hall and Dworkin wailed and Hawkins heard doors open downstairs. Then Dworkin tore his shirt, which was almost funny—two old men standing there with old-fashioned ribbed undershirts showing through torn shirts. Then Dworkin wailed something that sounded like "Aunt Sophie ... Auuuuuunnnttt Soooophieee." It was a shocking sound and, without warning, Luria slapped Dworkin's face. Luria swung again and Hawkins grabbed Luria's torn collar and shoved him hard against the wall; he lifted his fist high over their heads, but Luria didn't flinch. Dworkin pulled at Hawkins's arm, mumbling, "Please, please, Roger. He did right. I shouldn't talk like that. Please." Luria waited; Dworkin kept mumbling, and the phone rang in the apartment.

Hawkins lowered his fist and let Luria go. "Answer the phone," Luria said softly. Hawkins backed away, watching Luria. "The phone," Luria said again.

It was Ableson this time, calling to tell Hawkins that they'd gotten a tip and picked up five kids for killing Adam.

The kids were members of a gang called the Eagles. They met in the basement of the Lensky house on President Street. Hawkins made Baer stop in front of the club-house. The bank of ivy that was once Mrs. Lensky's pride was dying. The glass in the front door was dirty, there was litter in the basement entryway, and he knew the Len-skys were dead or moved away. Some time ago, too, from the extent of the neglect. The stairs down to the basement were cracked and someone had spray-painted "Fuck you" on the stone wall.

"Fuck you, too," Hawkins whispered.

The clubhouse had one window in front; on it gold decal letters spelled out "Eagles." Under that someone had painted a child's-nightmare eagle with huge claws and a tearing beak. At first the eagle looked ugly and cruel; it fed Hawkins's rage. Then he saw that the artist had painted each feather with ribs and outlined the talons on the claws. The painting was painstaking, almost loving, and against his will he felt something like pity for the artist. He couldn't help asking himself why they'd done it. Why five kids who met here to get away from packed apartments, family fights, squalling babies, and the con-stant pressure of being poor, came out of this little haven and stabbed Adam to death for thirty dollars.

It was crazy, like his friend Pinchik said everything was. "People're hot to kill," Pinchik once told him. "Don't be-lieve me, Roger, go see *Psycho*; watch the audience watch-ing that scene in the shower where he stabs her in the tits, the belly, the juice, and there's blood everywhere, and that knife's going into her with a crunch.

"The people don't look away. They watch with their mouths open, like they were watching a good fuck. . . . People're hot to kill," he'd concluded.

Was that it? Hawkins wondered miserably. Were they hot to do it?

* * *

"Maybe he didn't have enough on him," Ableson said. "Maybe they hated philosophy teachers. *Why*. Did you ever hear a reason that made sense?"

It was only midnight; the air conditioning was off for the night and the men sweated. Most of the windows had been sealed shut and last week Max Aronson had thrown his chair at one of them but succeeded only in cracking it. The cracked window made the room look raffish.

Hawkins took off his tie and jacket.

"Can I see them?"

"You better do it tonight. They'll be out by tomorrow night because no one saw nothin', no one heard nothin', no one says nothin'. I had half the street in here. It looked like the Puerto Rican Day picnic in here." Ableson twisted paper clips. "I 'interviewed' thirty-five of them. They were home when it happened. They live on the ground floor. It's hot, so they had their windows open—"

Hawkins cut in, "Let me see the kids."

"Okay. See 'em. Try and kill a couple while you're down there."

They were in the holding room on the third floor. Ableson called it the pen. They were sitting at tables, or on the molded plastic benches against the wall. They were active ... smoking, eating candy, twisting the handles on the vending machines.

Hawkins stopped in the doorway, confused because he couldn't remember what he'd expected to see when he opened the door. They were just a bunch of kids, sixteen, seventeen, and too lively to sit still. Hawkins crossed the room and pulled one of the kid's hands away from the knobs of a vending machine and smashed his back against the machine. The change inside jingled.

"No candy," Hawkins said.

The boy backed away from him to the others. They looked at each other, then at Hawkins, who was still in his tux with the strings of his tie hanging loose around his neck. He looked exhausted, his skin had a gray cast, and his eyes were bloodshot. He outweighed the biggest of them by fifty pounds and they looked scared.

"Adam Levy was my friend," he said.

"Who?" asked one. He was very thin and he had black-lashed blue eyes.

"Adam Levy . . ." Hawkins said. "The Jew on Sterling Street with thirty dollars and the plastic briefcase full of books. The short, thin, pale man . . . you remember," Hawkins said. The boys stared. "He had hay fever and carried pills for it. He was a philosophy teacher and carried books. It'll come back to you . . ." The boys pushed themselves back against the wall. "He had a father, a wife . . . the wife's pregnant, by the way. . . ."

One of them started to cry, and the others looked at him, then at Hawkins. Another one turned to the wall, and Hawkins was stunned. He stood still for a moment, then he went to the door and left the boys alone.

He had three drinks with Ableson, told Baer to go home, and got his own car from the lot. Then he drove into the Heights, parked and walked back and forth in front of Alma's house. Finally he found a phone booth and called her.

It was after one and only a few die-hard, run-down-looking hookers were left on the street. One passed the phone booth and oozed against the glass door so her breasts, pushed up in the street light, looked enormous.

Alma sounded sleepy.

"Where are you?" she asked.

"A block away."

"Anything wrong, Roger?"

54

"Bad night." Which was so inadequate he almost laughed.

"Okay, honey, come over."

Alma had a duplex on the promenade, overlooking the bay, the bridges, the whole city. Some nights he'd turn off the lights and sit there in the dark watching the city like he'd watch a movie.

Alma's ex-husband owned an insurance agency and he paid alimony on time. She broke dates to see Hawkins and she was sweet and funny and Mo said she was gorgeous. She was gorgeous tonight; her dark skin showed through her nightgown and her nipples looked black. He pushed her back and actually tore the nightgown getting it off. He was usually the gentlest lover; but tonight he was rough with her. For some reason he didn't want to see her face and he turned her away from him and pushed into her so hard she gasped. When it was over, she fell asleep almost at once and he felt bereft. He wandered through the dark apartment for a while, then took a shower, half hoping the noise would wake her so he wouldn't be alone, but it didn't and he left her asleep, got dressed, and went down the stairs to the lobby.

The lobby guard nodded at him and went back to his *National Enquirer.* Hawkins crossed the street to the promenade and stood alone in the dark looking at the river. He thought of Adam in the drawer at Kings County and of Rachel getting through her first night alone in the hot apartment with Levy unconscious in the next room. He looked back up at Alma's windows. If he saw a light he'd go back up there. They'd have a drink and maybe get really drunk together. She was lively and funny when she was drunk. Maybe they'd go dancing. There was an after-hours nightclub on Atlantic and they'd go there and dance until four. She loved to dance, her behind was full and tight, and she swung it subtly, barely moving her legs; the other men would stare at her, the way they always did, envying him. Then he'd take her home and make love to her again. Gently this time, taking a long time. The rest of the night. But the windows stayed dark and he walked back into the streets to his car. Shadows seemed to follow him, but when he looked back all he saw was full garbage bags lying at the curb. He walked a ways and looked again. There was nothing there.

He didn't get home until almost four and he undressed, hung up the rumpled tux, and got into bed. But when he closed his eyes, he saw Adam in the morgue, his face covered with slashes. That wasn't how Hawkins wanted to remember him and he made himself think of the first time he'd seen Adam twelve years ago.

They were in the International Arrivals building and the El Al flight had just landed. Levy was leaning against the rail of the visitors' balcony, his hands pressed against the glass as the people poured through the gate into the customs hall. Then Levy cried, "There, Roger. There he is," and Hawkins saw a short, slight young man who looked like Levy. He was tanned and handsome and he wore a yarmulke like Levy did. He looked up and saw his father; he waved so wildly the cap fell off. They went downstairs to wait; people came through the doors and ran into the arms of waiting relatives; the lobby was full of people hugging each other and crying, and Hawkins stood next to Levy, feeling alien and alone. Then Adam came through the automatic doors holding his cap and carrying a huge valise. He dropped the case and he and Levy ran to each other. Levy kissed the man's cheeks and eyelids. He held his son's head in his hands and started kissing him all over again while Hawkins stood apart. Then Adam had turned to Hawkins. He was laughing and crying at the same time, and he said, "You're black, so you must be Roger."

Hawkins had nodded awkwardly and put out his hand, but Adam ignored the hand. He threw his arms around Hawkins, stretched his body and kissed Hawkins first on one cheek, then on the other, then he just hugged him, while Levy watched them with tears running down his face.

HAWKINS HELD his hands over the basin on the table in the hall. Old man Oshevsky saw that they were black and looked up blindly.

"Who're you?"

"Roger Hawkins, Mr. Oshevsky."

"Roger Hawkins the cop?"

Hawkins nodded.

"Where were you last night, cop?"

It took him a little time to remember, then he said wearily, "I was at a party, Mr. Oshevsky."

Oshevsky's cheeks turned purple. "Adam Levy's getting stabbed and you're at a party!"

Behind him in the line, Sam Arkin yelled, "Shut up, Oshevsky. How could he know?"

"*Feh*!" Oshevsky yelled back, holding the pitcher away from Hawkins. Hawkins kept his hands over the basin.

"Pour the water, Mr. Oshevsky," he said, "or I'll go into the house with dirty hands."

The old man looked up at Hawkins while the others in line waited to see what would happen.

"It's getting late," Hawkins said, gently.

"Feh" the old man said again, but he poured the water

over Hawkins's hands, handed him a towel to dry them with, and Hawkins went into Levy's apartment.

The place was hot and crowded and smelled of onions and smoked fish. Used paper plates littered tables, radiator tops, and windowsills. Most of the men in the room had beards and all wore hats. Hawkins took a black yarmulke from a pile on the table at the door and pushed it down over his hair. Eli Pinchik was leading against the far wall of the foyer watching the crowd. The top of a small liquor bottle stuck out of his jacket pocket and his eyes were swollen and bloodshot. He saw Hawkins and grabbed his arm. "You didn't come to the funeral. Your best friend dies and you don't help bury him. Why?"

"Some of them wouldn't want me there, Eli."

Pinchik made a dry spitting gesture and looked through the arch at the men. "Because they're schmucks, that's why. . . ." He raised his voice, "Schmucks!" A few turned around but most ignored him. Pinchik sobbed and pulled out his bottle. "C'mon," he said, "let's get out of here."

"Not till I see Levy . . ."

"I'll be at the Union Dairy," Pinchik said, "we gotta talk." He went out the door and Hawkins looked over the other men's heads for Levy.

He was sitting low on a mourning stool and Luria, Dworkin, Walinsky, and the rest sat on chairs to make a closed circle. Adam had told Hawkins that they mourned for seven days. For seven days the family of the dead couldn't sit in chairs, shave, or cut their hair. They couldn't put on new clothes or greet guests. Hawkins got through the crowd, breached the circle, and knelt at Levy's feet so his head was almost level with Levy's.

Without counting, Hawkins knew that there were eight men in the circle; some of them liked him, some didn't.

Levy grabbed his hands. "You got the killers . . ." he said.

Hawkins didn't answer.

"Abe said you got my son's killers."

"We arrested some boys last night, Jake, but we had to let them go."

"You let them go. . . ."

"We don't have enough to hold them yet, but we'll get it. . . ."

"How?" Luria asked. Hawkins ignored him and talked to Levy.

"We'll get witnesses, evidence . . . blood on their clothes, knives, we'll get it." The men around him were quiet; he kept on talking to Levy. "There's five of them, Jake. That means we've got a chance. We pull 'em in at odd hours when they don't expect it; we push and keep pushing till we find the weak link . . ."

"Weak link?" That came from Walinsky, who leaned forward facing Hawkins.

"The one most likely to break." They all leaned forward to listen and for no reason Hawkins wondered which one was the weak link in *this* circle. Every group had one, no matter how solid it seemed. Dworkin with his warm, brown eyes would be it. But Hawkins didn't understand why was he thinking about weak links here. These men weren't his enemies. Levy loved him, he loved Levy, and the others wouldn't hurt him; some of them didn't trust him or any black and never would, but they weren't men to hurt anyone. Except Luria . . . he faced Luria and their eyes met and locked. Luria would hurt him; Levy rubbed Hawkins's hand. "The weak link," Levy said, "tell me about the weak link."

"We . . . work on him; we scare him until he avoids the others. Then we spread rumors that he broke and the others'll know he's weak and they'll believe it. Then they'll get scared that we'll make a deal and leave them out."

"Deal . . ." Luria's voice was flat, like his eyes. "What deal?"

Hawkins knew he had made a mistake.

"Tell Jacob about the deal," Luria said.

"What are they talking about?" Levy asked.

This time it was Walinsky who answered.

"They make deals, Jacob, like you'd make with Garfinkel for a diamond; they grab the *momzers** and they all sit in a chamber . . . lawyers in ties and the judge in his robe . . . and they *handel*.† You did first-degree murder, they say, but that's hard to prove and expensive to try and it takes too long, so even though we know you're guilty, even though you killed a man, or woman, or little child . . . plead guilty to second-degree, or third-degree. No jury. No big news trial . . . and *oy*, the money we save! The time! And at least we get your rat's ass off the streets for a year or two. . . ."

"A year or two?" Levy asked.

"More like ten," Hawkins pleaded. "Maybe twenty." If we're lucky, he thought. But they were young, there were five of them, and he knew twenty years was a dream.

"And with parole," Luria hissed, "good behavior, and aptitude tests . . ."

"That shit won't buy much time from a murder rap," Hawkins said.

Luria was ready. "But some, right? A year, six months. So what are we talking about, Inspector, six years for killing Adam, seven?"

Levy put his hands over his ears but Luria pulled them away. "Listen to it, Jacob. You can't hide now any more

* Bastards.
† Bargain.

61

than you could then. Tell him, Hawkins. Tell the truth. Seven years for murder . . . tell him!"

Levy appealed to Hawkins, "It'll be fifteen, won't it? Twenty . . ."

Suddenly it was an auction. *Do I hear twenty-five?*

"I don't know."

"Then they're right?" Levy was begging him, but he didn't know for what. Luria waited, the whole circle waited.

Hawkins said, "Maybe."

Levy looked at Hawkins for a long time, then said sadly, "Seven years isn't enough." A verdict he didn't want to come to, Hawkins thought, but he didn't know who was on trial for what. "Just not enough," Levy said, and the circle shifted and seemed to ease back.

"Time to eat," Dworkin said. He touched Hawkins's arm. Hawkins shrugged him off. "Jacob, we'll get them and they'll go to prison. Shit, Jacob, it's hell in there . . ." Levy wasn't listening and Dworkin's hand was back on Hawkins's arm. "You have to eat, Roger."

Hawkins didn't know what he'd lost, only that he had.

Levy said softly, finally, "Go eat, Roger."

Hawkins stood up. The men outside the circle were still talking and eating. They hadn't heard any of this. They weren't part of it any more than Hawkins was. He was dismissed. Alldmann and Roth moved to let him out; Dworkin kept a hold on his arm, and before he could say any more to Levy he was on the outside and Dworkin was leading him to the table. He looked back. It was a definite circle, seven men and one empty stool. A circle of men—a tribe in Brooklyn.

Dworkin filled a paper plate with salads, lox, and, sturgeon and held it out to Hawkins. He didn't take it. "Abe, why did Luria slap you?"

Dworkin held the plate. "He was very nervous," he said. "It was a terrible night."

"But you said something first. It sounded like Aunt Sophie."

"Aunt Sophie?" Dworkin asked.

"But drawn out . . . Aaaauunt Sooophie."

Dworkin looked down at the plate. "We have to find you some place to sit." He paused, then he said, "Listen to me, we come from the same village; we lived there for generations, maybe centuries. And after so long we're probably related. Cousins, at least. It's possible. So Adam was a cousin. More—a son, because he was so bright, and we could be so proud of him."

If they *were* a family, Hawkins thought, they didn't look like one. But even if they were, something more connected them. Family men compete, discuss, argue. These men didn't even have to talk to each other. They were quiet, but no one was uncomfortable. An outsider broke the circle, bent over Levy, and said something. Then he spoke to Walinsky; then he left the circle, and they relaxed, because it was only them again.

"We'll try the dining room," Dworkin said, and he went down the hall, waving at Hawkins to follow. But Hawkins stopped in the doorway to look one more time at the men in the circle.

Dworkin came back without the plate. "You must eat," Dworkin told him. Then in the kindest voice he said, "Customs last because they have a reason. You loved him, too, your grief is sharp and you feel empty. Eat, you'll see, the emptiness shrinks and with it a tiny edge of the sorrow. Lean down to me." Hawkins did, thinking Dworkin wanted to whisper something. But he kissed Hawkins's cheek gently, firmly, with what seemed great affection. Then he said, "I just cried out last night.

63

The sound was meaningless but it startled poor Isaac and he struck out blindly. You know how it is. . . ." He patted Hawkins's arm, then went back to his stool and sat down. No one greeted him, no one even looked up, but the circle was complete.

Hawkins passed the dining room where Dworkin's daughter, Golda Cohen, guarded his plate; Rachel wasn't there. He went to the bathroom. The place was so hot even the tiles were warm. He looked at himself in the mirror. What battle did he lose and Luria win? What was so hard for Levy to face then and now?

He opened the door and went out into the hall. Mrs. Rosenblatt was waiting. She patted him. "Good to see you, Roger. It's been too long . . . call." She went into the bathroom and he opened the door to Adam's room and went inside.

The horses looked down; young, beautiful Levy smiled at him from the bedside table over a big wedding *chalah*. He went to the aquarium; the fish sensed his presence and came to the top waiting to be fed. "Your master's dead," he told them. They hung there for a time, angels, and gueramis, the sweet black mollies with the bug eyes that never fought or bit other fish.

"Dead," he told them. Tears filled his eyes. Adam, he thought. Adam, my friend. I can't imagine what it will be like without you on this earth, without being able to think of you living somewhere. To call or see . . .

The fish had waited long enough, and they swam away.

He found Rachel in the big bedroom that had been Levy's; she sat on the bed crying and holding the edge of her skirt in a wad in her hand. The dress was black with long sleeves and a high neck, and a scarf covered her hair.

"I can't get up," she said. Her face was pale, shining with sweat and tears. The scarf pulled at the sides of her face, making her eyes slant.

"Help me," she said, rocking from side to side, still trying to get up on her own.

Her scarf was damp, and he wanted to take it off and dry her hair for her. He wanted to loosen the neck of the dress and help her take off her shoes and stockings. He suddenly thought of a French movie he'd seen with Mo when they were young. Jeanne Moreau was in it, and everyone said it was hot stuff because this guy went down on her on camera. He and Mo tried to get dates, and couldn't, but they went anyway. He could see the actress's mouth right now, fat, bitten-looking in the front. He could see her lying back on the bed, naked except for a string of pearls around her neck. He could see her in a white nightgown, walking through a field of tall grass with gauzy movie light shining on a lake in the distance. The graceful reeds bent as she moved, and her voice was soft and exquisite as she said in French, with the English printed in white on the gray screen, *Love can happen in an instant.*

"Help me," Rachel said again, and he crossed the room to her. She was white and Adam's widow, he told himself. Adam had been his best friend, and this was the day of his funeral. He stood in front of her and told her to bend her arms and hold them stiff. He tried not to look at the damp curls of her hair that escaped the scarf, or her nipples poking against the front of her dress. He looked over her head, cupped her elbows, and hoisted her up off the bed. Her belly brushed him, pressed lightly against his, and he got an erection. He knew she could feel it, and he stepped back quickly and crossed his hands in front of him preacher style.

She smiled at him. "We're moving," she said softly.

"Where?"

"Way out on the Island. Near Golda. We're buying a house and a shop with the insurance money."

"A shop?" he said stupidly. "You and Jacob?"

She nodded, still smiling at him. He sensed that she wanted to look down at his body. "It's hard to imagine a Brooklyn Yiddish bookstore way out on the Island," he said. They were whispering to each other.

"We'll carry stationery, too, and some paperbacks. We'll do all right. Jacob'll give you the address . . . you'll come to see us, won't you? There's a garden, and we'll be near the Sound. . . ."

A tear ran down her cheek. He reached up to wipe it away, but before he could touch her the door opened, light from the hall came into the dim hot room, and Golda Cohen marched in. She stared at Hawkins and he knew how bad it looked: he was alone in a dark room with Rachel, reaching for her; he was big and black, she was frail and white, and he still had the hard on, which felt solid and frighteningly free; it would sway if he moved.

"I thought you'd gotten lost," Golda said. He didn't answer. She tried to look stern. "There's fifty pounds of pickled fish waiting for you and my ass is melted." She turned to Rachel. "You look like shit."

He looked at that face; did she? he wondered. And how did she usually look? He remembered her as Adam's bride, lifting her veil to kiss her new husband who was blushing and had shining eyes.

"It's a hell in this place," Golda said.

Rachel was looking at Hawkins over Golda's shoulder.

"Come home with me," Golda said. "It's air-conditioned, you can sit by the pool tomorrow. . . ."

"I can't leave Jacob," Rachel said.

"They'll be here for seven days. He won't even know you're gone," Golda said.

Hawkins backed to the door.

"He needs *me*, Golda."

Golda shrugged. She had light red dyed hair, a big pleasant face, and eyes as warm as her father's.

"The invitation stands. Tonight, tomorrow night. Any night you say." Her voice was gruff but full of kindness. Then she turned to Hawkins. "You'll be glad to hear I threw all that crap out. There was enough salt in that fish to pickle your balls."

He got the door open.

"They put out a coffee urn, and some Danish," she was saying to Rachel. "and they spilled coffee on your *bubbe*'s* lace cloth. I put seltzer on it, but you can see the stain. We'll try vinegar."

Hawkins went out into the hall and closed the door.

Hawkins ordered coffee in a cup, not in the glass they usually served at the Union Dairy. Pinchik did, too, then took out the bottle and in plain sight of everyone poured vodka in the coffee. The cream curdled instantly.

Pinchik tried it. "Awful," he said.

"Awful," Hawkins agreed.

"Roger, we're moving."

Pinchik and Levy were moving; Adam was dead. Hawkins looked out of the window at the street. It was almost ten, but it was warm and clear, and the street was crowded with people. Fat Spanish women in flowered cotton dresses and men in shirt-sleeves passed the window. Some kids had opened a hydrant, and the water ran slowly in the gutter carrying leaves and litter with it. Jewish men in wide-brimmed black hats and long coats stepped care-

* Grandmother's.

67

fully across the river the hydrant water made, then walked on, arm in arm. Pinchik followed Hawkins's eyes, and he looked through the window, too, as he talked.

"I don't want to go," Pinchik said softly. "I was born two blocks from here; I was bar mitzvahed at Shaare Tikvah, and married at the Candlelight; I was gonna die here." He smiled wanly. ". . . to die in Brooklyn, in Beth Israel a few miles from here. In a semiprivate room with a view of the bay. A good room to die in . . . color TV, phone. In the morning I watch the tankers come in, in the afternoon I watch *As the World Turns*, at night, the stars, the ceiling, *The Rockford Files* . . . then die."

He turned his head away. "This was my hometown, Roger, as surely as if I'd come from Cairo, Illinois, or Ames, Iowa. People forget that when you say you're from Brooklyn. But it's true. My hometown. Now I gotta go."

"Just because of Adam . . ."

"*Just* because of Adam? Are you crazy?"

"No. Adam could have been murdered in Cairo, Illinois, or Ames, Iowa."

"But he wasn't. Christ, look out there, Roger. The streets are filthy and the nice old houses . . . Lensky's, Shirmer's, the del Pinos' . . . they're rooming houses with little hot plates in the bedrooms and one toilet for every floor. And the people are different. Oh, I know, we're supposed to love each other anyway. But they're different in ways that task me. I hate them, they hate me. My son is eight, and full of life, but he won't go out to play. He's scared, Roger. It's still light at seven, but he sits in the kitchen like an old man and stares out of the window. Five times this year they stole his lunch money. Five times! The last time, one of the little bastards kicked him in the balls. An eight-year-old kid. What should I do? *Nu*, tell me. I could teach him to fight like them, I suppose. But is the rest of the world like Flatbush and Bed-Stuy? Is it? Do I want an eight-year-old kid around who kicks other kids in the balls, or pounds them in the face or stabs them? Do I?"

Hawkins couldn't answer.

"No, Roger. I'm gonna figure that my son can get by without learning to kill. I'm gonna figure that there is civilization out there. And that's where I'm going."

"Where is it," Hawkins asked at last, "this civilization?"

"Riverdale," Pinchik answered. They laughed so hard that old Yoshe, the waiter, told them to shut up because they were disturbing the other customers.

He took Pinchik's new address and phone number and they promised each other they'd get together at least once a month.

Chaim Garfield had read about the murder of the rabbi's son. He tried not to think about it, especially now on Rosh Hashanah, but the details kept coming back to him. Stabbed twenty times, the paper had said. He stopped in the middle of the sidewalk, looked up through the branches of a tree, and prayed that Reb Levy had not had to see his son's body. Other people on the street looked curiously at him, and he walked on up Route 9A to 236th Street, then across to the river. It was late, the services were over at most shuls by now, and the people were home for dinner. Dinner was waiting for him, too. There would be chicken basted with honey and orange juice, *tsimmes* made with honey and apples, and honey cake. Everything sweet in hopes the new year would be the same. He walked with his head up like he always did, not looking where he was going, and he tripped on the uneven sidewalk and had to grab a tree trunk to keep from falling. He shook his head at himself and went on. He left shops, houses, buildings behind and reached the riverbank in front of a huge gray stone apartment building. There must be a hundred miles of hallways in the place, he thought; more. He didn't like this backdrop for the ritual he had to perform, but there were probably other people at the prettier river accesses and he wanted to be alone.

He wasn't usually a loner; he liked being with people. He'd been trained for the rabbinate by the rabbi of Vorka, and when they sent him to Theresienstadt, the "model" camp, the older men kept up the teaching. He wasn't sure anymore if there was a God, or how he felt about him if there was, but he'd stayed a rabbi when he got to America, first in Washington Heights, then in Riverdale. First because he liked people; he wasn't sure why else—inertia maybe. He wanted to be alone for this ritual because the others believed in it, or looked like they did, and he didn't. He was going to do it anyway. Again, he wasn't sure why. Maybe because he always had.

He half slid down the short bank and stood on a narrow stone shelf above the river. It was clear, the rain had stopped, there was no fog and he could see the lights on the Jersey shore and on the bridge. He stood at the edge of the shelf so the river was only a few feet below him, and he bowed his head. He didn't pray. He looked into the water instead and thought that sturgeon were living there again, and shad, then he turned out the pockets of his jacket and trousers, symbolically brushing sins out of his clothes into the water. He brushed lint out of them, and crumbs of tobacco; they made a small scum on the river, which was gone in an instant. He unrolled his cuffs and brushed them into the water, too, then took off his jacket and flapped it over the river. Then, still holding his jacket over the fast current, he said in Hebrew, "Cast all our sins into the depths of the sea; and may You cast all the sins of Your people ... the house of Israel ... into a place where they will not be remembered; or visited, or ever again come to mind."

Later that night, after his daughters had gone back home to Scarsdale and Hartsdale with their husbands and children and his wife had made her last phone call and gone to sleep, he went into the clean kitchen that still smelled of honey, and, with just the moonlight to show him where things were, he prepared a box of food—a jar of honey, a wrapped piece of honey cake, chicken, and a plastic container of *tsimmes*—to take to Ossining tomorrow, to his brother Meyer who was serving a life sentence for murder.

THEY FOUND knives in the lake in the park, but they were clean and could have come from anywhere. They searched the boys' houses while their mothers trailed them from room to room followed by a procession of children, and found nothing. They searched the clubhouse and found some grass, dirty pictures, comic books, beer, and a guitar with a broken string. Hawkins looked out of the basement window at the blank wall in front of it, and plucked the dead-sounding strings. It was the last day of formal mourning and after the search he went to Levy's.

The apartment was quiet except for Oshevsky at the door, and the circle of men. But the circle was smaller, and Hawkins realized that Luria and Fineman were missing. Walinsky said he didn't know where they were, and Dworkin was asleep in his chair with his hands folded in front of him.

Levy looked and sounded vague, except about moving. He had their new address and phone number written down for Hawkins and he watched while Hawkins put it in his wallet; then he went back to staring at the far wall over the heads of the other men.

Hawkins left the living room and went looking for

Rachel. She wasn't in the kitchen. The bedroom door was closed and he knocked on it, then opened it with his heart pounding, but it was empty. He went back down the hall to Adam's room. The pictures were off the walls, the books were packed, and the aquarium was gone. There was nothing left but the bed, surrounded by packing boxes. He shut the door quickly and stood in front of it for a moment, then he went back through the apartment. When he got to the little entry hall, he turned around for one last look. Jacob was still staring at the wall. He was pale, his eyes were half-closed. He looked like he was in a trance, but Hawkins saw him blink. The other men's heads were bowed, and the scene was oddly silent and motionless. It bothered him for some reason. He went out the front door and, without thinking, he let it slam, but he knew none of them would even look up to see who'd left.

He wrote Levy's new address in his book when he got to the office. He tried to work, but he kept thinking of the men in the circle. They'd looked like they were waiting for someone, except Levy, who'd looked like he was having a vision.

Hawkins went through the papers on his desk; the commissioner wanted an income/education breakdown on the new black rookies. He was supposed to write a speech for a PBA meeting, on anything he wanted, and he tried to work on it, but couldn't. He looked out of his window at people in the little park next to the buildings. He made up lives for them. The man with the striped red and black umbrella was a customers' man with three children. The harried look and conservative three-piece suit told him that much. But the umbrella was gaudy, and didn't fit. So maybe the man was a fag . . . a closet job. A squall came up, rain crashed down, and the people ran for cover; the drops hit hard, mud splattered the sidewalk and peoples' legs, and Hawkins thought of Adam in his fresh grave, the rain smashing against the dirt that covered him. He'd go to the grave today and leave a pebble as a token of his visit the way Adam had done when they'd gone to old Feldsher's grave. He would pray for his friend, even though he hadn't prayed since he was a kid and didn't remember any prayers. He'd ask Ableson to go with him, to help him.

He tried to call Ableson, but he was out. He tried again at four and at five, but Lerner hadn't heard from him and he sounded worried.

He tried again to work, but he couldn't forget that it was after five and Mo still hadn't called in. It wasn't like him. Mo was a rock, the most reliable officer in that precinct—or any other, Hawkins thought. If only they were all like Mo. Then where was he? Hawkins looked at the clock. Five-fifteen. It was getting dark earlier now and they couldn't go to the grave today. They'd go on Sunday, and maybe bring Alma and Peg. Five-twenty-five and still no Mo. Hawkins wondered if his old friend had found another woman. He wouldn't tell Hawkins if he had, because Hawkins was Peg's friend, too, and he'd hate knowing about it. Maybe Mo was getting it right now at the Granada Hotel across from the precinct.

At five-thirty-five Mo called on Hawkins's private line. "Roger, help me." He sounded sick.

"Where are you?"

"The clubhouse on President Street. Take a squad car. Use the siren." Incredibly, Ableson sobbed. "Get here, oh God, get here. . . ."

Every window on President Street was dark. Hawkins watched Ableson climb out of his car like an old man, holding the door frame and seatback to pull himself up. Gray mud or something was smeared all over the front of Ableson's jacket, his face was in shadow, and Hawkins had a sudden nightmare image of mud melting off his friend's face like gray acid, taking flesh and features with it, leaving clean, white bone behind. The people would come to the windows then, but they would have smooth, hairless stocking-mask faces with gauze eyes. Ableson reached him and raised his head; he was just Ableson, but very pale.

He said, "The boys in the clubhouse are dead."

Hawkins looked up the street. It was empty and silent; the rain fell steadily.

"All five?" Hawkins asked.

"All five," Ableson answered. The stuff on Ableson's clothes smelled of mold, mud, algae, and rotting vegetation, like a tidal swamp or pond bottom.

Hawkins looked into Ableson's eyes; they were glazed and open too wide. "Mo," he said as gently as he could, "Mo, we need help here. Call Lerner, then turn on the lights for me."

Mo grabbed his arm, and something in Hawkins shriveled at the thought of getting that stuff on him. "Don't go down there, Roger . . ."

"It's okay." He tried to sound soothing. "Just get me some light."

"Don't," Ableson cried. Hawkins repeated stubbornly, "The light, Mo." But Ableson didn't move. Hawkins went to the squad car and turned on the top light and the side spots. He even turned on the headlights. Red and white beams speared the rain. He went to the steps and looked into the well. Gray stuff streaked the walls, steps, and stone floor. The window was smashed and only the tip of the pointed eagle's wing was left on a long shard sticking out of the frame. The door was splintered and hung loose. The steps looked slick and Hawkins reached for the wall, touched gray slime, and snatched his hand back. He wiped it on the clean stone edge of the basement well until he'd scraped the skin. He got to floor level, left the turning light behind, and went through the wrecked door into the basement.

There was more mud here, and the smell was stronger, mixed with basement smell. He breathed through his mouth, but then he thought he could taste the smell. It was metallic and moldy and seemed to coat his tongue. He swallowed, trying not to gag, and pulled his flashlight out of his pocket. The rotating light from the car came through the window, but all it did was throw shadows, and he thought he saw a pile of pipes and conduits or broken furniture. Then his foot hit something soft, and he shone his light down. His shoe rested against a denim covered leg. He moved the light up. There was nothing where the leg should have joined the torso. His gorge rose but he made himself look. Femoral blood leaked slowly through the torn flesh, marrow oozed out of smashed bone on the muddy cement floor. He retched and dropped the light. It rolled, and shadows jumped all around him; then it stopped. He saw bodies in the light, tangled together, thrown against the wall and covered with gray mud.

Hawkins stood under the shower until his fingers puckered and the hot water faltered and ran out. He tied a towel around his waist, came out into the kitchen, and shoved all his clothes, even his shoes and his good raincoat, into a big plastic trash bag and carried the bag out back with the rest of the garbage. It was warm again, people's windows were open, and he heard talking and laughing. He went back and sat at the table his father had made, surrounded by cabinets his father put in thirty years ago.

His mother put on the TV in the den. Out on the street something fell with a crash and his head started aching. He tried to think about Levy, the circle of men, and the dead boys in the clubhouse, but the headache intruded and he gave up and just sat at the bare table, suspended, while background music to some TV show came out through the den door. The kitchen window was open, and the noise of his neighbors' TVs and radios echoed in the courts and bounced off the walls of the houses until the whole back of the block echoed. It was a trick of sound that reminded Hawkins of the courtyard in *A Tale of Two Cities* where Sydney Carton waited on a Sunday afternoon for Lucie Manette. It was summer, London was quiet, and Carton could hear footsteps on the street he couldn't see. As they got closer, they were magnified and multiplied by the courtyard walls until two people walking sounded like hundreds rushing. The echoes had foreshadowed the future.

Hawkins listened to Walter Cronkite intoning the news, a game show audience screaming, the twang of country music, men saying lines in a movie or play, and lugubrious background music, and he wondered if the babble presaged some chaos coming. He thought of the basement and the bodies thrown around like trash. He wondered which one of the dead boys was the one who'd cried, and the pain in his head got so bad he pushed the sides of his skull with his fists. The noise got louder for a second, then the wind started up, the dead air that fed the volume moved, and the din subsided.

He tried to eat, but couldn't. He took aspirin and went to bed, praying that the headache wouldn't be there in the morning, but it was.

"WHAT ARE you going to say about Levy?" Ableson asked.

Hawkins wet some brown paper towel and pressed it against his eyes.

"Why should I say anything about Levy?"

"It's going to come up, Roger. Adam was Levy's son."

Hawkins wet the towel again.

"You got a hangover?" Ableson asked gently.

"No."

"So what about Levy?"

Hawkins kept his eyes covered. They were bloodshot and burning and his head still pounded. He'd never had a headache like this before.

"What do we say about Levy and the rest of them?" Ableson asked again.

Hawkins didn't have to answer because Joe Turner pushed open the men's room door.

He smiled when he saw Hawkins and the towel, a nasty smile that Hawkins was used to.

"They's waitin' on you, darlin'. All the brass of this fair city. Waitin' on *their* man." Turner was black and he hated Hawkins. White man's nigger, he called him, and whenever Hawkins would pass him and some of the other black detectives talking in a bunch in the hall or lounge, they'd get quiet and watch him go by with smiles on their faces. Hawkins rubbed his head.

"Got DTs?" Turner asked.

"Shut the fuck up," Ableson said.

"Dear, dear . . ." Turner said. He went out and Hawkins and Ableson followed him down the hall to the press room.

The place was hot and crowded. Stringers and steadies lined the walls and packed the back of the aisles. There was a mike set up at the front, and Pescado and the chief stood in the front. Turner led Hawkins and Ableson to two empty folding chairs in the back row.

"What'd I tell you, honey," Turner said. "The fairhaired boy's here, and they can start. . . ."

Suddenly Hawkins grabbed Turner's arm and squeezed it until the other man gasped. People nearby turned around.

"One more word, Joe Motherfucker," Hawkins whispered loudly, "and press or no press, I'll punch your yellow eyes out."

Turner yanked his arm free and left the room. Ableson stared at Hawkins in amazement, so did Mary Ryker who was in the row ahead. Hawkins sat down and tried to concentrate on Pescado and the commissioner on the podium.

Pescado was at the mike first. The boys had been beaten to death, he said; they'd put up a fight, but either they were outnumbered two or three to one or the killers were much bigger. The dead boys accounted for the blood types identified, which meant that either their assailants had the same blood types as the boys, or they weren't injured enough to bleed. The press wrote, and Pescado waited for questions. One of the stringers asked about weapons; Pescado said they hadn't found any except the boys' knives; then a *News* steady said, "We saw mud all over the place."

Fluorescents on the ceiling speared Hawkins's eyes.

"Yes. . . . But we don't know what it was doing there. It's just clay. We're checking, but I don't think we'll be able to pinpoint it. It's too common."

The chief came to the mike. "Right now, we're operating on the assumption that the clay was used as a gesture of contempt."

A short, very thin, dark man stood up. He had light blue eyes, like the Eagle that Hawkins had seen in the station the night they murdered Adam. "Giorgio," the little man said, "*Times*." The commissioner and Pescado waited.

" 'Gesture of contempt' implies a rival gang," Giorgio said. "Is that how you see it?"

Pescado and the commissioner nodded in unison, and Hawkins thought they looked like dummies on strings.

"Any line on which rival gang?" Giorgio asked.

The chief answered, "No, uh . . . no idea . . . at this time."

Oliver Ames from the *Journal* stood up next. He was the best crime reporter in the country. Hawkins knew what he was going to ask and he wanted to get out of there, but the aisle was packed, people stood against the door, and he was trapped.

Ames said, "The Eagles were arrested for murder last week."

The chief nodded.

"Then what about the family of the man they were arrested for killing?"

Hawkins put his hand over his eyes.

"Roger—" Ableson whispered.

The chief said, "There's only a father and wife. The

father's over sixty and the wife's seven months pregnant."

The pain in Hawkins's head turned into a sick headache, and if he didn't get to the toilet he was going to throw up on the floor. He pushed his way through the crowd and made it to the men's room, but wasn't sick after all, and when Ableson found him, he was half sitting on the combination radiator and windowsill.

"That was some performance," Ableson said.

Hawkins didn't say anything.

"They probably think you were drunk or scared for Levy."

Hawkins stared out at the tops of the buildings downtown; he was frowning, and Ableson noticed a deep line that ran between his eyebrows to the bridge of his nose. Hawkins wasn't so young anymore. Neither was he.

"Why should they think that?" Hawkins asked softly.

"Because everyone knows Levy's your friend; and Adam was his son."

Hawkins looked at him. "So he's capable of beating five kids to death?"

"There's Luria, don't forget, and Walinsky and the whole *mishpochah*.* Luria's capable of anything. Besides, Adam was Levy's *son*."

Hawkins threw his cigarette in the toilet. "If you say that again, Mo, I'll tear your fucking head off."

Ableson drove up the ramp into the City Hall section, then up the Bowery to Third and through the tunnel to the LIE. He felt dirtied, like the kid who sees his daddy making love to the maid, and he knew it was because Hawkins—his best friend, his idol almost—had acted like a stranger.

* Clan.

Hawkins wasn't like Turner. He didn't hate anybody, and Ableson had never seen him lose his temper. He was so big, only men who were too drunk to know what they were doing called him nigger. But even when that happened, he wouldn't fight.

Like the night, years ago, when this big red-faced rummy wanted to take Hawkins on with everyone watching. He was as tall as Hawkins, and bigger. He had a bright red face, a belly that hung over his belt, and arms like a bear. He sat next to Hawkins and Ableson at the bar and he kept calling Hawkins nigger, as if it were his name. *Nigger, who do you like in the NFL playoffs? . . . Nigger, lemme buy you a beer*, shit like that. But Hawkins wouldn't break, and the drunk got so frustrated he pushed Hawkins hard in the chest, and Hawkins had to hang on to the bar to keep from falling on the floor. Hawkins and the white man slid off their barstools and faced each other. Everyone stopped drinking to watch. The place was dead silent, and Ableson saw a look of triumph in the white man's eyes as he squared off. But Hawkins raised his big hands fast, grabbed the man's shoulders, and held him stiff-armed so the drunk couldn't get any closer. Sweat ran down Hawkins's face, and the drunk strained against the hands that held him, but he couldn't move. Then Hawkins started talking.

"Let me tell you about this book I'm reading," he said wildly. "It's called *Oblomov* and it's about this guy who can't get out of bed. No, I mean it. All he does is lay in bed, day and night, and then he meets this woman and she falls for him. Shit, I can't remember her name . . . I'll look it up and tell you later. Anyway, he falls for her, too."

The drunk stopped struggling and stared at Hawkins. Hawkins went on.

"And he's got this one chance to live, see. To be alive. All he has to do is get out of bed. . . ."

The drunk started to weep and Hawkins let him go. He stumbled blindly out of the place, still crying, with Vinnie and everyone else watching, and Hawkins got back on the barstool next to Ableson. He was sweating with rage and it took him a minute to talk. Then he said to Ableson, "If it weren't for Levy and the books, I'd've killed that asshole."

"You should've," Ableson said.

Hawkins turned to look at him. "Should I, Mo? Then what?"

He didn't turn violent the night they arrested Calladay either. It was way out in Bay Ridge, the coldest night of the year. The bay looked frozen green, and the bridge was covered with ice. They'd gotten a tip that Calladay was there, in this little house at the end of a crummy block, with his girl friend, and they'd come in the middle of the night, closed off the street, and surrounded the place. Nothing happened for hours, and they were all cold and miserable, hating the man who was keeping them there, and Ableson thought they'd start shooting as soon as the door opened. But Hawkins had the horn, and when the lights came on in the front, he got out of the car and stood next to it. Ableson took his gun out, and he knew the others were ready to kill like he was. But when the door opened, Hawkins said through the horn, in a voice so gentle and clear Ableson could still hear it if he tried:

"Don't, Mike. It's so fucking cold."

It was that simple, Ableson thought in amazement. No one wanted to die in that cold, to fall dead in the stiff filthy snow. And after a second, Calladay raised one hand high over his head, and then the other, and they arrested him without firing a shot.

83

That was the man Ableson knew. Not the nasty son of a bitch who threatened to punch Joe Turner's eyes out and tear Ableson's head off.

Ableson pulled into the Adventurer's Inn off the Expressway and ordered a brisket sandwich on a roll. He ate and tried to understand how this could happen to his best friend, the best man he'd ever known, in only one night. He decided it was Levy's fault. Hawkins loved Levy, and he had to know, like Ableson knew, that somehow Levy had killed those kids. So maybe he was afraid they'd catch Levy and Hawkins couldn't help him. Or maybe he was afraid that if Levy could do such a thing, even to avenge his son, then everything Hawkins thought about Levy . . . all the love and trust and gentleness . . . was a lie.

Ableson finished the sandwich and stuffed the paper plate and napkin into a litter can. Then he got back on the Expressway and headed home, cutting easily in and out of the early afternoon traffic. He was past Lefrack City—the ugliest place in the world, he thought—when Lerner called him.

"Get Roger," Lerner said, "and get in here. We got some guy in the pen who says he saw who killed the Eagles. . . ."

Chapter
6

LERNER CONDUCTED the interrogation in a small dingy room on the third floor of the precinct. Hawkins and Ableson sat to the side, Hawkins close to the wall, a little in the shadows of the room. Ableson watched his friend. He could see the tension in his back, and Ableson knew what he was thinking. This man—Juan Comera was his name—had seen the men who killed the boys in the basement. What if he said he saw some old men with black skullcaps and beards? What if he described Levy? Ableson watched Hawkins shift in his chair, trying to relax. He'd known Hawkins so well, and for so many years, he could almost hear the other man's thoughts.

How much did he really trust Levy, Hawkins would ask himself. Totally would be the answer. Then why was he nervous? Could Levy really kill five young men without a trial or any chance to speak for themselves? Not just kill them, but beat them to death and cover their bodies with mud? Could Levy plan that and then do it? Never, Hawkins would answer. But his body still wouldn't relax.

Lerner started the interrogation.

"What kind of car did you see?" Lerner asked Comera.

"It was a van, not a car. A green Dodge van," Comera answered. He was twenty-four. He was wearing clean chinos and a blue sport shirt that had been washed, ironed, and mended too many times.

"What about the plates?"

"I couldn't get the number," Comera said, "but I think they were New York. They were orange and black like ours."

Lerner nodded. Hawkins shifted in his chair.

"Can you tell us any more about the van?"

Comera shook his head. "Only that it had curtains; a lot of them do. I don't know what color."

Good, Ableson thought. The man was a clear, to-the-point witness.

"Fine," Lerner said encouragingly. "Now just tell us what happened. Everything you can remember. And try not to leave anything out, no matter how silly or insignificant it seems.

Comera nodded. "Where do you want me to start?"

"What made you look out of the window in the first place?"

"Noise," Comera said.

"What time was it when you first heard it?"

Comera said, "About five-thirty. I work in the Bond Factory in Long Island City. I get out at four-thirty, it takes about forty minutes to get home. My sisters and father weren't home yet. My mother was in the kitchen, and I'd opened a beer and turned on the TV. The local news. They were talking about the weather, which was lousy, and the traffic, and I fell asleep—at least I think I fell asleep—and when I first heard the noise I thought I was dreaming about home. I'm from Ponce," he said, "in Puerto Rico. Outside the town. And a lot of the people there keep their own animals. Pigs, chickens, a cow or two. And in the fall they'd slaughter them and you could hear the noise they'd make. And I hear this noise like animals screaming . . ."

Ableson looked at Hawkins. He was leaning forward in his chair.

". . . and I think I'm dreaming that I'm back in Ponce and someone's killing pigs outside. But I open my eyes, see the TV, and I know I'm in Brooklyn, not Ponce. Only I still hear that noise."

"You went to the window then?"

"No," Comera said.

"Why not?"

"I was scared." Hawkins didn't move, the tape slid through the recorder.

Lerner prompted, "But finally . . ."

"Yeah, finally I did," Comera said. "But I kept down, right at the sill."

"Why?" Lerner asked.

"You wouldn't ask that if you'd heard the noise; I didn't know what was going on or who was doing it, and I didn't want anyone out there to know I was watching."

"What did you see?"

"The van, and three guys standing on the sidewalk."

"Describe them, please."

Hawkins looked out of the window and Comera said, "Two were short, one was tall. Very tall. They were wearing plastic raincoats, the kind that fit in a bag, and rain hats, like sailors or fishermen wear."

"Slicker hats?" Lerner asked.

"Yeah."

"Did you see their faces?"

Ableson forced himself not to watch Hawkins.

"No," Comera said and Ableson heard Hawkins shift in his chair.

"Not at all?" Lerner asked.

Comera shook his head. "But I think they were white."

"Had the noise stopped?"

"No, man, it went on and on. Not just yelling . . . wood split, glass broke, stuff crashed. I thought that house would fall down."

"So the rest were still in the basement."

"What rest?" Comera said. "There was one more guy."

Ableson and Hawkins looked at each other.

"One man caused all that racket?" Lerner asked.

"That's all I saw."

Lerner thought, then said, "Maybe the rest didn't leave until you stopped watching."

"No. I saw them drive away and no one else came out."

No one knew what to ask next. Then Lerner said, "Go back to when the noise stopped."

"It just stopped. Like a stuck horn stops. Then the three on the sidewalk go down the stairs and I couldn't see them. Then they come up in a minute, and there's four of them."

"Could you see the fourth man's face?"

"No. He was wearing a big plastic poncho with a hood pulled down."

"Then what?"

"They opened the van panel, helped the fourth guy in, then they got in and drove away."

"Why did they help the fourth man? Was he hurt?"

"I don't think so. I think he was just big and clumsy."

"How big?" The question came from Hawkins. It was the first time he'd said anything.

"Real big," Comera said, "the tallest of the four."

"You said one of the three outside was very tall," Hawkins said.

"The fourth one was even taller."

"How tall was the third man?" Lerner asked.

Comera considered and looked at Hawkins.

"Maybe as tall as him."

Lerner said, "Stand up, Roger."

Hawkins got to his feet. He looked enormous in the low-ceilinged room.

"Try to see him in relation to the van," Lerner said. "Was the third man that tall?"

"Yes," Comera said softly, staring at Hawkins. He looked scared.

"And the fourth man was even bigger?"

Comera didn't answer; he was still staring at Hawkins.

"How tall are you, man?" he asked.

"Six three," Hawkins said.

"Oh God," Comera moaned. "Oh my God, the fourth one was bigger . . ." He held his arms wide to show them how much, then he looked at the spread and widened it even further. "Two feet . . . oh my God . . . three feet."

Pescado shut off the recorder and looked at Hawkins. His face was red and he was holding a peeled orange in one hand.

"I came all the way from Brooklyn to hear this shit," he said. "And it's total shit. No one's nine feet tall."

"Maybe he was only eight three," Hawkins said mildly. He still had the headache and everything in the room looked out of focus. He'd tried to call Levy three times, but Luria answered every time and said Levy was sleeping. He'd asked to talk to Rachel then, but Luria said she was busy. Alma kept calling, but he hadn't called her back, and the speech which he was supposed to give day after tomorrow was only half finished.

"No one's eight three either," Pescado said, sectioning the orange as he talked. "You gotta come up with something better than that." Orange juice dripped on Pescado's trousers as he leaned forward. "In the first place your witness is lying or crazy. There's no way one un-armed man could beat five other men to death. No way in the world."

"Maybe he was armed," Hawkins said.

"He wasn't. Did your genius witness see any weapons?"

"No," Hawkins answered.

"Right. Because there weren't any."

"So maybe they took them away or hid them . . ."

"They didn't. Weapons leave tracks. You know that, Roger. You show me a stab wound, and I can probably tell you if it was made by a butcher knife, a bowie knife, a nail. You hit someone with a baseball bat—it looks like you hit him with a baseball bat."

"Okay," Hawkins said warily, "no weapons."

"Not unless they were made of clay."

"Is there such a thing?" Hawkins asked.

"I never heard of it," Pescado answered.

Hawkins was quiet and Pescado opened his copy of the *Post*. There were pictures of the outside of the club-house, and of the basement room after they'd taken the bodies away. Hawkins didn't look at it. Pescado said, "Roger, one of the boys was torn apart."

Hawkins remembered the leg on the floor. He closed his eyes and breathed through his mouth.

"How did they do that?"

"I don't know," Pescado said. "I never saw anything like it. There's more."

"I'm waiting," Hawkins said quietly. He kept his eyes closed.

"The boys had their knives out. All of them."

"So?"

"If they had their knives out, they must've used them. Right?"

Hawkins didn't answer.

"But there was no blood on them, Roger."

Hawkins opened his eyes. "That's crazy," he said.

"Yeah, crazy."

Hawkins tried to think. A man six nine or seven two could look huge on a rainy evening in the street light. There might be weapons that Pescado never heard of . . . maces of wood or clubs made out of clay. But the bloodless knives didn't make sense, and never would, no matter how many witnesses they found or how much evidence they uncovered. The headache pounded and he stopped thinking and pulled the speech to him. The last paragraph read, *"We have to prove more than the cops before us. They just had to prove that they were regular guys because no one believed that they were. We have to prove . . ."* He pushed the speech away and picked up the *Post.* There was a picture of the basement room on page two, and yearbook and communion pictures of the boys. The one who'd cried was Jorge Ortiz; he was fifteen and a freshman in high school. The *Post* said the funeral was that afternoon, at one.

He called Levy again, but now the line was busy. Why had the boy cried? Because Adam had a father? Or because his wife was pregnant? Hawkins looked closely at the picture. He had been a handsome kid, trying to grow a mustache. He looked again at the clock. It was twelve-ten. He put on his jacket, told Betty, his secretary, she could get him on the car phone in an emergency but that he was going to a funeral and didn't want to be disturbed.

The church was yellow brick, big and ugly, and looked like it was meant to house a swimming pool. It was in a section of factories and gas stations mixed with asphalt-sided houses built to fit odd-shaped lots. A few trees came up through holes cut in cement. The murders made page one in the *Post* and *News*, and TV cameras waited at the foot of the church steps to catch the glistening of tears on the mothers' faces, or even better, on the fathers'.

Hawkins put on the plain sunglasses he kept in the glove compartment; he couldn't see too well with them, but it was a disguise of sorts. He kept to the side of the steps as he eased his way through the crowd and into the church. The families were in the front; the women were mostly overweight and pretty and they sat together in the first row, weeping and rocking. The men were in the second row. They wore shiny dark jackets with tight shoulders and sleeves that were too short. Hawkins stooped at the end of the row. One man saw him and nudged another, then another, until they were all staring at him. The looks were hostile, and he wondered weakly if it was because he was black or because he was a cop. He also wondered if they'd feel better if they knew how bad his head hurt. He smiled at them, but none of them smiled back and he went to the back of the church and stood to the side, while the priest went through the service for the dead.

The service was in English, but the sermon and eulogies were in Spanish so Hawkins couldn't understand what they were saying about the dead boys, about death itself. He leaned against a bilious-yellow stone pillar and looked out over the dark heads of the people. Almost all of them were from San Juan or Ponce, or villages on the coast. They lived within a few blocks of each other, went to the same butchers, vegetable stands, movie houses. They had bright painted plaster statues of the saints at home on false mantels or dressers or windowsills. They had souse for wedding feasts and trumpets for funerals. The trumpet started now, a beautiful moaning sound, and a drum came up under with a slow Caribbean beat. The pallbearers lifted the coffins and came up the aisle toward him, their tight jackets hiked up.

He left the church with the crowd and stood to the side at the top of the stairs as they carried the coffins down the stairs to waiting hearses. Sobbing mothers followed their sons' coffins, the cameras moved in to catch them coming down, and Hawkins turned and thought he saw Jacob come out of the crowd and head down the street. He didn't want to attract attention by calling, so he pushed through the crowd and down the stairs to the sidewalk, keeping the mass of people between himself and the cameras. The black-coated man walked fast toward the subway entrance at the end of the block and Hawkins went after him. He reached the head of the stairs just as the man went through the turnstile and Hawkins ran down the stairs, feeling in his pockets for a token. He didn't have one and there was no agent on duty to buy one, so he jumped the turnstile and ran into the passage to the westbound trains. The passage was empty. When Hawkins got to the southbound side he saw the man standing at the center of the platform with his back turned. Bare low-watt bulbs shone from the high arched ceiling. Dirty white tile walls caught the light, threw it back, making the air look misty. There were no trains coming, the station was silent and empty except for the two of them, and Hawkins knew as soon as he reached the platform that the man ahead wasn't Jacob. The man turned slowly, and Isaac Luria faced Hawkins.

"It's Jacob you want, isn't it?" Luria asked softly.

Hawkins couldn't answer.

"You can't have him," Luria said, "because he's leaving you. Right now, he's saying good-bye to the shop, to the streets, the people. To you. Say good-bye back, and I'll convey the message."

Tears of desolation filled Hawkins's eyes behind the flat dark glasses. He saw an empty room with dust balls rolling across a bare floor.

The train pulled in and Luria stood in the open door waiting for Hawkins to say something. When he didn't, Luria shrugged, "Good-bye then, Inspector, you should leave us alone now." The doors closed and the train pulled out of the station.

Hawkins made it from East New York to Flatbush in ten minutes. He stopped at the shop, but the window was empty, the stacks were gone, and so were the little folding table and chairs. He raced around the corner to Sterling and saw the moving van still standing in front of Levy's building.

He got out of his car and was halfway across the street when something made him turn around. A dark green Dodge van like the one Comera had described was parked three cars ahead of his. He crossed back and went around the front of the van. The license plates were orange and black, like New York plates, except that these were issued by the state of Minnesota, Land of a Thousand Lakes. Without thinking, he went back to his own car, opened the trunk, and found the long flat blade he carried in case he lost his keys or had to open a strange car. He went back to the Dodge, slid the blade between the window and door, felt the blade catch the lock mechanism. He pulled, the lock button popped up, and he opened the door. Two movers came out of the back of the truck and watched him. He sat in the front seat, closed the door, and inhaled. He smelled pine air freshener, stale smoke, and under that something else. A moldy, damp, muddy smell. The pond-bottom smell he'd never forget. He opened the glove compartment and found the registration. The car was owned by Rachel and Adam Levy. He put the registration back, got out, slid back the rear panel door, and felt the floor. It was slightly damp, as if it had been washed recently. He brushed at the carpet and gray powder came off on his fingers. He took out his handkerchief and wiped it off; it showed up clearly on the white linen.

He knew there was someone behind him, and he turned. It was Levy. He looked at the open van doors, and the gray streaked handkerchief in Hawkins's hand. He was pale, his yarmulke was pushed off-center from packing and moving boxes, which he shouldn't have been doing, and the front of his jacket was covered with dust. Hawkins waited for Levy to look at him, to explain. And if he couldn't, if there wasn't any explanation, Levy would talk to him in that quiet voice Hawkins loved listening to. He'd tell him what they'd done, and how. He'd plead for understanding, and Hawkins already knew he would understand. They'd work something out. Levy was old, so were the others. They were mad with grief over Adam. They'd never go to jail. . . . Hawkins waited for Levy to talk. But Levy looked down at the dust on the front of his jacket. He brushed at it, frowning. When he did speak, his voice wasn't halting or remorseful, it was clear and strong.

"What did you expect?" Levy asked, then he looked right into Hawkins's eyes without pleading or guilt. "What would you have done?" he asked. He waited, but Hawkins was too stunned to answer. Levy stared at him for a while, then turned and crossed the street. He didn't look back, and Hawkins watched him until he disappeared into the building.

Hawkins slammed the door of Ableson's little office. The walls shook.

"Levy did it," he said.

Ableson didn't say anything.

"The van belonged to Adam. They tried to clean it up, but this was still there." Hawkins pulled out the handkerchief. Ableson looked at it, then away.

"They did it," Hawkins said again.

Ableson nodded.

"Say something," Hawkins shouted.

"What?" Ableson asked mildly.

"Tell me how you're going to pin it on them."

"Tell me how they did it," Ableson said.

"We'll find out, Mo. . . ."

"*You'll* find out, Roger."

Hawkins looked murderous. "Get Lerner in here."

Ableson shook his head. "Adam was a Jew, the kids were Spanish," Ableson said. "A quarter of the men here're Jews, ninety percent are white . . . They'll lose tapes, Roger, reports'll get filed in the toilet. . . ."

"What the fuck are you talking about?"

Ableson went on in the same mild voice, "Those kids killed an innocent man with a pregnant wife and a father who'd been in the camps, and no matter who got them, or how, every man here is glad they're dead. You understand that, don't you?" Ableson asked softly.

Hawkins didn't answer, and Ableson opened his desk drawer and took out a telex sheet. "I found this by accident on Dan Schwartz's desk this morning."

He handed it to Hawkins. It was from R & I, a report

on a dark green 1980 Dodge van registered in Minnesota to Rachel and Adam Levy. It was dated three days earlier. "Schwartz said he meant to send it through, but he lost it or some shit. He had the grace to blush when he said it. And that's what'll happen to everything we get on this case. You want to hang them, Roger? I won't say you should or shouldn't, I won't say how I feel, because I swear to God, I don't know—but if you really want to hang them, take the report, tape, handkerchief, to that Ivy League bunch in Manhattan."

He took the cassette out of his drawer and held out both hands to Hawkins, one with the tape, one with the report. "Take it to the WASPs, Roger. Because if you leave it here, you ain't gonna hang nobody. They killed five kids without a trial, without even a chance to talk for themselves, and they're gonna walk for it unless you stop them."

Hawkins didn't move and Ableson's hands sank and rested on his desk.

"I'm sorry," he said, "I don't know what I'd do if I were you." He lifted the tape and report and held them out again. Hawkins hesitated, then took them and left the office.

"Hello, hello! Who's there?"

It was Pinchik's voice, sounding like it used to when Hawkins would call him Friday morning to see if he'd be at Vinnie's on Friday afternoon.

"What is it?" That was Rose Pinchik in the background.

"Some schmuck calls and doesn't talk," Pinchik said to her, then back to the phone, "Whatsa matter, schmuck, you can waste a dime to hear me call you names? *Nu? Shmekele . . . paskudnyak . . .*" Hawkins almost said it wasn't a dime, it was eighty cents and he needed help. But he couldn't talk.

"It's a breather," Pinchik told Rose, and he hung up. Hawkins stayed in the phone booth until a woman with a string bag and an umbrella banged on the glass. He showed her his badge and she yelled that that didn't give him the right to just sit in a phone booth when other people had to make calls. What about the call boxes that were everywhere the public phones should be. He wanted to open the door to tell her that he didn't have the strength to get up and even though she was a taxpayer she should let him sit here until his legs were steadier. But she banged on the door with her umbrella, and a few people stopped to see what was going on. Hawkins got the phone booth door open and walked stiffly out onto the street.

"He's drunk," she yelled at the people who'd stopped. "He's a cop. I saw his badge, and he's drunk." He made it to the wall of the building. It was a variety store and across the street was a sign in Arabic and strips of shiny pastry in the window. He was on Atlantic Avenue and he couldn't remember how he got there. He couldn't even remember getting into the phone booth in the first place. "Drunk!" the woman yelled.

The sun was over the Island.

It was morning and he couldn't remember where he'd spent the night. "And they give him a gun," she yelled. He kept his head down out of the light. He knew there was a bar half a block away that opened at eight-thirty. He went inside, out of the sunshine, and went right to the can. To himself he looked like an old black bum in the cloudy mirror over the sink, but Lerner would have to listen to him anyway. He had clout in Brooklyn, in Queens, and most of all in Manhattan with the chief and the mayor, and with or without Lerner's help he was going to start an investigation like they'd never seen.

He left the bar and found his car on State Street. He drove around the block, back toward the Expressway, but the sun blinded him and he forgot to turn and all at once he was in a little street he couldn't remember and the sun was so bright he couldn't see the signs. He kept going and made another turn that he was sure would get him back to Joralemon or Fulton, but instead he was under the Expressway, in the shadow of the bridge. The blocks were very short and he could see the bay to his left. He turned again and there was a stone church on the corner, with people just leaving mass, and across the street was a playground with kids in it, and nuns standing at the gates. Another turn and the bay was to his right. He didn't know these streets at all. The houses were strange, much poorer than in the Heights, and some looked empty. There was a vacant lot, and through it he could see a grape arbor in the backyard of one house. They made wine in the fall, and fruit brandy, and kept it all in the basement for Easter and for next Christmas. There'd be crucifixes on the walls, and pictures of Jesus with His heart neatly exposed, dripping blood. Hawkins turned and turned again, he drove faster around the corners, up and down the strange streets. He wanted to stop and ask someone to help him but the only people he saw were women wearing black dresses and scarves on their heads. They would be scared of a black man, and they wouldn't speak English. He tried to find some building or street that looked familiar, but all he found was the church with the steps, and the playground, empty this time.

He turned left doing fifty, the tires screeched, and an old woman jumped out of his way. He pulled over then and made himself breathe evenly until he calmed down. He was in Red Hook somewhere and if he turned left, then left again, and kept going, he'd get back to the Expressway. But he drove straight ahead to the river at the end of the street, left the car in an empty asphalt square, and got out on shaky legs.

He walked out on a sort of dock that was covered with abandoned clay conduits, broken cinder blocks, and steel drums rusting in the sun. The asphalt heaved up from the weather and years of neglect, and he had to walk carefully. There was scree further out on the dock and his feet scraped and slid, but he kept going until he was at the edge of the river where it widened to the bay, and lower Manhattan and all the bridges were to his right.

They were going to walk and he was the only one who could stop them. He could do it. The people on that block hated cops, but they hated Jews more, so they'd talk and he'd get a sane description of the fourth man. If he didn't, he'd do to the tribe what he'd planned for the kids, he'd find the weak link and push. Dworkin . . . little Dworkin with his soft brown eyes was his man. He'd pull him in at midnight and at six in the morning, at all hours, until the old bastard had his days and nights all mixed up. He'd pull him in on Friday nights and on Saturday morning, and there'd be nothing for him to eat but ham sandwiches. Hawkins grinned. He'd make sure the others knew what was happening and they'd push Dworkin, too, so he'd be getting it from both sides. In a week, a month at the most, the old fart'd break and deal. Jews were good at deals, Hawkins thought nastily, and he'd have his fourth man. The big one in the poncho, the key, and once Hawkins had him, he'd have the rest of them.

It'd be a big case, bigger than Son of Sam. *Vigilante*

Jews Kill Five Spanish Kids. Big news, big time. The case would make Hawkins's name and, best of all, the whole bunch of lying Holy Rollers would spend the rest of their lives in the can. Levy too. Especially Levy.

The prison barber would shave his beard and cut his hair. He'd wear blue work clothes like Meyer Garfield and he'd live like the rest of the killers. But for how long? How long could a skinny old man with skin like white paper last at Ossining? A year, Hawkins thought, maybe two. He'd die alone in his bunk with the toilet next to him in his cell. Or in that bare yard under the basketball hoop with a circle of murderers, rapists, and thieves for company. . . .

Hawkins bent double like a man with a cramp because he suddenly remembered that when Levy left the barber they'd take him to the showers. They'd strip him like they'd stripped the prisoners in the camps. Then they'd lead him, shivering and frightened, to the stone shower room. They'd give him soap like the SS had given the condemned and he'd stand alone on the cold floor under the shower head like all those other people had done, waiting for water or gas to come out of the holes in the rusting metal. Hawkins groaned again and someone touched his shoulder.

"You okay, man?"

A huge black man squatted next to him. He was sixty and overweight; he was wearing a light gray silk suit, gray silk shirt with a maroon tie, and gray alligator shoes. His face was coarse, deep lines ran down the sides of his mouth, and his hair was powdered with gray. But his eyes were large, soft, and kind, and his hand rested gently on Hawkins's back.

"You sick, man?" he asked.

Hawkins looked past him and saw a gray Cadillac

almost the color of the suit waiting at the end of the dock.

"Hey, boy," the black man said, rubbing Hawkins's back gently. "Nothin' kin be so bad. I'll git you a drink, a steak, find you a little nookie, you'll be okay, boy."

"I'm okay," Hawkins said.

"No, you ain't. You in awful condition . . . what happened to you?"

Hawkins looked at the other man's gentle homely face and said, "A man I love is a murderer, and I can make him pay for it—" he stopped. The man put his hand under Hawkins's arm and pulled him effortlessly to his feet. He brushed at Hawkins's jacket.

"A man?" he said. "A lover man, a frien', what?"

"Like . . . a father," Hawkins answered.

The man stopped brushing and looked very serious. "You can't bitch aroun' with yo' daddy, boy, no matter what he done."

The man let Hawkins go, and after a moment Hawkins took the tape and the report out of his pocket. The man watched him closely as he walked to the very edge of the dock. He looked down at the river that ran at his feet, crumpled the report into a ball, drew back his arm, and threw the tape and report out into the river. The tape sank at once. The report fell slower, held up by the wind. It hit the water, bobbed, then blended with the other litter and Hawkins couldn't see it anymore. Tears he couldn't control ran down his face and the other man took his arm, clucked with sympathy, and led him gently but insistently off the dock to the sunny street.

Chaim Garfield sat at the kitchen table with half the paper. He hadn't seen one since the holiday started, or heard the TV or radio. He was hungry, and before the formal cold meal to break the fast of Yom Kippur he had half a bagel smeared with butter and cream cheese and a glass of sweet wine. There would be guests soon, people from his shul who visited him every year at the end of the holiday, and his wife and daughters were arranging platters of cold fish and cheeses and hard-boiled eggs. One of his sons-in-law was across the table from him with the news section, the other had turned on the TV in the small bedroom, and his granddaughter was asleep in her portable crib in the big bedroom. The women talked quietly, the TV noise was only a murmur, and he chewed his bagel and looked out at the river, feeling, as he always did when this holiday was over, a great sense of peace. The feeling bemused him. He'd atoned for sins he hadn't committed in the name of a God he didn't like, and he couldn't understand why the experience gave him peace. He shook his head at his reflection in the window. No one noticed. His son-in-law finished the first section of the paper and they traded. The murder of the five boys was on a back page and he read the story.

He wondered how Jacob Levy would feel reading the same story. Maybe he was a vengeful man and the murders satisfied him. But then Garfield thought about the mothers of the dead boys and he tried to weigh the two sets of grief against each other, the mothers' for their dead sons, and Levy's for his. He knew he'd never be able to take sides and if he didn't stop trying he'd wind up feeling so lousy he'd have to go to sleep. Then he noticed the word *clay* in the story. It reminded him of something and he made himself think about that so he could stop thinking about Jacob Levy and the five mothers. He finished his bagel, had another glass of wine, and tried to think what it reminded him of, but couldn't. He read the story again. The article said the clay might have been used to express contempt, or as part of some esoteric ritual. Neither made sense to Garfield.

"Did you read the story about the five boys in Brooklyn?" he asked his son-in-law.

"Yeah . . . some mess."

"Dave . . . does the mud or clay remind you of something?"

"How do you mean?"

Garfield shook his head. "I don't know. Just something . . ."

Dave Schermer shook his head. "Sorry, Pop. I can't help. Don't worry, it'll come to you."

The doorbell rang. "*Oy!*" Ada cried, "they're here. Sara, put on water for tea, Chaim, put on your jacket. . . ." She grabbed the platter, rushed out of the kitchen. Garfield reluctantly folded the paper over the story of the dead Eagles. David was right, he thought. It would come to him in the shower some day, or when he was polishing the ceremonial silver, or saying a *brocha*. Hours, days, years from now; when he'd stopped thinking about it.

Labor Day weekend ended the best season in the history of Bianco Bros. Notions and Variety, and Louis Bianco decided to take his family to Nova Scotia for three weeks. It was a hot muggy day in the middle of September and he stopped by the store to get his deep-sea-fishing equipment, which was stored in the basement. The heat had seeped in through the stone walls, and the basement was hot and damp. He collected the rods, reels, and tackle box, then stood for a moment smelling the air. After a long hot spell like this, and when the air was very damp, he thought he could still smell traces of the big bottle of Prince Matchabelli cologne he'd broken thirty-five years ago. The stuff had soaked into the cement floor and the heat and dampness brought it out again. He breathed in. He could smell it all right, and he wondered where Abrams was, and Pearce. He'd meant to call Abrams or write to him. He still had his address in the old leather book they kept next to the phone. But the address was as old as the faint smell around him and Abrams had probably moved away years ago, or maybe died. Pearce was in his seventies, if he was still alive. Speiser was dead and so were most of the men on that list by now, Bianco thought.

" 'Hardly a man is yet alive . . .' " he said softly. Then he tucked the rods under his arms and carried them and the tackle box up the stairs.

By the time he got back home, the story of the boys' murder in Brooklyn took up two paragraphs on page thirty of the *Post* and there was nothing in it about clay.

Rachel Levy

Chapter

1

RACHEL HEARD murmuring; she thought it was part of a dream. In it she was carrying Adam, who was amazingly small and light, to a canoe, like the one they'd rented when they went through the wilderness park in Minnesota. She carried him easily at first, then as the woods got deeper, and the sun started to go, his body got heavier, and soon she was staggering along the trail, toward the canoe that waited at the edge of one of the lakes. He was alive and awake, his eyes were bright, and he talked to her, to make the trip go faster. She didn't listen to what he said, but the sound of his voice was a comfort, and before long she reached the canoe, laid him in the bottom, careful not to bang his head on the slats. Then she got into the stern, and with a sweet movement that no one who hadn't portaged could appreciate, they slid across the shallow end of the water and out into the lake. He couldn't move, but he talked as she paddled, the murmuring of his voice spread over the flat water.

She woke up and opened her eyes, but the murmuring went on. She had a pain between her legs, her back hurt, and she knew she'd had the baby, and that it was Jacob sitting next to her bed, praying or just talking to himself. She was glad to be alive, not on the lonely lake with her paralyzed husband. She turned her head to smile at her father-in-law, and saw Isaac Luria sitting on a chair next to her bed, his lips moving, his fingers rubbing something flat and silver in his hand. He saw she was awake, and he stopped talking and put the silver whatever in his pocket.

"The baby?" she asked.

"A little girl," he said. "But perfect. Seven pounds four ounces." He looked at her like he always did, with the same flat look he'd give a chair or piece of meat. Yet, she thought, he'd been praying for her, or over her, or something, and she smiled at him. He didn't smile back, just regarded her without any expression on his face.

Suddenly she wanted him out of her room.

"Jacob . . ." she cried.

"He's eating," Luria said. "He's exhausted and needs to eat."

She lay still, watching the ceiling, then the snow that blew against the window. She asked him when she could see the baby, and he said he didn't know. Then she asked where Golda was, and he told her Golda was with Jacob. His voice was soft, and she knew he was trying to sound kind. They didn't say anymore to each other and she tired to fall asleep. She closed her eyes but couldn't forget he was there; she even thought of trying to get out of bed, when the door opened and she saw Jacob. He threw his arms wide and shouted so loud nurses came running down the hall.

"It's a little girl, Rachel. The prettiest baby in the whole world."

Rachel and Levy learned how to take care of the baby together. Golda showed them how to bathe her and she recommended brands of powder, paper diapers, cotton, baby oil, even though she'd never had a baby herself. She said she'd read a lot, so they listened to her. They called the little girl Leah. She was born with hair, which was thick and black, and curly by the time she was three months old. Her eyes turned hazel, then brown. She didn't get fat enough to suit Levy, and he worried, even after the doctor said she was fine.

On Fridays, Rachel lit the Sabbath candles according to Jacob's instructions. She shielded her eyes against the glow the way he taught her, and with him and Leah watching, she held her hand flat and waved it around and between the flames in an odd Eastern gesture, the meaning of which was lost, but Jacob said women did it anyway.

She cooked, kept the house, helped Levy in the store in the afternoons with Leah in her playpen next to the cash register. She played cards on Tuesdays, went to the movies on Saturday with Golda or Barbara Fineman, and thought that it would have been a good year if she could sleep nights.

Getting to sleep was the problem. It was quiet and she was used to noise. In Minnesota, other professors had parties, or played Bach, Mozart, Scriabin until late at night. In Brooklyn, trucks ran all night between fisheries on the bays and the bridges. When she was growing up, people walked under her window from Central Park to Columbus, talking, laughing, yelling until late, and buses ran all night. But in Laurel, it was quiet. She tried to imagine that she could hear the surf on the other side of the Island, or the sea birds, but the quiet defeated her imagination and she stayed awake until she heard Levy leave his room, which he did every night, and go into the baby's room. Then she'd fall asleep. If she didn't, she would think about Adam, and that was dreadful because she didn't remember him alive, diminutive, vibrant, and with the brightest eyes she'd ever seen; she remembered him in his coffin. Levy had warned her not to look. Orthodox Jews never looked at their dead, but she had insisted. He had been too sad to argue, and the mortician, after a few hours of preparation, lifted the simple coffin lid and she looked into her dead husband's face. Pancake makeup covered dry rubbery-looking gashes from the knives, and the lids covering the protruding eyeballs looked too thin to keep out the light.

Before they killed Adam, nothing frightened her; now, if the baby coughed, she called the doctor. If she ran a fever, Rachel wanted to take her to the hospital. She paid the mortgage on the twenty-fifth and had the van tuned up every three months. She bought five pounds of coffee at a time and ten pounds of sugar because she was afraid of running out. She bought a whole case of toilet paper and in the middle of wrestling it down to the basement, the absurdity of what she was doing hit her and she sat on the basement steps and cried until Leah, in her crib, started crying too. The worst, craziest fear was of the doorbell because when it rang, she thought automatically of the story *The Monkey's Paw* and she had a glancing image of opening the door and looking into her husband's dead face, the eyelids blown away like spider webs and the poor bare eyeballs staring at her, weeping from the light they couldn't shut out.

She lost weight, got dark rings under her eyes, and decided that what she needed was fresh air. She started driving out to the beaches with Leah. Leah loved it; she screamed when the waves broke, and clutched wildly at the sea gulls that flew over their heads. Rachel looked out over the gray water toward Europe; Finland was there, she thought; Norway, Russia. "Home," she whispered to Leah. But she knew if she ever found that flat ice plain her grandmother had told her about, it would be covered with factories. Ten thousand factories, all making rubber boots. "Rubber boots," she told Leah, who waved her hands and cried "ubbah." Rachel started back to the car, then saw a black man in fishing boots standing in the water almost up to his knees, casting into the waves. He had the same strands of white in his frizzy hair that Roger Hawkins did, and even though she knew it wasn't Hawkins, something about the figure was reassuring; she crossed the pebbles and stood near him; he didn't move away.

"Did you get anything?" she asked, wanting to hear his voice.

"Not yet," he said. He didn't sound like Hawkins, except for the soft timbre some black men's voices had.

"What's running?" she asked.

He shrugged. "Blues maybe."

He kept his back turned and she left him alone. When she got home, she looked for Hawkins's name in the address book. It wasn't there and she called Levy at the shop. He was quiet at first, then he asked, "Why do you want his number?"

"He was Adam's best friend and we haven't heard from him for almost a year, Jacob."

"He's a busy man, Rachel. When he has time, he'll call," Levy said and he hung up. She went out to the Florida room and stood next to the window wall and looked out for a long time, trying to figure out why Jacob should sound so cold about calling Roger Hawkins. Hawkins had been Adam's best friend. "If I was in trouble," Adam had said once, "I'd call Hawkins. I feel safe with him. We used to go to Astoria, to the Italian section where they hate blacks and Jews the same, and we'd sit in any bar there, with the whites trying to look like they were going to kill Hawkins because he was black and me because I was a nigger-lover, or a Jew, and either way they hated me. I'm a little guy and they smirked when I stood up to go to the can or order another beer but I always felt safe with Roger. Not just because he was big. Though he is. One of those men who never seem to stop standing up. He says he's six three. I think he's taller.... But anyway, it wasn't just that. It was this gentleness about him. A wall of gentleness and humor. And pretty soon he'd smile at the wops at the bar and their eyes would lose that hard look, and I'd remember what handsome people they are, and I'd be smiling too. We made friends, just like that. If I'm ever in trouble, Rache, get Roger Hawkins. If you're ever in trouble and I can't help, get Roger Hawkins."

Was she in trouble? She couldn't sleep and she longed for company that wasn't Jewish and female. Or Jewish and a dentist from Centerreach or a psychiatrist from Glen Cove.

She called information. She knew he lived in Queens, but she didn't know the street. She knew he lived with his mother, which seemed crazy, since he could have lots of women, but she didn't know his mother's name. There were three R. Hawkinses listed in Queens. The second number she called was his. His mother answered and gave her his office number. His secretary answered there. Rachel held on while the woman went to get him, and she realized that she was looking forward to hearing his voice so much that she was a little breathless. But it was the woman who came back on, saying that he was busy and he'd call her back. She hung up and thought that after all this time he could talk to her at least for a second. Or tell her himself that he was busy and would call later. She heated up the soup, sliced the roast.

He hadn't called back by seven. Leah was asleep, Levy was in the den watching the news; Rachel finished the dishes, went back to the sun porch and, feeling sneaky for some reason, she called his house. He answered himself. Her heart beat faster.

"Inspector Hawkins ... Roger ... this is Rachel Levy. Adam's wife ..."

"I know who you are." His voice was cold. "What do you want?"

No hello, how's the baby. He didn't ask if she'd had a boy or girl.

"I just thought ... I had a daughter, and we didn't hear from you for so long ... I wondered ..."

"Don't wonder," he said, "ask Jacob. On second thought, don't ask him because he won't tell you." He hung up and left her holding a dead phone, staring out at the snow still falling.

She didn't know what to do. Ask Jacob, he'd said. She went into the den, but he was asleep, sitting upright with *The MacNeil-Lehrer Report* going on PBS. She left the TV on to mask the quiet and went back to the porch. Something scampered in the attic. Mice, Golda said. All houses have mice.

She thought of writing to him but he didn't have to answer and she could wait months and not hear from him. She walked back and forth across the porch. The program changed and she heard ballet music. Finally she called Queens information again and got the number for the only Moses Ableson listed. He was the right Ableson, but didn't want to talk.

"Call me tomorrow at the precinct," he said, "or come in. I'm there between—"

"It's personal," she told him.

"I don't know what could be personal, Mrs. Levy." He sounded wary and a little drunk. In the background Rachel heard a woman call that something was getting cold.

"You and Roger Hawkins were Adam's friends, weren't you?"

"The best," Ableson said softly, "the very best."

"I just called him and he wouldn't talk to me, he sounded like he hated me."

"Did he?" Ableson said softly. "Did he indeed? And you want to know why, is that it?" His voice made her skin crawl. She didn't say anything and after a moment Ableson sighed and said, "I'll tell you what I think, Mrs. Levy. I think Hawkins wanted to be Jacob's son and Adam's brother. Part of a family he could respect. And maybe he thought Jacob could make that happen somehow, and he would be transformed from a lonely black man of no special ties to a Polish Jew who belonged to the village. And maybe when you left him behind and took it all with you, maybe he realized that he'd never known or understood you people and maybe he thought he'd gone too far to come back and now wasn't one thing or the other. Which maybe, he thought, made him nothing." Ableson was quiet for a moment, then he said, "But that's a lot of cheap-shit psychology, isn't it, Mrs. Levy?" Now he sounded angry.

"I don't know," Rachel said.

"It is, because there's a better reason." Ableson took a breath. "He thinks your father-in-law and his *mishpochah* killed the kids on President Street."

"That's crazy . . ." Rachel cried.

"Why?"

"They couldn't."

"Someone saw your car there. Parked in front of the clubhouse. A dark green Dodge van, right?"

Rachel didn't answer.

"You still got that car?" Still no answer. "Sell it, give it away. It's *tumah*, that car. Corrupt."

He was sounding a little crazy. His wife said something about soup and he told her to shut up.

Rachel said, "Don't get upset, Lieutenant."

"Upset!" he shouted. "Do you know what they did to those kids ... do you know what we found in that basement? Revenge is one thing, lady. I'll go with it, maybe. But this wasn't just that. This was hate like I never saw or imagined. They beat them to death, all five of them. They tore one to pieces and, oh God, that's the one that haunts me still. Can you imagine? I mean, how long did that kid live with parts of him missing? Did he pull his torso along the floor with the one arm he had left? Did he see his own leg lying next to him? What was it like for the kid, Mrs. Levy?" Rachel sobbed, but he didn't stop. "And that wasn't enough. They hated them so much that they threw dirt on the bodies. Clay. Why clay? Where'd they get clay? And why didn't they just shoot them or stab them—anything."

"Shut up," Rachel screamed and slammed down the phone.

Levy came running out to the porch. "Rachel, what happened?"

She wanted to tell him what she'd just heard, to scream it at him, the way Ableson had at her, but even asking about it would give it some credence and she couldn't do that. Instead she yelled, "What happened with Roger Hawkins?"

The question stopped him.

"He never called," she kept yelling. Leah woke up and started to squall. "He never came to see us. Because of you. Why?"

She raced through the kitchen to the garage. He followed, and Leah cried louder in the background. Rachel slid open the van door and looked inside. It was clean and dry, but she knew it would be. They'd had the inside shampooed a long time ago.

"What did you do with my van?" she yelled. He

looked helpless. It was cold in the garage; he was in his shirt and trying not to shiver. She started hating herself but she couldn't lower her voice. "What happened with Roger?"

"A misunderstanding. A terrible misunderstanding."

"Tell me."

"Please, let's go inside."

She felt like a harpy and wanted him to get angry at her, to yell back, but he said quietly, "It's too cold to talk here."

She followed him back to the kitchen, feeling like she'd lost momentum.

"What did you hear on the phone?" he asked.

"Just tell me what happened."

"It's not so easy to *know* what happened. Maybe if you tell me . . ."

She was silent. He said softly, "Is our trust so fragile, Rachel?" She was still quiet, and he said, "Maybe it should be. Why should we trust each other after only a year? . . . Maybe your suspicion makes more sense." He wasn't looking at her. "Okay," he said, "what I know is that Roger met Isaac at the funeral of those boys." Now he looked at her. "I don't know why Isaac was there, maybe to gloat, maybe he felt some sorrow. He met Roger there and he told Roger that I was going away that day, and he should leave us alone." He was looking into her eyes. "Isaac shouldn't have said it. But he did." He looked out the kitchen window and his voice got so soft she had to lean forward to hear. "Roger must've believed him and maybe he blamed himself for not being able to try the men who killed Adam, and thought we blamed him, too."

He kept looking out the window. "I think that's what happened," he said. There were tears in his eyes, and she thought he probably didn't want her to notice them.

What he said made sense. Besides, she thought, eight old men together couldn't beat five young men to death. Hawkins was wrong and Ableson was crazy.

Levy watched his granddaughter sleep. When she was awake, she looked like Adam; when she laughed, she looked like Rachel; but asleep, right now, she looked like his dead wife, Leah, and he closed his eyes and let himself imagine that it was her after all. She was wearing the linen nightgown he had had made for her in Sosnowiec and she was half lying, half sitting on their bed, waiting for him to strip and wash in the icy water. It was so cold he was trembling and, still a little wet, he got into bed next to her, naked, and she held him, using her body to warm his. When he stopped trembling, they made love, and late at night, after she was asleep, he awoke and had to get up and put on his socks and nightshirt.

He heard a whistle and woke in a panic. Then he saw the ducks appliquéd on the curtains and remembered that he was in Laurel, not Dabrowa, and that the whistle was a freight running from New York to Greenpoint and not the relocation transport from Krakow to Belzec.

EVERY TIME it rained after that, she thought about clay, then the dead boys, then of Shabbes school for some reason, and the big colored picture book she had then. She couldn't see the connection and she tried to find the book but it wasn't on the shelves downstairs and she didn't want to look for it in the attic, which was cold and still full of mice for all she knew.

She kept going back to the beach but by the middle of November the stretch of pebbles and water was empty, gray, freezing, and she gave up and took to spending the afternoons after work in Golda's kitchen, which was bigger than Rachel's living room. It had a fireplace, a work island, and a microwave oven that everyone was scared of using. The oven hung black-faced and neglected in the wall, and Rachel felt absurdly sorry for it.

Golda poured vodka for herself and coffee for Rachel. She lit the fire, put her hands on either side of Rachel's face, and turned it toward the firelight.

"Still not sleeping?" she said.

"Not too well," Rachel said.

"You know what you need?"

"What?" Rachel asked.

Golda kissed her friend's cheek. "You need a man," she said, "and I'm going to find you one."

Rachel thought of Hawkins. She could almost see him against the flames, looking embarrassed and gentle at the same time, covering himself by folding his hands. She felt an unexpected rush of tenderness, and then, before she could stop herself, she thought of Ableson, the dead boys, the clay.

Golda gave a New Year's Eve party and Rachel dressed for it under Golda's direction. Golda took her to Port Jefferson to Maurice's, and there Rachel bought a long maroon velvet skirt, and silk blouse to match, and Maurice himself stood in the door of the dressing room with his hand flat against his cheek, looking at Rachel. "*Oy oy oy . . .*" Maurice said, "she's som'pin . . . *vay iz mir*, that face . . . but who does she look like?"

"Like herself," Golda said.

He shook his head, "No one looks like themselves. . . ."

He left while the seamstress pinned up the skirt and Golda beamed at her, then he was back, pointing at Rachel: "I got it!" he said, "Gilbert Roland!"

The night of the party, she looked at herself in the full-length mirror on the back of the bathroom door. She was too thin. Her chest was almost flat in the silk; but the maroon reflected some color in her face, and with her hair combed to the side the gray was partly hidden. When she went into the living room to show Levy how she looked, he stood up. "Some *bura**," he said softly. They looked at each other for a moment; she was Adam's wife, dressed up to go out without him.

"Don't come home too early," he said.

* Beauty.

When she got there, Golda led her to a slender man standing in front of the bowed window.

"Allan—here she is!" Golda crowed. The man turned, saw her, looked surprised and pleased at the same time. Golda took their hands and held them together, and Rachel looked at the heavy gold chain that stretched from one of his vest pockets to the other. It had a key on it, but she couldn't tell for what honor, or fraternity, or if it was simply a piece of jewelry. Then she looked at him. He was tall enough, she thought. He had fine blond hair and a long face with thin features and wide blue eyes. He was handsome and she wondered what he was doing on New Year's Eve waiting for a blind date.

The old Slavic bluntness came out before she could stop it.

"Why don't you have a date?" she asked.

He laughed impulsively, and everyone turned around to see what was going on. Golda blushed purple. "He just moved in, Rachel. The Burns's house?" It was huge. Allan-whoever had money. He was still holding her hand.

"Allan Siegal," he said, and she nodded. "I don't have a date because I just got divorced. What's your reason?"

"Didn't Golda tell you?" She turned to Golda, but she was edging away into a group of other guests.

"She said you're a widow."

"Yes."

"Recent?"

"*I* think so."

He nodded; his eyes were kind. "And no one else does."

"Something like that."

"How long?" he asked.

"A year or so."

She didn't look at him, he didn't let go of her hand.

"What happened?" he asked, and she thought of Adam stabbed, bleeding, falling. Weeping naked eyeballs, gashed face full of pancake and rouge. And dead bodies thrown around like trash, broken, pulled to pieces, covered with clay. She didn't even have the *best* stories. She should send him back to her house to hear Jacob's stories about Belzec, or Luria's. Or out into Golda's kitchen to listen to Abe Dworkin's. *What happened?* was the wrong question to ask in Laurel. She laughed and he looked startled.

"Excuse me," she said and headed for the kitchen. Abe Dworkin was there with Marge O'Shea, a black woman who'd answered Golda's ad in the *Irish Echo* ten years ago and had worked for her ever since. Marge was putting triangles of lox on toast points already smeared with cream cheese; Dworkin was preening.

"How do I look?" he asked Rachel, smoothing back his thick white hair on either side of his cap.

"Spiffy," she said. "Got a date?"

"Yeah." He deflated. "At Isaac's house, watching TV and playing *clabiash* with the old cockers."

Rachel said, "Stay in the kitchen with me. We'll get drunk together." He smiled. Rachel had started to help Marge with the lox when she saw the kitchen door open, and she knew it was Allan Siegal. She ran out to the back porch where Golda kept her second refrigerator and her deep freeze and stayed in the shadows while Siegal pretended to look for ice. He said something to Marge, took a canapé, and left. Rachel wanted to stay on the porch but it was cold and all she had on was the skirt and blouse. She went back inside.

"*Nu*, you staying with me, you ain't staying with me?" Dworkin complained.

"I ain't staying with you."

"I didn't think so," he said, buttoning his coat.

She went out into the hall, keeping close to the stairs, but Siegal was watching for her, and when she reached the foyer, he left the people he was talking to, and started toward her. She went up the stairs. She didn't know why she was running away from him, but she couldn't stop. The den door was closed, but she heard the TV and she thought she could go in there and watch the New Year in with the kids, surrounded by the guests' mink coats. But when she opened the door, she saw Gerry Samson and Selma Rubin on the couch; Selma's head was back, her legs were spread, and Gerry's hand was under her skirt. Selma was panting and the movement of Gerry's hand made something in Rachel's insides turn over. She backed out and closed the door softly.

The next door was the bathroom, and she went in there and washed all the makeup off her face and wet her hair. When she came out, Allan Siegal was at the foot of the stairs. Gerry was probably on top of Selma now, his pants down, his bare backside green in the glow of the TV screen.

She went down the stairs and faced Allan.

"I was sick. I'm sorry, but I think I should go home."

He reached up and touched her hair. "You better wear a scarf," he said.

"I will."

"Golda told me what happened to your husband, Rachel. I'm sorry."

She almost said, *it's all right*, but she stopped herself in time.

"I don't suppose you'll let me take you home," he said.

"I . . . I'd rather not," she said. In this light, his hair was silvery gold.

"What are you afraid of?"

"Nothing!" she answered sharply. "Nothing at all," and she fled.

New Year's Day she walked in the yard, through the snow. Siegal was right, she was scared. But not of him, she thought. The worst that could happen between them was that they'd make love. Nothing scary there. Even if it was more, even if she fell in love with him or he with her, what was so terrible? She brushed the snow off her tulip tree and watched the tree branches rise, released of the weight. What scared her had nothing to do with Allan Siegal or sex. With what then? The clay. She looked up and saw Jacob at the sliding glass door.

Jacob ... clay. Suddenly she remembered a color picture of a village street. Not in this country or time, because the street was cobbled and the houses had leaded glass windows, and the second stories hung over the street. There was a man on the street . . . a rabbi, like Jacob, dressed all in black and wearing a high rabbi's hat. Next to him fell a shadow of something. The shadow darkened the cobbles and came up the wall. Melting snow dripped on her bare head, but she stood still, concentrating, trying to remember. . . .

"Rachel . . ."

She tried to ignore the voice, but Jacob called her again and slid open the door.

"Telephone, Rachel. An Allan Siegal to talk to you."

She gave up and went inside.

"Will you have dinner with me tomorrow?" Siegal asked when she got to the phone.

"Where?"

He laughed, "Will the place decide whether or not you go?"

125

"I have trouble getting into the city," she said, then thought bitterly, *My car is corrupt.*

"Not the city. Centerreach. You can meet me at my office."

The firm of Siegal and Kammerer took up the top floor of a three-story office building in downtown Centerreach. His office, the senior office, was lovely. Two of the walls were solid glass, the carpet was thick beige wool, and the ashtrays were Steuben glass. He had his own bathroom, which he showed off proudly, with a sauna. She sat on a huge beige leather sofa while he made calls. She tried not to be annoyed by the opulence of the place, but she remembered Adam's little bare office in Minnesota with plain, steel files and books piled everywhere. She managed to drop one of the Steuben ashtrays, but it hit the rug and didn't even chip. He introduced her to his secretary, a gray-haired black lady, and to his partner, Bill Kammerer, who looked her up and down and whistled silent approval to Allan, which made Rachel want to throw one of the antique vase lamps through one of the window walls.

He took her to a marina restaurant, and she had lobster for the first time in years. It wasn't as good as she remembered, strings of it stayed in her teeth, and he got them both toothpicks and Irish whisky to go with their coffee. He asked if she'd kept kosher while she was married to Adam, and she told him she hadn't after they'd left New York. Adam didn't care much one way or another.

"A rabbi's son who doesn't care?" Allan asked.

"He cared," Rachel said, "just not about being kosher."

Allan raised his hands in a truce gesture. "Rachel, I'm not looking for trouble with you." They drank their whisky without talking for a moment, then he asked, "What about now?" She was getting high.

"I keep kosher, now."

"Two sets of dishes ... the whole *shmeer*."

"Four sets of dishes; two for Passover."

"Right. I forgot."

His family had been Orthodox, too, he told her, until his grandfather died. They quit then and he thought he'd be relieved, but he found he missed it. The dishes, the ceremony, checking out restaurants and hotels. "It made everything special," he said. She nodded.

"My mother was glad, though," he said. "She hated the bother, she hated getting up to go to shul on Saturdays." Then he asked, "Does it bother you?"

"I don't go," she answered.

He looked surprised. "Doesn't your father-in-law insist?"

She just stared at him, and after a moment, he laughed and shook his head. "No one insists on anything with you, is that it?"

She still didn't answer, and he changed the subject with the same easy good humor.

They had two more whiskies and left to go home. As they drove, he told her about his wife, the JAP of all time he called her, from Bronxville. They had two kids, a co-op on lower Fifth Avenue. Ninth Street. One hundred acres of the Poconos, a dog, and two cars. He smiled and said he'd gotten one of the cars.

His voice was pleasant, she was high and tired, and she leaned back and just listened. At one point she thought of asking him if he knew anything about how clay fit in with cobblestone streets and crooked houses, but he was talking about his wife. Their divorce had only become final last week, and until then, he said, he'd been faithful except for one drunken night in Chicago where he'd picked up some tart in a bar. He actually said *tart*, and that struck Rachel as a kind word, better than slut or cunt or whore. Only a nice man, she thought, would call a bar girl a tart. She watched his profile, and that lovely silvery hair that came down the side of his face in short sideburns. He took her to his house, one of the most expensive in the Sutter section of Laurel, and from the moment he turned off the motor and lights and looked at her, the air was full of that sexual suspense that she hadn't felt in years. That she'd forgotten existed.

"I thought we'd spend some time here," he said.

She didn't answer. She wanted to see the house, she told herself. After all, it probably went for two hundred twenty-five thousand. It had a pool, a cabana, five bedrooms, four baths, a Florida room, a country kitchen. Golda would never forgive her if she didn't at least look at the house.

The living room was empty except for a huge sectional sofa of soiled light-colored velvet. As far as she could tell it was the only furniture in the place. Their voices echoed in the beautifully proportioned foyer; the dining room was empty. The fireplace was cold and unswept, with bottles of liquor lined up in it. The glasses he poured the Irish whisky into were dusty.

"I just moved," he apologized. "And I wasn't kidding, she did take everything." When they finished the drink, he turned out the only lamp and in the moonlight he put his arms around her. She was sure she'd leave as soon as he tried to kiss her, but he rubbed his thumb against her bottom lip, which was unexpected, and Rachel felt a gut-turning excitement so intense she caught her breath. He heard her.

"It's been a long time for you, too, hasn't it," he said

softly. Then he kissed her, and after a while he took off his clothes. He wasn't self-conscious, and she watched him. His body hair was as gold-silver as the hair on his head; Adam's had been black on his pale skin. Allan was thinner than she thought, not as tall. Shorter than Hawkins, taller than Adam, perfect, she told herself as he helped her take off her clothes. Perfect.

It was, too, except at the end, when she was afraid that she'd imagine that it was Adam in her instead of this man; not living Adam, holding her with that odd, intense gentleness she'd never forget, that no one could match, but Adam's corpse the way she saw it in her worst moments: fish-green skin sunk on its bones; round, jellied, lidless eyes staring; corpse fingers like claws holding her. But she didn't. She imagined she was with Roger Hawkins in the bedroom in Brooklyn. He was naked and excited. She was naked, too, and they were standing next to Levy's big, old bed, with their bodies barely touching.

In Laurel Jacob Levy celebrated Havdalah* with the other men. They had a cold feast of rolls, butter and pot cheese, tea and whisky. A braided candle gave the only light. Levy poured the wine and blessed it. He opened the silver box of cloves and cinnamon, blessed it, breathed in the scent, then he passed it to Luria who sat next to him, and he smelled it and passed it to the next man. Finally Levy raised the cup of wine and drank most of it as was customary, then passed it so each man could have a sip. The cup came back to him and, with divided feelings—sorrow at the end of the Sabbath, and gratitude that it happened at all to give him this sense of peace—he extinguished the candle in the few drops of wine left in

* The end of the Sabbath.

the cup. In the dark, he dipped his fingers in the wine, then ran them tenderly over Isaac Luria's eyebrows. Luria smiled, and all the sternness left his face. Then Levy leaned over and kissed his friend. "*Shabuoth tov,**" he said, "*Shabuoth tov.*" They all embraced each other. A little light came through the basement windows and in it Levy saw Dworkin go to the light switch. In a second there would be light and the Sabbath would be over.

For Levy, this was the most solemn moment. He remembered again, as he did every Saturday night, that the dead candle he held was supposed to be held by a child and that the symbol of the Sabbath was a woman, a queen, a bride. But there had been no women with them in the camp and the two little boys who had been inside the barracks weren't children at all after a while. The men got used to being alone together and children were never invited to Havdalah. All men they were; like the long-house Maori of New Zealand. Levy smiled at the thought, and then suddenly he longed for Adam. Or even Roger. He used to hope that someday, when Luria was older and calmer, Hawkins could come to Havdalah, share the wine and their little feast, and watch the dancing. . . . Dworkin reached for the switch and, in the last seconds of darkness, Levy remembered that in the old days, in Dabrowa, Levy's father used to pretend to lead the Sabbath Queen out of the house and down the narrow village street. They would all imagine watching until she was out of sight, saying good-bye in their hearts until next week. That custom died in the camp, too. But lately, as he got older, Levy imagined he could see her, tall, beautiful, stately, going through the basement door and out into the snow.

* Good week.

Dworkin turned on the lights and the Sabbath was over.

In Riverdale, Chaim Garfield and the men from his shul also celebrated Havdalah with the braided candle, the silver spice box shaped like a fish, the cup for wine, the dish to go under it to catch the overflow because it was tradition to fill the cup too full in hopes that the week would be full. The lights were dim, the way they were in Laurel, the men solemn. But in Riverdale, at Avaarith Israel, the candle was held by a little boy because the men here brought their sons with them, and at the end of the ceremony, when the Sabbath Queen left them, they didn't eat and drink or dance together. They embraced, shook hands, wished each other *Shabuoth tov*, and went home to their families.

Simon Leshman walked two blocks with Garfield. As long as he was with his friend, Garfield was comfortable and animated. Then Leshman turned into his street and Garfield was alone. The cold hit him and went right through his clothes. He wrapped his muffler around his mouth and chin and hurried along the quiet street. The trees were covered with ice, the river was silver-colored and looked like it wasn't moving. He was freezing and lonely, and he would have liked a son to walk home with on this night.

When he got home he ate while Ada dressed. They were going to Hartsdale to their daughter, who was having a card party with her husband's parents, some friends, and the Melnicks from their old building in Washington Heights.

Ada had put on a soft wool dress, in the new sleeker style, and he thought how slim and pretty she still was, and he told her in Yiddish that she looked so good he'd fuck her if it was earlier, and she smiled as if she believed him. But he was sixty, tired, and still cold and he was glad it wasn't earlier. She bent to put on her boots, the dress caught in the crack of her behind and he wondered if she was glad, too; if they were both getting old.

He'd been in Theresienstadt from 1940 to 1945. The Nazis had taken that five years and probably another five at this end. Too much abuse, Dr. Frank had told him. "The body's not meant to take it. I know some live to be eighty, ninety, but most . . ." He'd looked at the lines on the first EKG. "Well," he'd said, "we'll see. We'll see."

"That's for sure," Garfield mumbled, and when Ada asked him what he said he kissed her cheeks and answered, "Nothing, nothing." Her English was terrible and even her Yiddish wasn't so good. But in Russian his wife was a poet, a marathon talker. Every month when they got the phone bill, he was grateful that more people in Riverdale didn't speak Russian.

When they got home from Hartsdale, Ada went to bed and he went into the kitchen and filled a large lunch box with a jar of creamed herring, a small hard salami, butter cookies, a container of *ikra baklazhan,** a slice of halvah. Milk and meat all mixed up, but he didn't care. No one would see but Meyer, and Meyer didn't care either. In the morning he filled two Thermoses, one for himself for the drive back and one with a cranberry drink that Mrs. Rostov made.

When he got to Ossining he had to wait ten minutes while the guard, Carver, examined the contents of the lunch box. Carver opened the Thermos flask and sniffed. "Cranberries?" he said. Garfield nodded.

"God, that smells delicious." He paused delicately.

* Eggplant caviar.

Garfield said, "You can't have that, Meyer's waited for a month for that stuff. Next week I'll get some more."

"Sure do appreciate it, sure do."

"You're a *shnorrer*, William, a real *shnorrer*."*

"Sure am," said the guard. "Sure am." He was opening the bag of cookies. "Take one," Garfield said. He tried to dislike the man but couldn't. He *wanted* William Carver to have a cookie, to enjoy it, and that was crazy. But he couldn't help himself. One night at a meeting of the Habonim,† thirty-odd years ago, he'd had two cigarettes left and a man asked him for a smoke. The man had been in a camp, too, his false teeth fit badly, and even though he was still young, he was already getting bald. Garfield took out his pack of Camels and while his comrade Tepel watched in amazement, he gave the man his last two cigarettes, lit one for him, and thought, as the man drew the smoke deep into his lungs, that he enjoyed that smoke as much as the man with the cigarette. Tepel shook his head. Extreme generosity, Tepel had said, was the first sign of insanity.

Meyer was waiting; he smiled and kissed his brother. He opened the lunch box, took out the plastic container of *ikra* at once, opened it, and breathed in the smell of garlic, olive oil, green peppers, and eggplant.

"A *mechaiah*," Meyer said, "a *mechaiah*."‡

He closed the container. "Later," he told Garfield. Next to him on the table was a large box of Hershey bars. Garfield smiled.

"The inspector has been here."

"Yeah," Meyer said, "faithful as always; every sixth Sunday."

* Chiseler.
† Youth organization of the League for Labor Palestine.
‡ Joy.

"Someday I must meet him."

"Why?" Meyer asked. He wasn't being contentious, he really wanted to know, and Garfield said, "Because you love and respect him."

"Don't get too excited," Meyer said. "He tried to save David's life, so I owe him. That's all."

Garfield decided to drop the subject and he asked, "What else is new?"

Meyer laughed. "This is the slammer, Chaimele. What could be new? I didn't take it in the ass, I didn't give no blow jobs. . . ."

Chapter
3

Tʜᴇ ᴅᴏᴏʀʙᴇʟʟ ʀᴀɴɢ.

"Don't answer," Allan groaned. He held her down on top of him; he was so close to finishing he barely moved. "Please . . . Rachel, Rachel . . ." He kissed her, the bell rang again. Leah woke upstairs and started to cry. Rachel tried not to laugh and Allan moaned, "Shit . . ." It rang again and they both laughed. "Oh God, answer it," he said.

He held her another instant, still not moving, then he let her go.

She straightened her skirt and looked back at him from the living room door. He was lying on his back on the couch grinning at her, his erection pointed up, shining in the sun.

"Hurry," he whispered. "For God's sake, hurry," but she had to run back to him to kiss him.

"Don't move," she said.

The bell rang again and she went to the door and opened it. A tall fat man stood on the threshold holding his hat.

"Sussman," he said, holding a card up like a police badge, "Mort Sussman of Sussman and Raines. We're brokers for this section, Mrs. Levy. We sold you and the other members of your . . . ah . . . community these houses." His face was heavy, he had big pores in his nose, and he looked greasy even in the cold. "Can I come in?" he asked.

"It's not convenient. . . ."

"Ah, I should have called. But what I have to say won't take long, and it's extremely important."

There was something wrong with the deed to the house and they were going to lose everything. She knew it was immigrant thinking, her grandmother's thoughts in her head; they'd closed on the house with lawyers, and brokers, deed searches and title insurance. But the fear stayed and made her feel savage. She wanted to take this fat, ugly man right into the living room, to see Allan lying back on a chintz couch in the sun, member out and gleaming, pointing at his chin. When she was young, she'd have done it, out of defiance.

They said she did everything out of defiance; her mother said she married Adam out of defiance, her father said she beat up her brother Danny for the same reason. She would trap Danny in the park, in a tent of willows at the foot of Seventy-ninth Street. He was bigger and older but he wouldn't fight, and once she got so enraged she bit him hard enough to draw blood. When her mother saw the wound, she sent Rachel to her room without supper, and Rachel sat on her bed without moving until her father came in with his glass of brandy. He sat in front of the window and looked at her for a long time. Then he said, "I love you, Rachel."

She didn't say anything.

"Do you love me?" he asked. She nodded.

"Then why do you hurt my son?"

Thoughts came to her—because he won't fight and he went to Hebrew School and had to go to shul on Saturday whether he wanted to or not. But no one cared if she was there Saturday, Sunday, or any other time. In two years, Danny would be bar mitzvahed, even though they weren't religious, and she would be nothing. Fighting her meant recognizing her. He was strong and she knew he'd beat her good. But that wasn't the point. Combatants were equals of a sort, and that's what she wanted. But she didn't know how to say any of it, so she was quiet.

Her father waited, then said, "You hurt Danny, to defy us, why?" She still didn't answer.

"Where does it come from—all this defiance? Do me the kindness to explain. . . ."

He'd said the same thing when she decided to get a Masters in philosophy. They were in the kitchen. Her mother was ironing, her father looked out the window at the boys running after each other in the park. "Why philosophy?" he asked. Her mother listened.

"I could teach," Rachel said.

"Do you want to?" her father asked.

"No."

"Then why?" he asked. Then said again, "Do me the kindness to explain."

This time she could tell him why, and she told them about one night . . . one night only . . . that decided her. She was studying Hegel's lectures on history, all alone in her room before exams. Everyone slept, except her, and she read the words over and over and thought they could have been broadcast from another planet for all the sense they made to her. Yet she kept trying. Defying the language that wouldn't be understood, defying her adviser who said Hegel was very difficult for women, defying Hegel himself, who'd probably hated women and Jews, and she was both. Good. She'd beat him; she'd make sense out of the stilted German-into-English if she sat there until she was an old woman. She read commentaries and explanations. She read the notes she'd taken at Adam Levy's lectures. His lectures were wonderful and if Levy were there, talking only to her, he'd make her understand. Then she was glad he wasn't; she wanted to do it on her own. She went back to the words themselves. She paced the apartment and had a shot of her father's brandy. Then she went back to her desk and started again. The text, the commentaries, the notes, and suddenly, as if he were in the same room with her, she heard Adam Levy's soft voice with its faint accent.

"Hegel is about relationships," he was saying. "He tells us how things relate not only to the elements that give them character, like the sugar in a sugar bowl; but also to all the things they are not. A sugar bowl relates to a cream pitcher by *not being* a cream pitcher. Thus in some sense it incorporates the *idea* of a cream pitcher. He goes further. . . ." She remembered how Adam's eyes shone as he explained to them. "He says that the seed of the tree contains all its processes, germination, growth, maturity, death, decay; but he says even more." He looked right at Rachel then. "That same seed also contains all the things it will never be. That seed, by being the seed of a tree and not of a flower, encompasses the *idea* of flower. . . . In other words . . ."

In other words . . .

"That seed is as much what it's not as what it is, as much what it will never be as what it will." Her head rested on the desk sideways. She raised it and looked at the text again with Adam's words for a guide, and right then she sort of slid into understanding how the explanation came out of what she read. She read it again. It made sense. She jumped and ran around, her feet pounding the floor. Downstairs, Mr. Rubinstein yelled and banged on the ceiling, but she couldn't stop. She hopped and danced, then she ran back to the desk, terrified suddenly that comprehension was temporary. But she read Hegel's words again, still understood, and knew absolutely that she would never again not understand what he wrote. She ran to the window, threw it open, and she leaned out over Seventy-second Street. A brightly lit bus waited forlornly at the corner of Seventy-second and Central Park West, which was the end of the line. The bus driver stood next to it and she shouted to him.

"I got it!"

Beneath her, Mr. Rubinstein shrieked and the bus driver laughed and yelled back up to her, "Never let it go."

She told her parents that she'd felt more joy that night than she thought possible. She would feel like that again, she told them, and she had ideas. For instance, what did it mean to perceive objective . . . but she'd lost them. Her father was looking out of the window and her mother said, "Joy, shmoy, she's doing it for that Adam Levy."

Her mother hated Adam. He stayed with his father on the Sabbath, so Rachel never had a date on Friday night, and his father was a rabbi; not like Rabbi Rosten with good dark suits and shiny shoes. Adam's father was from Brooklyn, leader of some village sect, and he probably wore a beard and side curls.

Rachel's mother listed Adam's flaws at Friday night dinner. His hair was wild, his clothes were shabby, his voice was too soft, he was short and skinny.

"But he's got the biggest cock in New York," Rachel snapped. Her mother gasped and started crying. Danny hiccuped and his girl friend, Madeline, stared.

"We've never met his family," Rachel's mother sobbed. It was the only safe thing she could think of to say.

"His mother's dead," Rachel said.

"He's an orphan?" Danny asked.

"No, asshole," Rachel said, "Jewish boys have fathers, too."

At this Rachel's grandmother laughed out loud, spraying vodka.

"Then we can meet the father?" her father asked desperately.

"Yes, but it can't be on Shabbes, and he won't eat here, so it has to be some place kosher if we do eat. I mean if *he* eats," Rachel said. "We eat anything, don't we?"

Rachel's mother passed her hand across her forehead. "Please, Rachel, please." Her mother's hand trembled, Rachel saw it, felt guilty, and started clearing the table to make amends, but on her way into the kitchen she bumped the server and chipped the wall mirror again. Her mother closed her eyes.

"We'll go to Alter's," her grandmother said, still laughing. "Steak, brains, *karnatzlach*, all kosher. My party . . ."

Mr. Alter kissed her grandmother's hand, brought the white wine, seltzer, pickles, and sour tomatoes himself.

Rachel sat next to the window looking out on Second Avenue. Rappaport's was still there. The baths were still on Houston, the gypsies were still on St. Mark's Place, and the Ukrainians on Eleventh, but the people who moved past the restaurant window like spirits wore beads, sandals, jeans, and looked like they came from Colorado.

She looked up and saw Adam and his father coming toward them. The father was beautiful, which made her realize that Adam was, too. Their noses were thin and straight, their eyes were dark and wide-set, they had thin nervous pale faces, with full, chiseled lips. The father had a short thick beard and Adam was clean shaven and had a cleft in his chin.

At first Rachel's father worried about drinking in front of a rabbi, but Levy drank, told jokes in Yiddish, and laughed so helplessly that everyone laughed with him, even Rachel who didn't understand Yiddish. She relaxed in his company, and for once she didn't spill or break anything.

Her father got drunk and talked about the old country. He told Levy about the village he came from and about his older brother being killed on the village street. Then he asked Levy where he'd been born and Levy answered, "Poland."

"What about Adam?" her father asked. Her grandmother leaned forward.

"Poland, too."

Her father was confused. "When was he born?"

"Nineteen forty-one," Levy said.

"Nineteen forty-one in Poland?" her grandmother asked.

"Yes," Levy said. "Adam's mother was transported—I don't know where—and a Gentile wine merchant who knew us hid him until 1944, then helped get him out of there to Palestine."

Danny—it would be Danny, Rachel thought—asked, "Where were you all this time?"

"Belzec," Levy answered.

Suddenly all of Rachel's concerns and decisions—should she marry Adam, get a Ph.D., teach or write, or get a job—were petty. Something heavy turned in her stomach that wasn't the food she'd eaten, and she felt awe for this man and a terrible shame that she hadn't shared his fate. Everyone at the table felt the way she did. They were silent . . . ashamed of how little suffering they'd done, and overwhelmed with respect for the man who'd done so much. He looked at each of them, then started to laugh. He poured wine for everyone, added seltzer, then leaned across the table and kissed Rachel's father on both cheeks. Rachel's father blushed purple and Levy went on laughing, his dark eyes reflecting the lights in the restaurant and the lights out in the street that came through the window until his eyes and face looked full of light.

"You all look so grim," he cried, "you'd think I'd perished in the ovens after all. I didn't," he cried exultantly, "I'm here." He raised his glass. "To being here," he said. They all drank.

Sussman and Allan waited in the living room while Rachel made coffee. She brought in a well-filled tray and put it on the coffee table. She poured for them and handed them plates of cookies and dried figs. Sussman ate while he talked, crumbs stuck in his mustache, and fig seed was trapped in the corner of his mouth.

"I'm not an alarmist," he said, "but you people have hundreds of thousands of dollars invested in your homes."

"We paid eighty," Rachel said, and Allan listened.

Rachel poured more coffee.

"Eighty, ninety, two hundred thousand," the fat man said. "It isn't the amount that matters, but the fact that the money represents your life savings . . . unless, of course, you're rich."

Rachel said quietly, "Get to the point, Mr. Sussman."

Sussman put his plate back on the tray and looked hard at them.

"The Rosses who live half a block from here have just—against our advice—against, I may say, our pleas . . . sold their house to a black family."

He paused again and in the silence Rachel laughed. Sussman stared at her; so did Allan. She felt her face get red and that old terrible anger crept up her neck like a flush.

"Are you signing people up for fire-bombing?" she asked.

"This isn't about race," Sussman said, "it's about property values. . . ."

Throw him out, Allan, she prayed. *Throw this fat motherfucker out of my house.*

But Allan sat still and Sussman went on. "Right now we're talking about nice people. He's a doctor. They've got two sons, one fourteen, one seventeen, good boys, good students. Wonderful. If Dr. and Mrs. Garner were all we had to worry about I wouldn't be here. But what happens when the Cohens want to sell, or the Raskins. Some nice family from Huntington or Hempstead comes out here and sees two black teen-agers tooling around in their daddy's Cadillac. Do you think that family's gonna put out two hundred thousand dollars for a house when their next-door neighbors are black? Do you?" Neither of them answered. "Would you?" Still no answer.

"*Nu,* Mr. Siegal." Sussman concentrated on Allan. "What'd you pay for your house?"

Allan shrugged. "Two fifty," he said.

"If you gotta sell, you want your money back, don't you? Plus maybe a little profit. Isn't that what you want?"

"I suppose so."

Sussman nodded; he didn't look at Rachel. "But we get five black families in this whole section and you won't get your two fifty. And she won't get her eighty, and the Cohens won't get their two hundred."

"What do you suggest we do?" Rachel asked hoarsely. "Have the black family murdered? . . . The flush on her face made her eyes sparkle. She looked lovely and they stared at her. Allan had never seen her angry; he didn't know what to expect. He hoped that she would give up and start crying in a second. But she didn't. She held the coffeepot in one steady hand.

"Of course not." Sussman tried to sound soothing, but Allan realized that he was a little scared of Rachel Levy.

"The blacks have bought, the Rosses are moving next month. That's that," Sussman said.

"I'll ask you again," Rachel said, "what do you suggest?"

"Sell me your house. That simple. I'll give you a fair profit."

"Where do I and my family go?"

"I got lots of houses, Mrs. Levy. Some further out, some closer to the water, bigger, nicer. I can give you a terrific house for almost the same dough you get for this."

"And what do you do with this house?" she asked. *With my tulip tree and the mice in the attic.*

"I'm going to tell you the truth," Sussman said; "I up the price ten thousand on this place and sell black. I do the same with Mr. Siegal's house, with the Cohens', Raskins', everybody. Turn the whole area over. I make a pile, everybody in the old neighborhood gets better houses; so, by the way, do the blacks. Better houses, better schools, everybody's happy . . ."

"Get out," Rachel said.

Sussman was stunned. "I'm not talking about race, Mrs. Levy. I swear to God . . ."

"Get out or I'll throw this in your face." The coffeepot steamed.

"Rachel, for God's sake," Allan cried.

Rachel stood up and tilted the coffeepot so a small stream of hot coffee hit Sussman's thigh. He jumped up.

"You're crazy," he screamed. "I'll sue you . . ."

But he backed away from her, up the steps still going backward and into the foyer. She found his coat with one hand, holding the pot with the other. Allan's eyes were wide with amazement. Sussman turned to Allan helplessly. Allan shook his head and Sussman said in his most soothing tones, "Mrs. Levy. I know how you feel. I swear to you, I'm no racist." Rachel drew back the pot to throw and he ran out the door, down the path. She stood at the door with the pot raised until he started his car and drove away.

When Allan told Jacob what happened, he laughed and shook his head. Rachel ladled out soup.

"Extra noodles?" she asked. He nodded and they exchanged a look of conspirators while Allan said, "It's not funny, Jake. Maybe Sussman's a boor, but that doesn't mean . . ."

Levy said, "Allan, a man I love deeply and who once loved me was black. . . ."

Roger Hawkins. Rachel spilled some of the soup she was ladling out and mopped up the drops.

"And I'm not going to run away because people of the same color live a block away."

"What if you live next door? What if they live all around you?" Allan asked.

"What if they do?"

Allan shook his head. "Look, Jake, I don't mean to sound like this, I swear I don't. But some of what that guy said made sense."

"About the property values?"

"Yes."

What about moral values, she expected Levy to ask. Should my money mean more to me than my conscience? He was one of the few people she'd ever known who could say things like that without sounding pompous. But instead he said quietly, "Allan, I've left Poland, Germany, Cyprus, Palestine, and Brooklyn. I'm not going again, and that's final."

It wasn't final then, but by the end of the evening it was. Levy called a meeting and by eight-thirty Luria, Dworkin, Alldmann, Fineman, and the rest had gathered in Golda's finished basement. Outside it was snowing again. They could hear the wind off the Sound; branches and limbs creaked and would break and leave windfalls all over the lawns and roads. They couldn't help contrasting the outside storm with the warmth of the room they sat in. Golda made sandwiches, sturgeon salad on thin sliced rye, with sliced tomatoes and black wrinkled olives. The men drank tea, ate the sandwiches.

It was Walinsky who came to the point. "So—we pack and move and have to start over someplace else, or we stay and lose money. Some choice," he said bitterly.

Dworkin said, "When do we lose this money, Sam? When we sell the houses in twenty years? You planning to live that long?"

"Sure not," Fineman said, "but our kids will. So *they* get screwed."

They all looked at Levy. Levy said, "Sussman wants us to think like that." He smiled. "You know who he reminds me of?" They waited. "Leo Cohn," Levy said. Leo Cohn had been a kapo. He'd been fat and sadistic and had oily skin. He took bribes and rarely delivered.

"What happened to him?" Walinsky asked.

Alldmann answered, "They shot him when they cleared out." The men smiled and Dworkin said, "So we

146

should worry because *he* tells us to? Where does it say that one black family—a doctor, mind you—is gonna cost us money? We cut and run and all we do is have more heartache and put money in that fat bastard's pocket. Besides, black people can move anywhere. It's the law, am I right?" Most nodded. "So where does *drekkopf* guarantee that it won't happen in Wading River or River-head? . . ."

Levy turned to Luria. "What do you say, Isaac?"

Luria laughed and shook his head. His laugh was infectious and they all smiled. "I wouldn't move if Martin Bormann bought the Ross house."

"Martin Bormann is white," Dworkin said. "Blacks bought the Ross house."

"I don't give a shit for blacks one way or the other," Luria said.

"Why then did I have the impression that you hated Roger Hawkins?" said Walinsky.

"Because he was a *putz*," Luria said. "Black or white, he had the soul of a *putz*."

"Don't say that," Levy said, sharply.

"Why not?" Luria asked. "After all the years you were friends with him he never came to visit. Did he?" Luria's eyes sharpened. "Did he?" he asked again.

Levy stood up and Walinsky said quickly, "He visits, he doesn't visit, who cares? The question is, what do we do about this."

"*You* hate blacks?" Luria asked. Walinsky shook his head.

"Any of you hate blacks?" He looked around the room at all of them. One by one they shook their heads.

"So we stay?" Luria asked. They all looked at Levy, who nodded.

* * *

"Those old guys're okay," Allan said to Rachel. They were at an Italian restaurant in Port Jefferson. "I mean they really put their money where their mouth is." He drank wine while the waiter cleared the table and they ordered coffee.

"For principles," he said. "Shit . . . that's remarkable." He shook his head. "I mean what kind of folk in 1980 would actually . . ."

Rachel wasn't listening, she was thinking about the men's decision to stay in Laurel. She knew they didn't hate blacks or Puerto Ricans or the Yankees from the south side of town. They didn't like them either. They didn't care about them. To Luria, Dworkin, Fineman, and the rest (she didn't include Levy) they were all outsiders. To them you were a Jew from Dabrowa or you didn't count. The Raskins didn't count, neither did the Rosses. Allan didn't either.

"Rachel," Allan called her back, "you want rum cake?" She nodded, he ordered, and as soon as the waiter left Allan took a velvet ring box out of his pocket, and put it on the table in front of her. He was smiling and his eyes shone. Rachel felt faint and she put her head down to try and get some blood back into it.

"Rachel . . . hey, Rache," he called to her over the roaring of the blood in her ears. "I just want to marry you. You know, home, kids, furniture . . ."

She opened her eyes. The ring box was still in front of her along with a large slice of rum cake. She sensed disaster and thought of Persephone opening the pomegranate. But she couldn't stop herself and she opened the box. It was a three-carat emerald-cut solitaire in a fine platinum setting. It caught the light, fractured it, reflected the spectrum against the walls in the dim restaurant.

She put the ring on and stared at it fascinated. It would

snag her stockings and sweaters but it was beautiful. He grabbed her hands and kissed the backs, then turned them over and kissed the palms. "When?" he asked, "when?" But she couldn't say when.

She took the ring off before she went to bed that night. It was too big and her grandmother would have loved it. Her grandmother had been Russian and nothing was ever too much for her. Rachel remembered having breakfast with her one morning in the enormous kitchen of the old apartment on West Seventy-second Street. Everybody else was out of the house. The old lady ate groats for breakfast with butter and she would talk about anything during the meals. Smallpox and the pogroms were two of her favorite subjects, and at breakfast she could be devastating. Rachel ate fast but not fast enough and as she cracked her boiled eggs, the *bubbe* opened her paper and cried "*Oy . . . oy, vay iz mir. . . .* Look at this."

She shoved the paper right in front of Rachel's face and there, on page one, was a news photo of a trolley accident in Chicago that the wire services picked up and printed across the country, and here it was on Seventy-second Street in front of her eggcup. The trolley had hit a gas truck and the truck exploded. Rachel couldn't stop reading. Flame engulfed the trolley, the driver's head was burning, the conductor was dead, and only the passengers in the back lived long enough to try to get out. And that's how the cameraman caught them, mashed together at the exit door where the sheet of flame got them. They looked like sticks, all black stalks and angles, except for their heads which were charred ovals. The heads were all touching—as if they were telling secrets at the end. Rachel pushed the paper away and took her egg to the garbage can. Her grandmother took the paper back and looked steadily at the picture over her bowl of groats.

She read slowly, moving her lips. Finally she looked up and smiled at her granddaughter.

"There was a Gordon on the trolley," she said. "*Andrew* Gordon. Sam Gordon or Nat Gordon might be Jewish, *might* be. *Andrew* Gordon, never." She folded the paper, satisfied. "There were no Jews on that trolley," she said.

Chapter
4

THE ROSSES' house stood alone and forlorn already, the windows were dirty, the grass needed cutting. Golda and Rachel looked out through Golda's kitchen window for a first glimpse of Sutter Lane's only black family.

"Bet he wears white silk suits and sells numbers," Golda said.

"He's a doctor," Rachel said.

"Who moonlights as a pimp. Imagine being a pimp in Laurel." Golda poured coffee. "If he's smart he'll sell the men . . ." she looked up at Rachel, "for instance Allan. Plenty of broads around who would pay good money for Allan."

"Stop it, Golda."

"He's waiting to set the date, Rachel . . ."

"Adam's only been dead . . ."

"One year, six months, three days, seven hours. How long you gonna wait? Even the Talmud says eleven months is long enough."

A moving van pulled into Sutter Lane behind a black Cadillac. Golda was going full steam and didn't notice.

"Okay, you're almost young and still pretty, but how long will that last? Jacob can't live forever and what happens when he dies? You could be forty by then, Rachel . . ." She'd be forty in a few years anyway. "Forty, and broke, with a kid that someone's gonna have to spend thirty thousand dollars to send to college, or twenty thousand to marry off. You'll really be a bowl of shit then, Rachel . . ." Rachel expected Golda's eyes to look cold and bitchy, the way Rachel's mother did whenever she talked about men or money, but Golda's eyes were soft, full of concern.

"They're here," Rachel said. Golda ran to the window and stood next to Rachel as the van and car pulled into the Rosses' driveway. A tall black man got out of the car and looked up at the house, then a woman got out. They stood still, then he took her hand, and all at once Rachel started to cry. "Rache, Rache," Golda said, "I'm sorry. But everything I said was true. He's a lovely guy, Rache. I envy you." Golda looked out at the couple and suddenly she remembered the black cop . . . Adam's friend . . . in the dark room, reaching for Rachel. Who knows what they'd said to each other in that room before Golda opened the door. Who knows what Rachel felt then and what she remembers. He was black, true, and a shitheel cop who probably only made twenty or thirty thousand a year. But he was the sweetest-looking man Golda had ever seen and there were, after all, some things that couldn't be measured in money.

Dr. Garner answered the door. Golda smiled, all teeth.

"We're not the welcome wagon," Golda said, "but we got a whole bottle of brandy and I bet a drink sounds pretty good about now."

He smiled and opened the door all the way. He was wearing wash slacks and a frayed dress shirt with the collar cut off, but he was the kind of man who looked neat no matter what.

152

He led them down the hall to the kitchen calling "Willa . . . Willa, company . . ."

The kitchen was already unpacked, empty boxes waited next to the back door, and Rachel thought the place looked and smelled cleaner than it ever had when Temma Ross lived there. She put the coffeepot on the stove as Willa Garner came into the kitchen. She had on a loose housedress-smock, bright cotton, still crisp after all the unpacking. She was much taller than Rachel, about Golda's height, and a little overweight, with a handsome round face and big firm arms, and she moved slowly and confidently, making Rachel feel jerky and nervous.

They had coffee, cake, and brandy and they talked easily. The Garners came from the city. They had two sons, one seventeen, one fourteen, both living with Tom Garner's mother on East Ninetieth Street until the school term ended. He'd bought a good practice in Lake Grove, and there was a good hospital nearby. He was an orthopedist. " 'Orthopods,' we call ourselves," he said, smiling. He walked around the back of Rachel's chair and she smelled his sweat, sweet and sharp, and she thought of Hawkins again. The doorbell rang and for one crazy second she imagined that when Willa Garner opened the back door, she'd see him at last. But it was Reverend Ryder (she didn't know his first name), pastor of the First Congregational Church. He was carrying a big, flat cake box and smiling.

"Cookies," he said. "My wife baked them." He was blushing and, standing right there in the middle of the kitchen, he raised the lid of the box and peered inside.

"Pistachio," he said. "Peanut. Chocolate. They're delicious, which I can vouch for personally since I ate half the top layer on my way over here." He thrust the box at Willa, then sat down at the kitchen table next to Rachel.

"My, that coffee looks good." Tom Garner poured some out and held up the brandy.

"Better than cream," Garner said, and Ryder nodded.

"I've seen you in the bookstore," Ryder said to Rachel. Rachel nodded and he held out his hand to her. "Ed Ryder," he said. His skin was pink and his eyebrows and lashes pale blond. He leaned back, drank, ate the cookies, and talked to the Garners, but managed to include the other women. He told them where the church was, then brought out two wrinkled pamphlets.

"They're about the church," he said shyly. "Not the religion . . . the architecture. Our little church is well thought of . . . architecturally, that is . . ."

It got dark and Rachel knew she should leave. Levy had had Leah all day. It wasn't fair for him not to have a hot dinner waiting. But she was comfortable here even though they were all strangers trying to get to know each other. She liked Willa, and Ryder's shyness was appealing, and she could have put her head down while they were talking about the church, the deacons, and what Tom would have to do to join. . . . She could have laid her cheek against the pine-topped kitchen table and slept more peacefully than she had in months.

But she stood up, her eyes heavy and burning.

"I have to make dinner," she said. Then impulsively she leaned down and kissed Willa on the cheek. "Call me tomorrow. Or come over. I live at number seventy, two blocks down toward town. . . ."

Willa Garner knew how to age cheese, pickle beef, and weather-strip windows. She could lay a slate floor and use a stone chisel. She knew things from another time. That adding a pinch of salt to wash water kept clothes from freezing on the line. That storing brown sugar in a tight jar with a slice of bread kept it moist. She knew how to garden and she taught Rachel. Golda wasn't interested, but with Willa's help Rachel planted zucchini, lettuce, broccoli, and ten tomato plants. She watered and watched the garden and, in June, when the first shoots of lettuce showed through the soil, she was so excited she ran the two blocks to Allan's house and brought him back.

"What did you think would happen?" he asked.

"I don't know," she said, "I honestly don't know."

But Levy acted as if no one had ever grown anything from a seed before. He got down on his knees in the dirt and clucked over the shoots, and when he asked which was which Rachel realized that she'd doubted the whole process so thoroughly she hadn't bothered to label the rows.

She wouldn't set a wedding date and, except for gardening, she drifted. She took Leah to Golda's or Willa's pool and she lay on her back out in the water listening to Leah laugh. Willa's sons, Tom Jr. and Eric, came home in June and they drifted, too. The white children didn't shun them, but they didn't seek them out, and Rachel sensed in both of them, especially in Tom Jr., a pride that kept them from making the first move. So they lay by the pool, too. They swam, barbecued, read, played some gin. Tom Jr. wore a big Afro, thin at the ends, so his hair seemed to float around his head. Leah stood on her toes to reach for his hair and when he'd pick her up and let her touch it, she'd bury her small fat hands in it and get a look of perfect peace on her face. He let her crawl all over him. She pulled his hair, bent back his toes and fingers, punched him, and loved sleeping on top of him. When he lay on the grass on his stomach, she sprawled across the small of his back. When he lay on his back, she curled up on his chest like a cat.

*   *   *

In August Rachel and Willa took some extra vegetables to Reverend Ryder. At first Rachel felt shy about going inside. All her friends were Jews or atheists or had gotten married in a garden or on the side of a hill and she'd never been in a church before. She'd seen pictures of churches with beaked and taloned gargoyles clinging to fluted columns that rose into the stone ceilings, and when she went inside the plain frame Congregational church she thought she'd see the Virgin, draped in chiseled stone, melting eyes raised to heaven in torment, and a stone or stained-glass Jesus crucified, with blood running into his eyes from the thorns gouging his forehead and into his groin from the wound in his side. She expected Roman *grand guignol* with griffins and demons, writhing serpents, and saints in agony trapped against the walls, embedded in stone, staring out of perpetual gloom.

But the sanctuary, if that was what they called it, was high-ceilinged, light, and plain. The walls were white plaster, the windows were mullioned clear glass with sunlight coming through in bars, stripes, and rectangles. She expected to smell old books and incense. Instead she smelled beeswax and bayberry from the thin green candles in pewter sticks at the front of the church. They were the only decoration, except for a simple, elegant, maple pulpit and a milk-glass bowl of autumn flowers. She stood at the head of the aisle for a moment, then followed Willa, who seemed at home here, down to the platform-altar and up two steps and through a door to the reverend's office.

Reverend Ryder gave them tea and he and Willa talked about the Harvest Bazaar, whatever that was, while Rachel looked around the room. The shelves were full of books by Calvin, Zwingli, Jonathan Edwards, and someone called Laud. There was a photograph on Ryder's desk of a blond woman holding a boy and a girl on her lap. And another photograph of a fishing boat called the *Lady Helena* out of Montauk. In the case behind his desk she found books by Dorothy Sayers on religion, a complete set of her Lord Peter Wimsey mysteries, and a set of Chesterton and John D. MacDonald. The reverend had more mysteries than religious books. He saw her looking at them and said, "They have more ideas for sermons than all the tracts put together. For instance . . ." He took down Sayers's *The Unpleasantness at the Bellona Club.* "In this one a man is murdered at his club and his body sits upright in his chair for two days before anyone notices. *Two days.* Of course, you can see the implications . . . the young woman who gets murdered on a street in Queens while thirty or forty or a hundred people refuse to notice. Or the poor old man who gets ill on the subway and falls off his seat while people snap open books and papers, terrified of noticing. But to do good you have to notice—" He stopped and laughed.

"You just heard the gist of last May's prize sermon," he said as he put the book back.

That afternoon she found a copy of *Bellona Club* in the shop and read it and for the next few weeks she read all the Wimsey books: *The Nine Tailors, Murder Must Advertise, Whose Body?* They were funny, sometimes good, sometimes silly. The deeper moral lessons of most escaped her, except that the code of honor of upper class England won out in the end.

In September she and Willa decided to pickle the extra tomatoes and Rachel went up to the attic to look for her father's recipe. She found her old textbooks and her lecture notes. She pushed them back and closed the box because the lectures were Adam's and the books were full of his margin notes. In another box she found her father's recipes, all of her Jane Austen novels, and her old Shabbes school book.

She took it out, blew dust off the cover, and laid it flat on the floor in the light from the dormer window. Then she opened it and there in the centerfold, was the picture the clay had reminded her of. She saw a crooked, cobbled street and crooked, ugly houses with blank leaded windows that reflected nothing—she saw the old man in his rabbi's hat. There was the twisting alley, and a shadow of something was coming up it. Something so huge its shadow blacked out the wall. The shadow was in the shape of a man, but too big to be a man.

Rachel read the first few paragraphs.

It wasn't a man, but a monster shaped like a man. It was called a golem and it was made of clay. *Clay*.

That was the connection, Rachel thought. A child's horror story that must've given her nightmares, and that came back to her when Ableson said clay. That simple.

She went back to the beginning and read the whole story . . .

An angel visited the great Rabbi Judah Loew of Prague late one night. The angel carried a glowing sword and wore a golden robe. He appeared against a backdrop of the ocean with waves rolling in on a lonely beach. As he came closer to the rabbi, the ocean disappeared. The rabbi saw his own bedroom wall behind the angel and he knew that he wasn't dreaming. The angel came up to the rabbi's bed and leaned close to him.

"On the first night of Passover, the Gentiles are going to attack the ghetto," the angel told the rabbi. "Only you can save the Jews of Prague."

"And how am I going to do that?" the rabbi asked gently.

The angel smiled and the whole room was filled with light. "You are going to build a golem."

The rabbi resurrected ancient cabalistic formulas from the clues the angel gave him that night. Leaves appeared on the trees, grass turned green, and Passover was coming. The rabbi took two men—a Levite and a Kohen—to the banks of the river, away from the city. There they dug the river clay and molded it into the shape of a man. When they were done, the rabbi incised the sacred word on the forehead of the thing, and the three men followed the formulas the rabbi had unearthed. The figure glowed red, the glow faded, and then, slowly, painfully, a huge gray form rose up out of the mud and stood mute before them in the moonlight.

Rachel's skin prickled as she read.

Three men had gone to the river, four came back.

They led the golem to the great Altneushul. They took it up the stairs to the shul attic and the other two men left the rabbi alone with the golem.

The rabbi studied his creation. It was huge, superhumanly strong, and mute. It shambled when it moved and seemed to have no mind of its own or capacity for feeling. He decided that the golem was more frightening than the Gentiles. He left it in the attic and spent the next days praying that he would never have to lead it down the narrow stairs.

But on the first night of Passover the Gentiles worked themselves into a frenzy and massed at the ghetto gate. They carried clubs, torches, swords. They killed the gatekeeper, battered down the heavy wood gates, and stormed into the ghetto. They found the Jews in their houses celebrating the first Seder, and they dragged them out into the streets. They beat them and beheaded some and set some on fire.

There was a picture of a wrecked house. It showed the broken door and through it the ruined Seder table. Chairs were overturned, wine glasses broken. The Seder plate lay in pieces on the floor and candles burned in the empty room. Rachel turned the page and kept reading.

The great rabbi saw the massacre, ran back to the shul, and led the golem down the stairs and across the empty sanctuary in the flickering torchlight that came through the window. The rampaging Gentiles had reached the synagogue. They were piling wood around the foundation to set it on fire when the rabbi opened the front doors and led the creature out. The rabbi released his hold on it and said to it, "Save us." The golem stood without moving for a moment, its head raised. A hush came over the crowd in front of the synagogue as they saw the being that was shaped like a man, but too big to be one. The torches burned and everything was quiet while the golem and the Gentiles confronted each other. Then the golem took a step toward them. The ground shook when his foot came down and a terrified murmur started in the crowd. The golem took another step, then another. The murmur in the crowd turned to screams and they broke and ran, trampling the people in the back who didn't move fast enough. In full panic the mob raced back through the narrow ghetto streets. Most made it over the wall, but the monster caught a few on the ghetto side and killed them by smashing in their heads or breaking their necks. The people on the other side of the wall listened to the shrieks of their companions and trembled, but they stood where they were, thinking they were safe. The golem reached the wall, stopped, and stared out over the top of the crowd. The Gentiles felt secure enough with the wall between them to raise their torches, shake their swords, and yell at the creature. It didn't move; its huge head was a black mass against the gray night sky. The people got bolder, and a wave of them moved closer to the wall; but as soon as they did that, the golem raised its enormous fists, locked them, and brought them down on the top of the wall. With one blow it demolished the stone barricade that had enclosed the Jews of Prague, and, with defiant fury, it charged the city itself.

It pounded through boulevards and side streets, killing as it went. It broke down the walls of houses to get to the people cowering inside. It broke lamps and upended stoves and soon the city was burning.

The cardinal, who had instigated the raid on the ghetto, stayed in his palace. His advisers pleaded with him to make peace with the rabbi. At first he was proud and resisted; then he saw the light of the fires, and he went out on his balcony and saw the cobbles of the streets of Prague covered with blood. He dressed himself in the red robe of his office and rode through the streets of the city toward the ghetto. What he saw on the way appalled and humbled him, and by the time he reached the Altneushul where Rabbi Loew prayed alone in the dark, he was a shaken man, and even though he'd hated the Jews and been their chief enemy for years, he swore to the rabbi that the Jews of Prague would be safe forever if the rabbi would stop the golem. In spite of everything he had done, Rabbi Loew felt sorry for the cardinal. He explained as gently as he could that he would have stopped the golem hours ago, but if he set foot outside the ghetto, the citizens of Prague would kill him on sight. The old cardinal looked crafty. "Would the golem die with you, rabbi?" he asked. "Aren't you, after all, the spirit of the thing?"

Loew looked into the man's eyes and, still in a gentle voice, said to the prince of the Church, "I don't know. But if I die and the golem doesn't, it might, since it has gone mad, destroy the world." Then the rabbi told the cardinal that if he couldn't stop the golem the cardinal should order his guards to kill him in the hope that the monster would die with him. The cardinal wept when he realized what a good man the rabbi was.

"I'll go with you," he told the rabbi. "You'll be safe with me."

The two men, one in black, one in red, left the ghetto together to look for the golem. They passed the bodies of the people, even children, who'd been smashed against and walls by the creature. Some of them were still alive . . .

Rachel looked at the picture of them, covered with blood, arms and legs at crazy angles.

. . . and they reached out to the rabbi and cardinal as they passed. They followed the trail of corpses and dying through the city to the river, and there at dawn, Rabbi Loew found his creation.

The monster held the body of a child over his head to throw it in the water. The baby wailed and the rabbi cried at the golem to stop. The golem paused, still holding the child in the air, and the rabbi was afraid he'd lost his power over it. But then the golem put the child down without hurting it and followed the rabbi meekly back into the ghetto and up the stairs to the shul attic. The rabbi commanded the golem to lie down, and when it did, he covered the clay man with prayer books, then spent the rest of the day alone with it in the attic. At sundown, the Kohen and the Levite came to the attic. The three men reversed the process of creation, and the golem was turned back into lifeless clay.

And forever after that, the Jews of Prague lived in peace.

Rachel turned to the front of the book and looked at the date. The book had been copyrighted in 1932 and reprinted in 1940. Where were the Jews of Prague now, she wondered. She turned the pages back to the golem story, ignoring the others. She sat in the dusty sunlight surrounded by boxes of her old books and notes, and Adam's things, and looked at the pictures again. They were vivid and gruesome, and she wasn't surprised that they'd stayed with her in some corner of her mind all these years and had come back when Ableson said *clay*. There was something especially frightening and unwholesome about the illustrations. About the whole story. She shut the book and carried it downstairs. The weather was still mild and she put Leah in her stroller and, carrying the book, walked the two blocks to the little house the men had bought and converted into a shul. The sun was bright, the vestibule of the shul dim, and she was blinded. She saw the box of books and clothes the congregation collected every month for the children's hospital in Tel Aviv, but she didn't see Isaac Luria sitting in the corner of the lobby at a table. She put the book in the box and left. When the door closed, he put down the silver spice box he'd been polishing and went to the box.

By January Rachel still hadn't agreed to a wedding date, and Allan lost patience with her.

"Rachel, what do you want? Tell me what you want."

She didn't answer. Allan stood in front of her and held his arms away from his nude body.

"I'm young ... youngish." He looked down at himself. "Handsome, rich; look at that gut." He hit himself, trying to be funny, but she wanted to cry, and he came back to her and sat on the bed next to her and took her in his arms. "What do you want, baby, try to tell me. I want to understand ..."

"Adam's only been dead ..."

"Long enough, Rachel. Even the Talmud says it's been long enough ..."

He stood up again and crossed the room, keeping his back to her.

"I'm lonely, Rachel. I work hard and come home to

this mess every night too tired to clean or to even call someone to clean. I don't like it. I love you, but I want a wife; if it can't be you, then at least tell me and I'll . . ."

"Marry Barbara Michaels?"

He turned around. "Maybe," he said very seriously. "Maybe I will." She ran across the room to him, so scared she could barely breathe. She led him back to the bed, kissed him, did everything to him; but she didn't feel anything except fear. Even so, she couldn't say she'd marry him on May fifth or June first or any particular day. After they were finished, he fell asleep, and she got out of the messy bed, got dressed, and went downstairs through the abandoned-looking foyer and out into the empty road.

The snow stopped, the wind died, and snow covered the houses and hedges. Branches creaked, then stopped, and in the sharp cold air she thought she heard music coming from a block or so down toward town. Her boots squeaked in the snow and she stopped walking to listen again. It was like the music her father used to play when her mother was out playing bridge, Eastern music with a sighing kind of rhythm that she remembered from weddings and bar mitzvahs. It didn't belong with snow and fake gaslight streetlamps or the ersatz New England architecture. It sounded like it came from the little shul and she walked toward it.

The first floor of the shul was dark, and the path up through the hedges was forbidding, but the music was coming from there, and Rachel saw a bar of light on the snow from the basement window.

She'd gone to service here once; she'd sat behind the drape that separated the men from the women; and in the middle of the service, as Reuben Alldmann had lifted the Torah from the ark to carry it around the shul, she had an attack of claustrophobia so intense it turned to asthma. She gasped for air she couldn't get and, clutching Golda, she'd staggered out onto the porch into the open air where she could breathe again. She hadn't been back since. Now she went up the spooky path to the light, squatted down in front of the basement window, and looked in.

The basement was finished, with track lights on a celotex ceiling. But the room was lit by candles, twenty or thirty of them, and in their light, the Sutter Lane elders of Laurel danced; they hopped and swirled, sashayed and skipped, the candle flames jumped in the draft of their bodies and cast wild, leaping shadows on the walls. Their jackets were off, their fringed shawls and their shirts shone in the candlelight. Luria was the biggest and handsomest; his shirt and shawl were wet with sweat and clung to him, outlining his muscles. The music climaxed, the circle broke, and the men danced in couples, singing, holding each other's arms, circling each other; then Luria danced to the center of the room and stretched his arms and body. The others stopped to watch and he closed his eyes, let his head drop back, and he began a slow heavy dance that should have shook the little house but didn't because he was so graceful. The light caught his hair, his beard; his feet came down without a sound and he danced faster. The music followed him; his white silk shawl came out of his belt and whirled around him, the fringes catching the light.

He whirled, singing; the light caught the edges of his teeth and his voice was moaning but full of joy at the same time. Rachel held on to the sides of the window as Luria's song reached a sobbing climax and he froze for an instant; very tall and heavy, his body stretched as high as it would go; then he broke the pose and ran across the room to Leah's crib and picked the little girl up. Rachel held her breath; he hugged her against his chest and kissed her. Leah laughed, squealed, then reached for her grandfather who was standing next to him, and hugged him, too. Leah be there when they danced, but Rachel couldn't. They wouldn't let Leah in either once she'd reached puberty. Rachel watched her little girl and knew she'd be hurt then, and wouldn't understand, and Rachel wouldn't be able to explain because she didn't understand either.

Luria leaned over, because he was so tall, and Jacob was so short, and he kissed Jacob. Everyone, including Leah, watched them. Then the men broke apart, and Luria said to Jacob, "*Shabuoth tov.*" Then the other men kissed and hugged each other, all wishing a good week.

Someone put on a record of slower, sadder music, and the men began to sing. Rachel left the window and, walking as quietly as she could, went up the temple steps and inside. The sanctuary was right over the men in the basement, the floor was wooden, and she took off her boots so they wouldn't hear her. The celotex ceiling soaked up most of the singing, and the music was faint. She stood at the aisle, in front of the altar lit by the suspended lantern meant to symbolize the eternal light. The Torah was hidden by a panel. She went to it, slid the panel open, and there were the scrolls, covered in velvet that was embroidered with gold thread. A hammered silver plate hung from the scroll's handles by a silver chain. On it, a crowned lion held up stone tablets. She knew that if a woman touched the scrolls, they were considered defiled and had to be destroyed. She stood in front of the scrolls in the glow of the eternal light and thought about her father who was dead; and her brother, who was a podiatrist on East Ninety-second Street and bragged about fucking his patients. She thought about her mother who'd sold the handbag business, had bought bigger diamonds and a wardrobe of tight silk jersey dresses and had moved to Fort Lauderdale. Rachel had taken Leah there in the fall. But her mother played cards or mahjongg every day they were there, and the afternoon Rachel insisted on going to the beach, her mother stayed in a hotel lobby reading the *National Star* because the ocean wind gave her sinus. Rachel gazed at her reflection in the beautiful silver plate over the Torah. She had meant to stay with her mother for two weeks, but she'd left after one. She was sure the old lady was glad to be rid of her with her tourist's plans and her baby's needs. But at the last minute, as the cab pulled away from the patio of the condominium, Rachel saw a stricken look on her mother's face, as if she had just realized that instant that she would never see her daughter or granddaughter again.

Rachel wanted to touch the scrolls. She even reached out to them, but she couldn't bring herself to do it. She stood still in the dim light for a minute, then she slid the ark closed and left the shul.

It was snowing again, the air was silent and freezing. The street was dark and empty and she walked fast. The houses looked strange in the snow, and she was suddenly terribly lonely.

Her father was dead, Adam was dead. Her mother played cards and her brother was a fool. That left Levy, and the old men downstairs, because they were *mishpochah*. There was Golda, too, and Sam, and Allan. She couldn't count Willa or Tom. They were still strangers.

Rachel took a hot shower and went right to sleep. She dreamed she was back at the basement window watching Luria dance. Levy was dead and she was alone. She saw the muscles in Luria's arms and back straining his shirt. He was handsome, big, and sexy, the dance was suggestive, and she got excited in her sleep, but his features had softened and spread. She was scared and tried to wake up but couldn't; clay covered his face and ran into his beard. It covered his body, and as he danced, faster and faster, clay spun off the ends of his hands and feet in ribbons that smacked against the basement walls until the composition paneling and vinyl floor were covered with it. Suddenly he stopped dancing and he pointed at the window, at her. Clay dripped from his arm and finger. She was sick with terror because he was coming for her, trailing clay like a snail, only now he was huge and lumbering and the clay ran at last into his eyes so he should have been blind but he wasn't, because he was coming right for her, and all at once the window was gone, and the wall, and there was nothing between her and Luria's clay-drenched hands reaching for her....

It was a nightmare, not just a bad dream, and she woke up covered with sweat, and still terrified. She forced herself to sit up and turn on the light. The room was empty, the snow was still falling. She got up, picked up the afghan which she must have kicked off the bed, and rushed to Levy's room to be sure he was all right. He was in his bed, sound asleep. Without him, she and Leah would be alone . . . except for Allan. She went downstairs, ate one of the butter cookies she and Willa had baked, and she looked at the calendar. Then she called Allan.

"Rachel . . . what's wrong?" he asked sleepily.

She held the calendar.

"I'll marry you on the twenty-first of June, Allan. If you still want me to."

"Yes," he yelled. "Shit yes . . . oh baby . . ." She listened to his voice, but not the words, and when he paused, she hung up without saying any more. She marked the date on the calendar; June twenty-first—the summer solstice—the longest day of the year. The million-year-long day, she thought.

Chapter
5

SHE ORDERED invitations, and bought a copy of *Bride's* magazine, but it was so insipid she lost her temper, tore it to pieces, and shoved the pieces into the dispose-all. It wasn't used to slick paper and it jammed and she had to dismantle it and pull the pieces out again. The sky and the Sound lost their gray look; the air was warmer, but damp and still sharp.

The invitations came, and she felt as if everything was settled. Her life, the neighborhood, the town. She thought of mammoths in ice, of insects in amber, of any creature trapped, settled, done for.

Everyone else seemed to like the settling.

Golda brought Rachel vacation brochures to plan her honeymoon, but all Rachel could think of was Labrador, some place cold and silent that would make her happy to come home to Laurel. Willa said she'd never been as comfortable any place as she was in Laurel, except for the busing issue in Claremont. Stupid, Rachel thought, because the kids were bused anyway, but the parents painted placards and carried them. A cross was burned on a black family's lawn in Port Jefferson, and fistfights broke out at the high school. Willa said it was nothing.

But Tom Jr. was upset, and the Saturday after the fight, he wouldn't come to Rachel's house. Leah waited for him. When he didn't come, she carried her stuffed seal from room to room like a little ghost. She wouldn't eat dinner, wouldn't watch TV.

Rachel called Willa. "What are we, Honkies now?"

"Sure, sugar . . ." Then Willa said, "Let it alone, Rache. He misses her, too . . ."

She was too busy to think much about it. Passover was coming and this year Rachel vowed to do everything right. Two weeks before the first Seder, she unpacked the special dishes and even though it was far too early, she went to the cabinets and separated the containers of cereal, flour, and all the starches so she wouldn't miss any when the time came. The market in Port Jefferson had a whole section of Passover foods, and she and Golda filled four shopping bags. When she got home, Allan was waiting; he'd just finished preparing a big case, and he was so tired his skin looked gray. She made him lie down on the couch and he fell asleep. His eyes rolled under the lids, his pale eyelashes looked golden in the lamplight, and she wondered if he was dreaming; she stood back and looked at his body, then came close to him, leaned down, and kissed his neck. He didn't move and she left him alone to sleep.

Their Seder plate was chipped and she bought a new one; she washed the windows, waxed all the floors, and took the flour and barley and the rest over to Willa's. She scoured the stove, and she cleaned the refrigerator to be sure there were no crumbs left behind. She washed the cabinets, put the regular dishes away, and stacked the Passover dishes in their place. Utensils, pots, and pans were put through the dishwasher twice. Golda said that satisfied Dworkin, it should satisfy Levy. She made gefilte fish from scratch for the first time in her life, trying not to gag while she cleaned carp and pike. Golda supervised and after it was boiled and the broth strained, Golda tasted it and said it was delicious.

She hid two bits of bread for Levy and Allan to find on the ritual hunt for leavened bread the night before Passover. She saw and bought an antique silver cup for Elijah which cost eighty dollars, but was so beautiful she couldn't resist. She knew Levy would love it. Besides, she told her reflection in the window of the antique store in Port Jefferson, you are going to marry a rich man. She stopped feeling frozen, she stopped dreaming about Luria or thinking about her father, and when she made love to Allan she thought about him, not Roger Hawkins. She even forgot about the clay. She was young . . . more or less . . . pretty, and getting prettier. And she was actually, for the first time, falling in love with Allan Siegal.

Three days before the holiday she bought the last of her supplies. She parked the car at the curb because it was easier than going up the narrow steps from the garage and, carrying one more shopping bag full of goods that were kosher for Pesach, she walked up the path to the house. The lights were on. Leah was with Golda and Levy was still at the store, so she thought it was Allan in the living room waiting for her and she hurried up the path, and opened the front door. Isaac Luria got up from his chair. His glasses were off, his eyes were swollen from crying, and his face twisted with grief. Jacob was dead, she thought. She dropped the bag and reached for the wall, but Jacob stood up from the couch and came toward her. He was crying too.

"Leah," she cried.

"Leah's fine," Jacob said. She hung on to him, trying to catch her breath. In the bag she saw that the eggs had broken. Yellow oozed out through the split carton. She picked up the bag and Luria hissed.

"Get her out of here."

"Please, Isaac."

"She doesn't belong here."

Rachel looked around wildly. They were all there. Dworkin, Fineman . . . Alldmann. Even the old man whose eyes were yellow all the time now, and runny. She backed against the door.

"This is my house," she said. "Tell that old fucker, this is *my* house. . . ."

Luria was on his feet coming toward her, the dream come true, but she came away from the door and faced him.

"Tell her," he yelled. "Tell her what her friends have done. Scum . . . tell her!"

"Which friends, what is he talking about?" Rachel yelled.

Jacob pulled her out of the door onto the path. Luria stayed behind, and her last view was of her shopping bag abandoned at his feet.

It was a beautiful early spring evening. Jacob made her walk to the end of the path, holding her arm. When they reached the curb he stopped and put his arms around her. They were almost the same height, and his body fitted hers perfectly. He held her close, almost like a lover.

"Go to Golda's," he whispered, "and stay there until nine. Leah's there, she's fine. . . ."

"Please . . . Jacob."

"There was a terrible fight in the school today. Two boys were killed, one white, one black. . . ."

"Not Tom . . ."

"No, not Tom, nor Eric. But Tom was involved. He and a bunch of other blacks were in on it. They hit

Michael Brodsky—a bad hit. Fractured his skull, Rachel. He's dead." He let her go and she sank against the car; Michael Brodsky was Isaac Luria's oldest grandson.

The funeral was on the afternoon before Passover eve. Esther Brodsky, Luria's daughter, screamed and clawed at her father, then sagged, ready to fall into the mud next to the grave. He held her up, his eyes bleak as they lowered the coffin. It was warm, the ice had melted all at once, and the grave site was a mire. Rachel's heels sank in mud. The coffin disappeared into the grave. Luria scooped up a handful of mud. It squeezed through his fingers and he opened his hand and looked at the lump of mud, then at Jacob. Dworkin looked up, and one by one, so did the others. When he had their attention, he nodded, then he pressed the mud into his daughter's hand.

"Throw it on the coffin, Esther," he said gently.

She did; then Myron Brodsky did the same, and the rest of the men. Rachel couldn't watch and she turned around just as the Garners got out of the Cadillac and came up the gravel path toward the group around the grave. Rachel saw them first, but a second later everyone else did too. No one moved or said anything. Mud dripped from the men's hands and the Garners waited. Tom didn't know to wear a hat; thin sunlight shone on his black hair. Luria let go of his daughter. She sank to her knees in the mud, wailing—the only sound. Luria held a ball of mud and Rachel knew he was going to throw it. She broke away from Allan and jumped and slid between Luria and Willa. But Luria's arm was already moving, he couldn't stop and the mud meant for Willa hit Rachel's cheek and neck with a smack, like a slap. Willa gasped, then cried out.

"Tom didn't hit that boy. Please, Mr. Luria, my Tom never hurt anyone. . . ."

"Rachel . . . Rachel," Levy called and started around the grave to get to her. Allan was too stunned to move and only Rachel and Luria seemed to know what they were doing.

Rachel almost wanted to take it back. But she faced Isaac Luria with mud clammy on her skin. Until then, whenever he had looked at her his eyes had been blank, but now they were full of life, full of wonder that anything like her existed, and then he smiled at her. It was the worst, most spiteful smile she'd ever seen. She wanted to cover her face and turn away, but she raised her head, stretched her neck, felt mud slide into her blouse, and smiled back at him.

"Why?" Allan asked. He sounded angry at her for the first time.

"Because he had no right to treat Willa like that. She came out of sympathy, to show her respect."

"The old guy just lost his grandson, Rachel. Her son was in on it—"

"No!"

"Maybe in on it . . ."

"It was an accident."

"You were there?" he asked.

She looked at him. "Do you think Tom killed Michael?" she asked softly.

"I don't know."

"But he's black, so he must've done something. Right?"

"I don't know," Allan said again. Then he shook his head. "The prejudice is there, Rachel," he said gently, "like it or not."

He was right. The prejudice *was* there. Adam had

known that, but he'd fought it and won. But Allan wasn't Adam, she told herself for the thousandth time. Suddenly she wondered if Roger Hawkins had had to fight the same feelings about whites. He must have, she thought, and won, too, or he and Adam could never have been friends.

Chapter
6

LEVY CARRIED his big black umbrella as he walked east along the shoulder of the highway. He was alone, there weren't many cars, and he walked with his back to the oncoming traffic and felt fairly safe. Dworkin said the river was called Wading River and it was perfect. He kept going. On one side he saw a clam stand, shut up, abandoned, gray and peeling. It was depressing and he looked up past the edge of his umbrella at the sky, hoping for some comfort. The sky was gray and he kept going. After a while gravel filled his shoes and mud caked the bottom of his trousers. Ahead to the east it was getting dark and he looked behind him at the last of the light. He had a flashlight with him, but it got dark too fast. He knew he'd never find the place. That was all right too. He didn't want to find it.

"What's the matter?" Luria had said in Yiddish, "only Adam is real? Only your children count?"

Levy had said, "I loved your grandson."

"Then prove it!" Luria cried and Levy had jumped out of his chair and grabbed big Isaac by the front of his jacket. He wished for an extra foot to lift this . . . this

177

bulvan* into the air so his feet dangled and kicked like a corpse on the end of a rope. He hated Isaac Luria that minute.

"Prove what? That I loved the boy, that I love you? How many times do I prove it to you?" He'd actually managed to shake the monster Luria and he pushed him, and Luria sat down hard. The other men were quiet and Levy said in Yiddish, facing the wall, not them, "My son was everything to me. I thought we were safe in Brooklyn, I thought we were safe here." He shrugged. "*Nu*, my father thought we were safe in Dabrowa, and who could count how many grandfathers, uncles, cousins thought they and us . . . were safe in one place or the other."

He looked at Luria. "More killing makes us safe?"

Luria had covered his eyes with one hand. "Yes," he'd said.

Levy saw a sign for Wading River, followed it, and a few minutes later he saw the small road crossing the highway that Dworkin told him about and he found the path that crossed it and followed it. His feet were soaked, so was the front of his coat and trousers. Only his hat under the umbrella was dry. The path ended at the river. The bank was covered with dead reeds, broken, beaten down into the mud by the rain. He went closer, too close; he slipped in the mud and his shoe and cuff got soaked in the water. He felt so miserable he couldn't think of anything to do but laugh. Rachel would laugh, so would Adam. A silly old man in the mud, in the rain, on the bank of the river, at dusk. The mud smelled, the river smelled, he was cold and wet and he knew it was ridiculous, and the past had been a dream. It couldn't work again, he didn't want it to work. Then, like a sign,

* Oaf.

a young buck came out of the reeds, and walked daintily along the edge of the river. A doe followed him. They were so close to Levy as they passed him that he could see the heavy soft tufts of hair in their ears, and the moss on the buck's antlers. The reeds barely bent as they went by, and it was so dusky they disappeared a few feet beyond Levy into the bushes on the same side of the river. Levy looked after them for a while, straining his eyes in the gloom to try to see them again.

When he was young the forests around Krakow were full of deer. Cabalists were everywhere then, and prophets cried through the village streets, like men with pushcarts, that the Messiah was on his way—the prophets were thin and ragged, as if no one would believe a prosperous man. But the Cabalists wore fur and shiny coats to their ankles. Some of them were fakes who said they could tell the future, cast spells, heal the sick, but some, like Aaron Levy, his father, were mystics who studied, meditated, and said that God emanated and that they could receive the emanations, be bathed in them, feel ecstasy from them. Aaron Levy would kneel for hours alone in the dark or with one candle in the room—meditating down the tree, he explained, from *Kether* to *Malkuth*. But his son Jacob liked people and by the time he was seven he had memorized the six hundred thirteen laws in the Torah and by the time he was twenty he knew the Talmud and its commentaries well enough to be consulted as a judge by the people of the village. Jacob didn't care about the world and about people, not about Zohar, Gematria, the Sefirot, or whether God in his infinite nothingness had gotten out of the way to make space for the universe. "You're not a mystic," his father told him sadly. Levy agreed. But when the Germans declared war on Poland and crossed the border, Aaron

Levy took his son to a *shtetl* near Sosnowiec to see the most famous cabalist in Poland. "In the world," his father told him. The old man lived four miles out of town on a lonely road that was just wide enough for the cart they borrowed. One room of the little house had only three walls; the fourth was open to the forest and the old man was in that room with the April wind blowing his caftan and beard. He sat on the packed dirt floor, in front of an unlit fireplace, and for the first few minutes they were there, he stared at the cold hearth without greeting them. Levy took a step, but his father restrained him. "He knows we're here," Aaron told his son, and Levy and his father waited while the wind blew everything around. There was a thin book on the floor next to the old man; the wind blew it open and ruffled the pages, and, as if that were a signal, the old man turned and looked at them.

Jacob wanted to hug the wall when he saw his face, but he made himself stand erect. The skin of the old man's face was so thin that veins running under it gave it a blue cast; his eyes were blue, like Isaac Luria's, but sunk into gray holes in his face, and his beard was yellow-white and thin and blew in wisps around his face. Strands of what was left of the hair on his head hung down from under his yarmulke, and only the black hair that stuck out of his ears in tufts seemed to have any life to it. He raised his hand and motioned Levy to come in; the fingers were still straight and long, and the skin on the back of his hands looked fresh, as if the old man's hands and the hair in his ears had stayed young while the rest of him dried up. Levy crossed the three-walled room and the old man gestured to him to sit on the floor across from him, next to the hearth. Levy did; his father stayed at a distance. The old man leaned toward Levy, and Levy had to keep himself from pulling back. The old man smiled; his teeth were still young too.

"You got a match?" the old man asked, which was so different from what he expected him to say that Levy almost laughed in the old man's face. He found his one box of matches and gave it to the old man. They were precious. He was afraid the old man would keep them and he'd be too embarrassed to ask for them back. But the old man used two to light the fire, then returned the box to Levy and sat for a long time looking at Levy, then at the fire without saying anything. The fireplace was so well engineered it heated the whole section of the room they sat in even though the wind kept blowing. When Levy felt so warm he thought of taking off his coat, the old man said quietly, "The Germans will be in Warsaw before long."

Levy said, "The Poles will fight . . ."

"They ain't such fighters," the old man said, "and the Germans will be in Warsaw," he repeated. Levy didn't interrupt him again.

"Now," said the old man, "sit back in the warmth of the fire . . . lean on the pillow there." Levy did as the old man said. "Relax and let thoughts come to you and you will know as well as I do what the Germans will do." Then he said to Levy's father, "Go into the house, Aaron. Make tea for yourself. We'll be a little while." His father left and after a while the old man said, "*Nu?*"

Levy had read the newspapers and commentaries. He'd heard the stories from Danzig, Czechoslovakia, and Germany. He looked at the flames jumping in the grate and came to the conclusion that everyone was avoiding. "They're going to try to kill us all," he said.

The old man beamed. "See, it's not so hard. That's what the Germans have been saying all along, but the Jews don't listen. Now," the old man sat up and Levy did the same, "Cabala isn't dumbheads looking at palms and calling up demons. Cabala is a method of trying to understand the true and profound nature of God"—he sounded like a teacher reading a familiar lesson—"and while there is no possibility of full understanding, of intimate union with Him, it is possible . . . common . . . to feel ecstasy in the attempt." Suddenly the old man's eyes filled with tears, and he reached across the space that separated them and touched Levy's cheek with his young fingers. "If we'd had time you would have felt that ecstasy, I promise you. But we have other work to do."

He handed Levy the little book. "Read this. It's only two thousand words." Levy turned so he was half facing the fire, half facing the land on which the house stood. The sun set, turning the grass in the west pink. The Germans would come from that direction, through the forest, to the little house. Levy picked up the book. It was called *Sefer Yezirah*, the Book of Creation.

His father stayed in the house and he and the old man lived in the three-sided room for four days while the Germans overran Poland. The old man told Levy what the book meant, and how to use it; and at the end of the time, Levy and his father took the borrowed cart back to the town and from there managed to squeeze on the Krakow train which was packed with Polish officers retreating to the East.

His father died in June, and a year and a half afterward Levy's name, along with the names of all the Jewish men in Dabrowa, was posted for transportation to Belzec. Levy held Leah against him all night; they made love so many times she tried to joke about not being able to walk in the morning. Then she cried and finally, exhausted, she fell asleep. He lay awake until dawn, then he took the book the old man had given him, crossed the village, and went out the gate, telling the guard that he had a gift for his father's grave. The guard let him pass, and when he got to the cemetery on the other side of the little river that crossed the fields, he prostrated himself on his father's grave. "I know what you want me to do," he said with his cheek against the dirt, "and I know what the old man wants me to do. But I believe that my soul will be in danger if I do it." He buried the book next to his father's grave, then he stretched out on his back, lying over the spot where the book lay, and looked up at the sky until he closed his eyes and fell asleep. It was the first peaceful sleep he'd had since they'd gone to see the old man; but when he woke up, and walked back to Dabrowa, the book's contents came back to him, along with what the old man had told him, word for word. He tried to forget it, but it stayed with him, like children's nonsense nursery rhymes. When he and the others were loaded on the train at the siding on the other side of the village, he heard it in the beat of the soldiers marching; when the train started, he heard it in the rhythm of the wheels contacting the rails. He told himself he didn't have to do it just because he couldn't forget how, but the day he'd gotten back from seeing the old man he'd told his best friend Isaac Luria about what the old man had taught him.

Levy bent and slid his palm against the muck. It *felt* right; stiff enough, not slimy like mud, but smooth, cool, and slick, like clay.

Rachel and Willa met at Laurel's one respectable cocktail lounge in the Cannery Shopping Mall. They got high, tried to laugh, and ended up crying. Rachel ordered a hamburger for them, and they cut it in half; Rachel ate her half, but Willa couldn't.

"What if Jacob knew you were here with me?"

"Jacob wouldn't care. It's Luria; that . . . that *pisher* . . ."

Willa laughed in spite of herself.

Then Rachel started to cry again and the women faced each other, crying, saw how they looked, then laughed, and the bartender and the two men at the bar shook their heads. Tom Sr. was in St. Louis, Tom and Eric were at the library, and Willa hated being alone, so they had another drink.

"Do you think things'll be calm enough by June for us to go to the wedding?" she asked.

"You're going, or I'm not," Rachel said.

"Luria—"

"Fuck Luria!" The bartender looked shocked, the two drinkers sniggered.

Afterward, they walked through the quiet little town, into the Main Street Extension. April was almost over, the thin tree branches were yellow in the street light, and the air was fresh, damp, cool. They walked close together, brushing each other from time to time, both glad for the contact.

Fog rolled in from the Sound, and the night turned heavy all at once, spooky. They heard their footsteps on the pavement. As they passed the shul, Rachel saw a light in the basement, but didn't think about it. It was eight-thirty, the boys wouldn't be home yet, so Rachel walked the rest of the way with Willa. The afternoon paper was at the door; it had been ten days, and the only mention of the fight at the school was half a column on page ten.

"Thank God," Willa said.

They had omelettes and brandy, and by the time Tom Jr. and Eric got home they were high all over again.

Tom Jr. stopped at the door when he saw Rachel. He still had the bruise from the fight on the right side of his face. It was yellow at the edges and a star of blood still showed in the corner of one eye.

"I didn't mean to hurt anyone," he said. "It wasn't me that hit him. I'm not even sure anyone did. That cafeteria's all chrome and glass and sharp edges. He could've fallen from someone shoving him and gotten hurt like that." Rachel was nodding. Tom started to cry; he was so tall, so well built, she forgot he was only seventeen. Still a boy.

"I didn't even know who he was. It was rousting, that's all. Just rousting. It was the white kid . . . the Brodsky kid had the knife. We wasn't even doing real punching till he pulled that knife . . ." he sobbed. "Oh, Rachel . . . I swear, I never hurt him. He was fifteen," Tom sobbed. "A little kid next to me. Shorter'n you. I never, never . . ."

"Michael Brodsky had a knife?" Rachel asked. Tom Jr. looked into her eyes.

"I swear it."

No one said anything about Luria's grandson having a knife. She'd tell Jacob; maybe he'd feel better about Tom. Maybe it would change things.

Levy was still up, and dressed, even though it was ten and he was usually ready for bed by now. He looked terrible, flushed and vague like someone with a high fever. But he said that he felt fine. He'd just started watching *Notorious* on the TV and couldn't stop. She sat with him and tried to watch too. But all the actors' gestures seemed bizarre to her, their problems trivial; she was going to tell Jacob about the knife, and she turned to him to do it, then saw that he wasn't watching the screen but was staring at the wall, concentrating on nothing, like a man in a trance. She sat back in her chair while Ingrid Bergman and Cary Grant kissed for what seemed like the last time in their lives, and she realized that it didn't matter about the knife. It wouldn't have mattered if Mike had carried a gun or a bomb. He was *mishpochah* and the Garners were not. The blacks could never be, and that was all the justice and reason there'd ever be to it. It wasn't justice that mattered to Jacob nor to any of them, it was … affiliation. In the movie, Claude Rains's Nazi mother understood that. Why should she, Rachel Levy, have so much trouble with it? She went upstairs before the movie was over, and fell asleep sitting up in bed with her book open on her chest and the lights on. At midnight, Willa called her.

"I'm sorry, honey, did I wake you?"

"Half and half," Rachel said. "Anything wrong?"

"No . . . just fog and feeling down and kind of spooky."

"Kids sleeping?"

"Yeah . . ."

"Want me to come over?"

"No, just talk a few minutes."

They talked about the wedding. Rachel wanted to wear a suit, Golda said she should wear a gown, but Willa said a short dress was best. Rachel was too short for suits, she said. Especially with the new big shoulders and short skirts. Ivory silk, Willa said, and as she said it, Rachel saw it, half full skirt, not too short, and a beige veil, maybe some sparkles on it.

"Sparkles," Willa laughed, then she said, "something just fell downstairs." She sounded scared.

"Go see, Willa, I'll wait."

The other end was quiet for a minute, then Willa said, "I think it's that exhibit Eric's building for the science show. He's got it propped up in the foyer."

"You okay?"

"Fine. I'll make him take care of it in the morning."

Rachel hung up, turned off the light, and fell asleep. She woke later, the fog was still thick against the window, and it must have turned cold because crystals of ice had formed in the corners of the windows. She sat up and listened. She thought she heard Levy's door close, and she got out of bed, wide-awake all at once, and opened her door. She felt the tail end of a draft and went downstairs; the foyer floor was freezing, she felt the cold through her slippers. She bent down and touched the tile. It was damp, too, but the heat was on; she could hear the furnace and the radiator was hot. Levy must just have opened the door. She opened it and looked out. The fog was freezing and so dense she could barely see. A light from his bedroom made a halo in the mist above her, and as she looked up the light went out. Fog settled on her hair, but something kept her on the doorstep with the door open, listening. It was just a feeling—the fog, the cold, the sense of the water on one side and the woods on the other. Willa was right, it was creepy. Fog moved on the road and she went in and shut the door.

She didn't fall asleep until three, and again the phone woke her; it was five and on the other end Golda was screaming; her voice mad, "They're dead, oh my God, they're all dead!"

"Who?" Rachel screamed back.

"Willa—the boys . . ."

Rachel slammed the phone and ran down the stairs. She flung her raincoat over her nightgown and ran across lawns and around hedges. The fog was gone, a cold wind

187

blew off the Sound through her coat and nightclothes and she shook and sobbed as she ran. She had to stop to catch her breath, and when she did she realized that Golda had been hysterical. They might not all be dead. One of the boys might have lived. Or Willa. Or all of them. What could kill three people all at once? Fire; but there was no fire. She'd have heard the truck, seen the blaze. What else? The furnace exploded; but she'd have heard that too. What else? Plague. Mother and two sons dead of plague on Long Island. She kept sobbing but she had enough breath to run the rest of the way, and she knew as soon as she saw the house, even from a distance, that no one was alive in there. It was a dead house; the door hung loose, the front windows were broken. The house had aged a hundred years overnight and was haunted now. A ghost house in six hours.

The whole Laurel police force was there, cars, a few men, and when they saw her, three came up to her. They were pale. One was young and handsome with thick blond hair; he talked for them.

"Were you a friend?" he asked.

"Best friends," Rachel sobbed.

The men looked at each other.

"What happened?" she asked.

"We're not sure."

"Are they dead?" she asked.

"Yes. Three people. A woman and two young men . . ."

Rachel nodded. Her mother would have screamed, her grandmother would have wanted to see. Rachel wanted to see and she pushed past the men and ran up the path toward that silent house. The blond cop grabbed her.

"You can't go in there," he said. He didn't expect her to resist or to be so strong, and she pushed him away and ran up the path. He ran after her, but she held her nightgown up and ran as if demons chased her. Up the stairs, across the brick porch-patio to the splintered door hanging loose, by a thread of hinge. She smashed through it, slipped on the slick floor of the entrance hall, fell and skidded. The cop reached her, pulled her to her feet.

"Please, lady, please," he gasped, but she was staring at the front of her beige raincoat which was streaked with gray. So was her nightgown, so were her shoes. She had slipped in gray mud that streaked Willa's parquet floor. The mud led away from the door, into the living room, across the celadon carpet.

She touched the front of her coat; it came off on her fingers and she rubbed them together and smelled clay.

Belzec

Chapter
1

HAWKINS LEANED on the windowsill and looked out at the promenade next to the river. It was eight-thirty Sunday morning, but the fags were already out in force. They walked arm in arm along the path against the backdrop of the Manhattan skyline. It was a real walk they took, a slow and stately march, like the women in hoop skirts and men in frock coats must have taken a hundred years ago. The baby carriages were missing, but the feeling was the same. A warm Sunday morning in April, after a night of balls, parties, at-homes, cruising the bars, drumming up trade; and no matter how the night had come out, they dressed up and walked out to show the world. Hawkins felt a wave of tenderness for them. They didn't care about the Puerto Ricans who swarmed over Red Hook and spilled into the Heights. They didn't get bitched off about busing and move to the suburbs.

He watched them for a while, then turned back into the room. Alma was still asleep. He kissed her and she murmured but didn't open her eyes. He lay next to her for a few minutes, then he got up, got dressed quietly, and stopped at the door to look back at her. They'd had a good time last night—good food and talk with Mo and Peggy. Just enough to drink and just enough good sex.

Most nights were good with her now and as he watched her in the morning light he thought that he liked her better than he ever had. Mo said that was all that mattered. Love was for afternoon TV.

It was warm outside, the first really warm day of the year, and the breeze that came off the river was fresh for a change. Hawkins drove slowly across Brooklyn to Queens, keeping to the side streets. He saw clusters of little girls dressed up like brides, on their way to their first communion. Their white dresses and veils blew in the wind and their families walked behind them, the women holding their hats. He smiled when he passed them, and waved, and one little girl in a swirl of white organdy waved back at him.

He hit the Expressway and even here the air was fresh. The bay didn't stink for once, the park along the abandoned fairgrounds had turned green overnight, and the little phony lake was blue in the sun. He started feeling absurdly pleased with himself.

He was making forty-five thousand a year. Alston said it was time for him to run for something. City Council, or State Legislature. Even Washington wasn't too far to go for a smart, handsome, black ex-cop, Alston had said. Hot stuff, Hawkins thought. The Congress, the Senate...

Of course, Alston had said, he had to get married. Single men had a hard time in politics. Everyone figured they were gay or fuck-arounds. Alma'd marry him, he thought. She'd have married him years ago, if he'd asked her. City Council meant good money. She wouldn't miss the alimony. Elections meant some celebrity, too, and his daughter might read about him and come to see him after all these years. Maybe they'd move to Manhattan....

He turned into his street and saw the van in his driveway. It was a Dodge, the same color inside and out, and

194

he couldn't believe it was the same but he knew it was. He remembered how much he loved Jacob, how he missed him; he thought of Rachel again and realized that he'd never really stopped thinking about her. He wasn't confident anymore, or happy. A second ago he could have told himself the whole story of the rest of his life. Now he didn't know anything.

He stopped in front of the door of the house and told himself he should go back to Brooklyn until Rachel Levy couldn't wait anymore and went home and forgot about him. But his hands shook as he put the key in the lock and he knew it was because he couldn't wait to see her. He opened the door and stood in the hall listening. He heard murmuring, but couldn't identify the voices and, with his heart pounding, he went to the living room and stood in the doorway.

His mother sat in her wing chair, a little white girl was sleeping on the couch, and Rachel Levy sat next to her, holding a cup and saucer and watching the door. Her hand jerked when she saw him, the cup rattled as she put it down, and she stood up quickly and came across the room to him. He couldn't do anything but wait for her to reach him. She looked older than he remembered, and very, very tired, but it was still the best face he'd ever seen. She got to him, and put her arms around him. Her face touched his, her cheek felt hot on his skin, and he could smell her hair. He couldn't hear the TV anymore, or see the shocked look on his mother's face. He raised his arms stiffly, like a man in a space suit, and with the feeling that he was finishing something he'd started a long time ago, he put them around her.

She wanted to talk to him alone and he took her into the dining room and closed the sliding double doors his father had built. He could see how nervous she was and he tried to get her to drink some brandy, or more tea,

195

but she didn't want any. He sat down across from her and waited for her to explain why she was there. She was so shaky he thought she'd have trouble getting it out. But she took a breath and, almost as if she were challenging him, said, "They killed a family in Laurel last night."

He didn't have ask who *they* were and he kept quiet and let her talk.

They were beaten to death, she told him, like the boys in Brooklyn...

The clay was there too. It got on her coat and nightgown, on her hands. She had been wiping her hands and crying and the cop was pulling her out of the house, but he didn't move fast enough and she saw Willa's legs sticking out from behind the grandfather clock. One leg was bent up casually, as if she could straighten it out, but the other was turned all the way around with the kneecap pressed into the carpet. Rachel gagged and the cop got her out of there. She thought she'd throw up and she bent sickly over the grass, taking deep breaths until she got some control. Then she looked up and saw Golda standing in her driveway watching, and Rachel shrieked and ran across the road to her. Golda flinched and would have run away, but Rachel grabbed her shoulder and shook her as hard as she could.

"What happened to them?" she screamed at Golda. A couple of the pink plastic rollers in Golda's hair came loose and fell. Her hair flopped in her face.

"I don't know," she sobbed.

Rachel shook her again. "What do you mean you don't know?"

The cop pulled at her. "Please, lady," he said desperately, "give her a chance to talk."

"Why did you call me?" Rachel yelled again, but she

let Golda go. Golda bent down and picked up the rollers. She was still sobbing.

"Something woke me up. I don't know what. Something. I thought it was the front door and I tried to wake Sam to go and see but he was out like a light. So I went. Our door was closed, everything was fine, and I went back ..." She wiped tears and cream off her face. "Then, just as I'm ready to get back in bed, I looked out the window. I don't know why, Rachel."

"What did you see?" Rachel asked.

"A light in Willa's house. Only a light. But something was wrong with it. ... And I knew I wouldn't sleep until I figured it out; I don't know why, I tell you. Just a feeling. So back I go to the window and this time I realize it isn't the porch light I see, it's a half-burnt-out-chandelier. ... But I couldn't see the chandelier unless the door was open, right?" Rachel and the cop nodded. Golda wiped her running tears with the sleeve of her robe. "But her door's not supposed to be opened at four-thirty in the morning. Still, I didn't want to be an asshole and call the cops in the middle of the night only to find out that she just forgot to change the bulbs and the door's open because she's taking out the garbage or walking in the garden 'cause she can't sleep. And then, oh God, the wind blew; and that door swayed sideways and I knew, even from here, that it was busted. So I called the cops."

Clay everywhere, Ableson had said. *He thinks your father-in-law ... your whole* mishpochah, *killed the boys in Brooklyn.*

Rachel stared at Golda, then looked up at the dark house.

"Is your father home?" she asked.

"Of course he's home."

Rachel turned and ran down the road. One shoe came off, so she took the other one off and ran barefoot. Golda and the officer yelled at her, but she didn't stop until she got to her house.

Everything looked the same. She went up to Levy's room, and stood outside for a moment, then she opened it slowly. He was sleeping on his back and breathing hard, like a man who'd had too much to drink. What if he and the others had gotten drunk, nothing else? What if he woke up and saw her standing barefoot with her hair tangled like a Medusa and her muddy nightgown flopping at the them. He'd cry out and cover his face. But the blue comforter over him rose and fell rhythmically and after a minute she came all the way into the room. She opened the closet; his dark jackets and trousers hung neatly, his shoes were on the floor in a row. She touched them quickly, then stopped and felt one pair again. They were wet. She turned them over and saw traces of wet mud in the stitching.

She left the room and stood in the hall for a minute, then she went downstairs, out of the house, still barefoot. She went around the side, opened the trash can, and saw something slick and wet inside. She pulled out a wad of gray plastic and unfolded it. It was a disposable raincoat that folds to fit a pouch and it was streaked with gray.

"The gray stuff was clay," Hawkins said.

Rachel nodded.

"So he was there."

"Yes."

"He killed them."

Rachel didn't answer. In the living room, Leah woke up and started to cry. Hawkins leaned across the table and asked softly, "How'd he kill them, Rachel?"

Out of nowhere she thought of the clay man in Prague, Rabbi Loew's golem. It was too insane to mention.

"I don't know," she said.

Leah started to scream and Rachel ran for the living room. He followed her.

"Why did they do it?" he shouted over the noise.

Hawkins's mother interrupted. "She's wet and hungry."

Rachel brought her tote bag and Hawkins's mother took it from her. "I kin handle her," she said. Her fingers were swollen and crooked from arthritis, her elbows were big knobs. Leah was quieting down and she picked her up and carried her into another room. Rachel saw a Naugahyde sofa and a TV set through the door. The old lady shoved the door shut with her foot and Hawkins grabbed her arm.

"In Brooklyn it was for Adam. What was it this time?" he asked.

"Luria's grandson. Some black and white kids had a fight in the high school and Luria's grandson was killed."

"The Garners were black?" His grip on her arm tightened.

"Yes," she said. She felt guilty, but didn't know why.

"One of the Garners killed the boy?"

"No . . . Tom Junior wouldn't kill anyone. It was an accident. They were all fighting in the cafeteria"—she remembered what Tom Junior had said—"and Michael fell or got pushed and hit his head. No one meant it."

"Then why?"

She looked at Hawkins. "I don't know. Michael had a knife . . . that's what Tom told me. And I wanted to tell Jacob. I almost did. But I looked at him and I knew it wouldn't matter. Michael was dead . . . one of our own. One of *their* own," she corrected herself. "That was all that mattered." She stopped, then said, "I don't know why they killed Willa and Eric. Maybe it was an accident too." She wiped tears out of her eyes. "I don't understand why they killed the boys in Brooklyn. I loved Adam. But I swear to you I wouldn't've killed them."

"Wouldn't you?" he asked softly, looking at her.

She was going to say no, but all at once she couldn't get the word out.

"Wouldn't you really?" he asked again.

She still couldn't answer.

Another program came on TV. She heard music and voices through the door, and Leah laughed. Hawkins picked up the phone.

"Who're you calling?"

"The Laurel police . . . the chief."

Someone answered the phone and Hawkins identified himself. Then he waited and the Laurel police chief came on the line. He was shouting and Hawkins had to hold the phone away from his ear.

"I've seen murder," the chief shouted; "even out here people get murdered. But nothing like this. One wasn't bad. It was like when some guy loses it and hits his wife with a baseball bat and it's a lucky hit. You've seen those. One clop and she's dead, and he just meant to scare her, to teach her a lesson. That's how it was with the little one. They threw him against a wall or something, broke his neck, and bang, the kid's dead. But the others . . . oh shit." The man coughed and Hawkins wondered if he was crying. "They beat them and beat them." The chief raved on. "They twisted parts of them . . . we were slipping in blood."

"And clay," Hawkins said.

The chief stopped, then said, "How'd you know about the clay?"

Hawkins looked at Rachel. "I have a friend who lives on Sutter Lane," he said.

"We don't know what to make of the clay. There wasn't enough to smother them or anything, but it was everywhere the bodies were. It was on the bodies . . ." The chief stopped. "I never saw such a thing. It wasn't enough to kill them, to beat them up like that, but to throw mud on them . . . oh my . . ."

"Where did it come from?" Hawkins asked.

"Wading River, Swan Pond, Linus Pond."

"Any way to tell which?" Hawkins asked.

"No. There's clay all over here. Riverbanks, streams, swamps."

"Any weapons?"

"We didn't find any. But there must've been."

Hawkins didn't answer.

"They couldn't do that with their bare hands."

Hawkins asked, "Is there any chance the husband did it?"

"No," the chief answered. "We found him at a meeting in St. Louis. He's on his way home." The chief stopped again. "Oh my God," he said, "that poor bastard. That poor, poor bastard." The chief choked again and this time Hawkins knew he was crying. Hawkins waited, but the man couldn't talk anymore and after a moment Hawkins hung up.

"Where did the clay come from?" Rachel asked.

"They don't know."

"Why was it there?"

He shook his head.

"It means *something*," she said desperately. "Some ritual."

Hawkins shook his head. "Ableson asked his mother's rabbi. He never heard of a ritual with clay. But he said

201

that some village sects had their own rituals, handed down for two or three hundred years, that he wouldn't know about."

"Who would know?"

"*They* would know. Or someone else from the same village." He looked at her. "Who else is from there?"

"No one," she said. "The Nazis killed them."

"All of them?"

"I think so."

She said it so calmly he realized that she was used to the idea.

"Who would know for sure?"

"Golda might."

"Call her," Hawkins said.

Golda sounded scared. "Rachel, where are you? The cops want to see you, there're reporters everywhere. My God, Rachel. Where are you?"

"Golda, you've got to help me."

"How?"

"Tell me who else is from Dabrowa."

"What are you talking about?"

"I mean who doesn't live with us. Who's not a"— Rachel searched for the right word—"a member."

Golda knew what she meant. "There's one man I know about. Two, but one's in Israel, I think. The one who lives here came to Adam's funeral."

"Did I see him?"

"No. They had you in the back when he came."

"Do you remember his name?"

"Relkin. Joseph Relkin, an importer of some kind."

"Do you know where he lives?"

"Northern suburbs, Connecticut or Westchester. I'm not sure."

Hawkins called Sam Hunt in Manhattan and a few minutes later Hunt called him back. There was only one

J. Relkin, he reported. Importer who had an office on Thirty-second and Fifth and a house in Larchmont. Three cars were registered to him, a Mercedes 300, a pimpmobile, and a Pontiac station wagon. "To go to the station, I guess," Hunt said. He had two speeding tickets from the sixties, both paid without protest. No arrests, no convictions. "He's clean," Hunt told Hawkins, "clean and rich."

Rachel called J. Relkin in Larchmont. He had a husky voice that reminded her of Walinsky's. When she told him who she was he was quiet for a moment, then he asked how Jacob was.

"He's fine," she answered.

"Good," he said, "I thought maybe it was another funeral." She asked if they could see him and he said he wouldn't be back until three. Then he asked who "they" were. She told him and he asked softly, "Trouble?"

"Yes," she answered.

He was quiet again, then he said, "Sure, wife of Adam. Beloved of Jacob. I'll see you."

MRS. RELKIN led them into the living room and they sat in front of the dying fire and talked about the weather, about Temple Emmanuel where Mrs. Relkin ran Hadassah and Mr. Relkin embarrassed her by never showing up. She asked about Leah, and about Golda. She answered her own questions. Rachel leaned back and listened to logs cracking in the fireplace, to the wind outside the big picture window that looked over the back acreage across the empty swimming pool to the trees. Aqua paint was peeling, the pool sides were dotted with dead leaves. Hawkins reached for his teacup and she saw the pale inside of his hand.

Mrs. Relkin raised the diamond-studded cover of her wristwatch: "He should have been here before now," she said. "I'm supposed to play bridge; I wouldn't mind, but they're counting on me."

"Go anyway," Rachel offered, "Mr. Relkin expects us."

Mrs. Relkin looked at Hawkins uncertainly.

"I could . . ." she said.

Rachel realized that she was afraid of leaving the black man alone in her house, as if he'd steal or break something.

She said, "We won't hurt anything."

"I didn't mean . . . of course you wouldn't . . ." She retreated out to the hall to get her coat. Then she came back, wrapped in mink. "I'm sorry the tea's cold. I don't have time . . ."

She left them alone.

Hawkins drank the cold tea.

"Are most people afraid of having you in their houses?" Rachel asked.

"Only white people."

She blushed and didn't say anything for a few minutes. It started to rain, and it was getting dark.

"Does it happen often with white people?" she asked.

"Not so much anymore."

"Why 'anymore'?"

"The gray in my hair. I even thought of growing a beard once, to make me look even older. No one's scared of an old nigger. But it itched and took too long."

The front door slammed, and Joseph Relkin came into the living room.

"She ran out on us, huh?" He had an accent, not as thick as Levy's, but the same dialect. "Bridge!" He came into the room and shook hands with Hawkins, but he kept looking at Rachel.

"*Shain*,"* he told her, his hand on Hawkins's shoulder. "*Zare shain*. Jacob Levy's daughter-in-law. Adam's widow."

Rachel nodded.

"How long now?"

"Two years," she said.

"Terrible thing. Terrible." He went to a cabinet across the room and took out a bottle. "Shitty weather. It's raining again. We'll have some brandy."

* Pretty.

205

Relkin brought them balloon glasses a third full. He was red-haired and big, bigger than Hawkins, and Rachel stared at him.

"Big 'un, right?" He laughed. "Big for a Polack . . . big for a Jew. Some Hun got in there somehow." More laughing. "Big man . . ." He stared at Rachel, his meaning clear, and for a second she was afraid that he was going to open his fly to show them how big, but he only winked at her, then sat down next to Hawkins so he could go on staring at her.

"I saw you at the funeral. You didn't see me, and they wouldn't introduce me, so we've never met. I'm Joe Relkin." He took her hand, squeezed it, kept smiling. "You were very mysterious on the phone, but I couldn't turn down Jacob Levy's daughter-in-law, could I?" He finished the brandy, then went back to the cabinet and brought the bottle with him. He raised his glass. "To the great Jacob Levy!" he said without irony, then drank. "Now, what could you . . . daughter of Zion . . . want with a rich outcast importer who hasn't been to shul for thirty years?"

Hawkins answered for her.

"You were at Belzec."

Relkin put his glass down.

Hawkins went on, "With *them*."

Relkin didn't ask whom Hawkins meant by "them." "I was at Belzec from 1940 until 1945."

He looked like he was in his late forties; he'd been a child in 1940, seven or eight. Rachel couldn't look at him.

"And you were from Dabrowa," Hawkins said.

"Yes."

"But you're not one of them."

Relkin looked surprised. "How do you know that?"

"You don't live with them, you don't dress like them, you don't talk like them. You're ... you're ..."

"An outcast ..." Relkin helped Hawkins.

"Yes." Hawkins sounded sorry for him.

"Don't sound like that; I *want* to be what I am, I don't have to pretend like that bunch of old *momzers*."

"Pretend what?" Hawkins asked.

"She knows what I'm talking about. Ask them about Dabrowa, and they'll make you think that Poland was Paradise!" He laughed harshly. "Paradise, full of Polacks. Now you know that can't be true. And they aren't the only ones; all the old farts ... singing *dy de aye di di*, hugging each other, dancing together like no one'd ever danced before ..." Alone in Luria's finished basement, Rachel thought, just the eight of them at night, dancing while everyone else was asleep.

"There're the Westchester matrons, too," Relkin said, "trying to love it all. To love and believe, the fat actors singing of the joys of being a Jew in a *shtetl*. To love and believe the artist who paints it with pink cows floating over the clean little houses and delicate brides. They don't want to remember that the bride had smallpox, and the *goyim* are waiting just off the canvas to rape her and steal the cow." Relkin laughed. "Don't take my word for it. Try to send them back and see what they do." Relkin took out a cigar and spit the bitten-off end into the fireplace; then he said, "Belzec's thirty-five years ago, who cares?"

"I do," Hawkins said.

"Why?"

Hawkins told him what had happened on President Street and in Laurel. Rachel looked out of the window trying not to listen. He got to the clay and Relkin paled and took out his handkerchief to wipe his face. But he didn't say anything.

Then Hawkins said, "I know they were involved, but I don't know how. All I know about them is that they come from Poland, that there's some kind of bond between them and you're like they are . . . yet not."

Relkin said quietly, "Why is this Jew different from all other Jews?"

"Why?" Hawkins asked.

"Because my mother married a communist who wouldn't kiss the *rebbe*'s ass. The *rebbe*, by the way, was Jacob Levy's father. So, one man won't kiss, pretty soon somebody else won't, and before you know it you can't get anyone to pucker up. Oh, they have reasons . . . the unity of community; safety in solidarity or some such bullshit."

"Why was it bullshit?" Rachel asked.

Relkin looked at her, surprised. "The Nazis sent us to Belzec anyway. Unity and all . . . the Unity only meant that we all went together . . ."

"They loaded us onto railway cars. . . . I don't remember too clearly, but I remember looking for my father and thinking he was in the next car. But he wasn't and I never saw him again.

"So there I was, alone with thirty-odd Dabrowa men who survived the trip and two other children; a kid who died the first month whose name I can't remember, and Danny Walinsky, who was a few months older than me."

"What happened to Danny?" Hawkins asked.

Relkin shrugged. "He lived; he changed his name to Uze Ben Ezra and sells phony antiques in his shop in Haifa. Danny Walinsky is a *vontz*. . . ."

"Bedbug," Rachel translated softly.

Relkin went on, "For a long time, nothing happened. Then one man, I don't remember his name, found out his wife was dead, and he screamed and cried the whole night. The others got impatient because he was interrupting their sleep. But Levy cradled him in his arms like a child, kissed him, crooned to him, rocked him, until the poor man finally fell asleep and had some rest.

"They took another young man away to the hospital and we never saw him again. Except for that, everything went along evenly. I know that sounds mad, but it's true. Danny and I learned Talmud. We played, had enough food to stay alive. The seasons changed and I remember standing outside, as cold as it was, and watching the snow melt. I actually felt joy when it did. Joy. It seems incredible to me now, but if I try I can still smell the dirt outside the barracks starting to thaw, even over the other smells. Of course I can't feel joy anymore . . . too old. Then that spring . . . the third spring we were there . . . two of the Dabrowa men were shot. I don't know what for. One was my uncle. He was older than the others. Maybe that was why. Maybe he faltered and couldn't work anymore . . . maybe . . ."

Relkin stopped and shook his head.

"Stupid . . . even now, when I know better, I still look for reasons. They shot him, that's all, along with . . . Abe Dworkin's brother. Oh God . . . the moaning and crying. It was Levy who did the comforting. I didn't feel sorry, except for Levy being so upset. But the dead men hadn't paid much attention to us, they never gave us food, so I didn't really care. I think if they'd hurt Levy, I'd've died. He was everything to me by then, mother, father, teacher. He cried with Dworkin and he helped me say *Kaddish* for my uncle. The men mourned . . . there weren't any stools, so they squatted, covered their heads with their shirts, and rocked and chanted.

"Only Luria didn't mourn aloud. He sat still on his bunk, legs crossed, and watched the others. Levy tried to get him to join but he wouldn't. He talked to himself, his lips moving silently. Once he cried aloud and Levy broke the circle to run to him, to comfort him, too.... Levy had so much comfort in him....

"The next night two of the guards started beating the man whose wife had died. He was the youngest, the handsomest, of the Dabrowa men. His skin was smooth, like a girl's, and the others used to tease him about not having to shave. The other men edged me and Danny behind them so we couldn't see what was happening. Then one of them, Chern I think, forced us to lie on the floor under one of the bunks. We couldn't see what was happening, but we could hear. The man screamed and groaned. We heard bones breaking and when they let us stand up again the man and the guards were gone." Then like a litany, Relkin said, "We never saw him again.

"After that everything changed. No more Talmud, as if it didn't matter anymore, and no more extra food, as if we weren't children anymore. After that all the men did was hold meetings. They clumped together in the back of the barracks, whispering or shouting. But all in Hebrew. Still, I understood enough to know that Luria wanted to do something Levy didn't, and the rest were with Luria. Only Levy was their rabbi's son. Traditionally they wouldn't act without his permission and they started hating him for not giving it, and finally they shut him out."

Relkin put his hand on Hawkins's shoulder. "I don't know what it means for a black to be shut out, but for Jews like us ... village Jews, ghetto Jews ... all we had was each other and some old books that only isolated us more. To be shut out was to die. Levy was a strong man, but think of it! Going to bed alone in silence and waking up that way, and all the time in prison, locked away with men who once loved you, but now turned away when you talked to them and looked down when you walked by.

"They even stole some of his food and soon he was thinner and whiter than anyone and I think he started to die. Not the inner man, you understand. He still folded his blanket and clothes neatly, he still washed himself. He undressed every night, no matter how cold it was, and I can still see him naked, white and skinny in the moonlight, his body hair thick and black in patches while he washed as best he could. After a time he began to shake, even when it wasn't cold. I pretended not to see what was happening and he pretended nothing was wrong. He even talked to them as if they were still friends. Oh, God, I can still hear him . . . 'Good morning, Michael, Good night, Isaac.' They grinned when he did it and kept their backs to him. I can still see the bones showing through the thin meat of their turned backs . . . like *binkas* . . ."

"Corpses," Rachel translated.

"Luria's *binkas*. I hated what was happening but, God forgive me, I didn't help him. To some of the others it was like a holiday. They had someone to hate who didn't carry a machine gun, and before long they started torturing him. Childish, terrible things; they stole his cup so he had to beg for another one. No cup, no water . . . no cup, no soup. They knew how important it was to him to be clean, so someone shit in his bed, and he had to clean it up with so little water.

"Then Walinsky stole Jacob's shoe, and I thought that would break him. You see, there was every kind of parasite in the camp, and many came in through the feet. If you lost a shoe you would surely get sick, maybe die. So I thought the stolen shoe was the end of Jacob. But he pretended it was only lost, and he searched the barracks

211

for it while they watched him, grinning. Me, too, I stared and grinned with the rest of them at our Jacob on his knees, looking under the bare board bunks for his lost shoe. Walinsky stood there watching, too, and I knew that he would never give back the shoe, that he would let Jacob die, even though he loved him . . . I swear he did. Go figure it out. It was Walinsky who loved Jacob most, who would watch him undress himself at night with so much pity in his eyes, and even some desire . . . the kind you have for the abused one, the kind that makes you want to hold him, comfort him. Tenderness, pity, desire. I saw all those in Walinsky's face as he watched naked Jacob wash himself at night." Relkin stopped talking and closed his eyes.

"Did he find his shoe?" Rachel asked.

"No. The next day, Luria, looking like a siren come to tempt him—Luria was handsome in those days—Luria came to Jacob and in front of everyone, he knelt to him, took off his shirt, tore strips from it, and took Jacob's bare foot in his hands, chanting as he did it . . . 'Jacob, Jacob, here's a splinter.' And then with all of us staring, he pulled out the splinter, then rubbed the foot to get the warmth back. You know Luria . . ."

"Yes," Rachel said.

"Then can you picture Luria on his knees to Jacob? Luria tending to Jacob's feet? Poor Jacob was so moved I thought he would cry at last, and I didn't want him to because I wasn't, even when I was only eight, the innocent your father-in-law is, and I knew Luria wanted something. 'Let's go outside, Jacob,' said Luria, 'just the two of us, and walk by the trees like we used to at home.' And he put his arm around Jacob and took him outside. They walked under the pines, heads bent together, talking. The guards watched them, but all they did was shoot a few branches off the pines, just to scare them.

Ah, those pines! They were covered with snow then. In the spring they were light green at the tips, and there was a soft bed of brown needles around them all the time. It was beautiful there. In America it would be a resort or a national park. *Nu!* Come to beautiful Belzec!"

He laughed, then stopped and shook his head. "I'm a bizarre man, especially my humor, and the people who know me think I'm brutal and a little crazy." He shrugged. "They're right. It's because of the camp. You've heard people say, 'I do so-and-so because I'm from the South or Midwest or North, or Italy or England or somewhere, and you understand, don't you.' The place has an effect. Belzec too. It's my hometown.

"Anyway, Luria and Jacob walked and talked as if they were on the village street coming home from shul, discussing a point of Talmud. Only Luria's bare-chested and Jacob's wearing Luria's shirt on his foot. And this time the *goyim* don't throw rocks and yell names, they stand silent and hold machine guns. And by now Jacob's wife is dead, though he doesn't know that yet. And Luria's young wife and his mother and sister. And Jacob's mother and sister. And all our fathers. No. Maybe some were still alive on that afternoon when Luria and Jacob went for their walk.

"I watched from the window. All the others watched, too. Then Luria and Jacob laughed and when they came back inside, I knew Jacob had given in. He still didn't like it. . . ."

"What didn't he like?" Hawkins asked.

"That they were going to kill the Krauts."

Rachel sat very still.

"Why should killing Nazis bother him?" Hawkins asked.

"Listen, if it were up to me, I'd've peeled their skin off slowly, slowly. They'd've died over and over again if I had my way. Burnt up," he laughed, "boiled, broiled, sliced, ground up . . ." He searched for horrors. "I'd've sandpapered them to death!" He laughed again, clapped his hands, then he subsided and patted Roger's knee. "But we're not supposed to feel like that. Until they sent Jacob to Belzec, he was religious . . . which is, according to some, that you don't kill. There're Jews who say we were that close to the Messiah because we suffered so much and that when we killed for Zion we lost Him. I'm not one of them, mind you. Kill the bastards is what I say. Keep what we've won, no matter what it costs, I say, because I know what it means not to have a place to hide and I know everybody'll kill everybody if they have half a reason. Forgive me, but the blacks'd kill the Jews if they could, wouldn't they?"

Hawkins didn't answer.

"Of course they would." He patted Hawkins's knee again as if to reassure him. "Jacob could have been the exception but they ruined him."

"Who ruined him?" Hawkins asked. "Luria? the Nazis?"

"All of them," Relkin said sadly.

Hawkins said, "So Levy failed the test and they killed the Nazis?"

"Yes."

"But the guards had machine guns and the Jews were unarmed."

"Yes."

"How did they kill them then, Mr. Relkin?"

"I don't know."

Hawkins leaned closer to Relkin. "What do you mean you don't know? You were there, you had to know."

"But I didn't. I only saw what was left," Relkin said. He seemed to be enjoying himself and he leaned toward Hawkins too.

"*What* was left?" Hawkins asked.

"Blood and clay," Relkin said softly, "just like in Brooklyn and Laurel."

Hawkins sat back slowly.

"Tell me, Mr. Relkin."

Relkin said, "They bought wood from the kapos. Kapos were Jew guards. They did it to stay alive, but I heard later, to my delight, that the Nazis killed them in the end, too.

"The men used the wood to make a long, wide box and they stood it on end in the back corner of the barracks. I thought they were hiding guns in it, or grenades, but when they killed the guards I didn't hear shots or explosions.

"You didn't see what they were doing?"

"No, they put Danny and me into a trunk and put something heavy on top. Maybe someone sat on it . . ."

"How did they know when the guards were coming?"

"They set it up."

"How?" Rachel asked.

"Dworkin strangled one of the kapos."

Abe Dworkin. Golda's father, who had a full head of gray wavy hair at seventy, about which he was vain, who couldn't save a dime, and who had a yen for creamed herring.

Rachel tried to see him strangling a turncoat Jew on a late spring night on the edge of a pine forest. But it was hopeless. She saw him at their kitchen table, drinking tea. She saw him showing their book of engraved stationery samples to the blond, tanned Yankee women from the south side of town who always wore tennis dresses or golf skirts, and who were kind to him in the way she imagined they were to hairdressers and saleswomen. What if they knew he'd strangled a man? Not with a scarf, no scarves there . . . she laughed and they stared at her. Hawkins looked worried and Relkin smiled as if he knew what she was thinking. She almost asked Relkin what Dworkin had strangled the kapo with and then she realized that Hawkins would think she was as crazy as Relkin.

"The murdered kapo set it up just right. The Nazis probably figured to have a real night of fun. Shoot us all, and maybe even bugger the little boys before they killed them. Oh, they'd done that before, too."

Rachel looked away from him.

"I heard a bunch of them come across the compound and I heard them open the door. Nothing happened for a second, then there was the 'boom' like a huge rubber mallet pounding the floor, and the Germans started shooting and yelling and then came the whoosh and a man screamed and they were all screaming ... screaming and screaming in terror, in agony . . . on and on until more came and they were shooting and screaming. Bullets hit the walls and I tried to get out of the box because I thought they'd use grenades and I'd be trapped and burn to death. But the weight was solid and I couldn't move. The booming went on and the shooting and a grenade went off just outside the barracks. There was a bigger explosion, like a bazooka or antitank grenade, and the booming stopped and I held my breath, afraid that the Germans had stopped whatever it was . . . it was silent a second and then it went again . . . boom, again boom! I cried with relief at the screams and I knew the crashing was their bodies hitting the walls and I waited for the sound ... crash, another dead, crash, another, and Danny and I hugged each other in the box and rocked with joy as the crashes came faster and faster. Then, above the screams and shots and crashing, I heard Dworkin start to sing." He finished his brandy and sang to them in a strong clear voice.

O Lord of the world, O Lord of the world!
Where can one find you?
Where can one not find you?
Wherever I go you are there, wherever I stand.
Only You, but You, always You, ever You.
You are here, You were here.
You are, You were, You will be.
In heaven, You. On earth, You.
Above, You. Below, You.
Wherever I turn,
Wherever I reach out—You!

In the dark with Danny in my arms, I sang—I, too, even though I hadn't sung those songs since I was practically a baby."

The memory was too much for Relkin. When he said the word *baby*, his voice cracked. Hawkins and Rachel didn't know what to say and Relkin stood up. His face was bright red and there were tears in his eyes.

"Excuse me," he said and he left them alone.

They were quiet after that. They heard water running in the kitchen, a cabinet door slammed, and Relkin came back into the living room and sat down. His brandy glass was full again and he took up the story as if nothing had happened.

"After that night the Krauts left boxes of food at the door for us and sometimes Danny and me got to open the cans. There was even canned meat. The first smell of it made the back of my mouth ache because by then it had been years since I'd had meat. We had as much to eat as the guards. More. The Germans in Berlin were starving while Jews in Belzec ate canned sausage." Relkin rubbed his hands together and smiled.

"Were you the only ones who got food?" Rachel asked.

Relkin nodded. "They were killing the rest of us as fast as they could by then," he said.

"Did you want to save the others? To include them somehow?" Rachel asked.

He looked at her and said, "You mean feed them and grow thin myself ... fight for them, die for them?" He smiled. "It never occurred to me. It did to Levy, though, toward the end when they were killing all the time, and Levy didn't sleep. He walked the barracks, and the path by the pines. The needles were covered with that ash and they turned dark and lusterless until it rained. Then for an hour or so they'd be green again and the sky would be clear.

"Finally Levy pleaded with the commandant. They were outside. Luria was there, too, and I didn't hear what they said but Levy actually kneeled to that *momzer— kneeled to him.* Speiser kept shaking his head, not angry, not contemptuous, but reluctant—like he wanted to say yes to Levy but couldn't. Luria was disgusted and when the commandant left he faced Levy and yelled at him and sneered like someone had just stuck shit under his nose. Then for the first time, I saw Jacob Levy lose his temper. His skin went white, his eyebrows and beard looked like ink on his face. He grabbed Luria's hand and with enormous strength for such a small man, he pulled Luria toward the electrified fence. Luria's a foot taller than Jacob, fifty pounds heavier, but no matter how hard he struggled, Levy was stronger, and he dragged Luria to the fence. Luria screamed and fell to his knees like Levy had done to the commandant, but Levy pulled him through the mud so his knees left a wake in it. He pulled Luria's hand so it was an inch from the wires. They wanted all the Jews dead by then, so the fence was really juiced up. Levy looked ready to hold that bare shaking

218

hand against the wire until Luria was fried. Then Luria starts weeping. I don't blame him, we were all weeping. I didn't care about Luria, mind you, but seeing Levy like that was awful. Levy saw the tears, the mud, his friend's hand shaking, and like the werewolf turning back into a man, Levy turned back into Levy. He let Luria's hand go and that was the end of it.

"Of course Levy had pleaded with Speiser for the lives of the others in the camp, and Luria told him he was a contemptible fool to grovel for any reason. Luria was right. You won't know that until it's your life or someone else's. But at night I would wake up and see Levy roaming the barracks, or walking the path at night, his face lit by the glow from the chimneys of the ovens that were going day and night now. After a few weeks he slept better and, by the end of the year, only a week or two before we were liberated, I realized that I hadn't seen him nightwalking for months. You get used to everything, Inspector."

"And you never saw what was in the box?"

"Never. One morning Danny and I woke up and it was gone. The floor under it was damp, as if moisture oozed from whatever was hidden there. The box being gone meant the Germans were gone. And I ran to the fence and thought I'd jump it or climb it and walk at last in the forest. But I stopped at it and looked into the woods the way I always had.

"Danny and I played near the barracks after that. Jacob taught us, we slept. . . . A few days later the Americans came."

"Then what happened?" Hawkins asked.

Relkin laughed. "Then? Like a story, eh? Nothing happened. They shipped us to Cyprus where we waited until the Zionists had killed enough Arabs or English or whoever so we could go to Israel—Palestine then—where the Red Cross found me. My mother got me and brought me here."

Hawkins didn't say anything.

"You want a happy ending?" Relkin asked. "My mother lived to be eighty. I'm rich and I drink and eat as much as I want. I have a beautiful woman to fuck and a loving wife. I have two daughters. One married a dentist, one a teacher. One just had a baby, so I'm a grandfather. *Nu?* The end!"

It was their cue to leave, but Hawkins said, "One more question, Mr. Relkin."

Relkin smiled. "Ask away. I got a whole night to kill." When he said that, Rachel realized how quiet the big opulent house was. She wondered where the children and grandchildren were spending Sunday afternoon.

"Was there a very tall man in the barracks?" Hawkins asked.

"Luria's tall."

"Taller than Luria."

"No," Relkin said, "Luria was the tallest. Why?"

"A witness saw a big man come out of the basement in Brooklyn where the boys were killed."

Rachel didn't hear the rest. The fire was suddenly too hot and she wanted to get out of there. She grabbed her purse and stood up.

"You want my advice," Relkin was saying. "Find a cabalist."

"What for?" Rachel asked sharply.

"Don't be a horse's ass," Relkin said gently. "What could it have been but magic?"

There was a thrill to the word, they all felt it.

"And who does our magic?" Relkin said, "cabalists. Go to Brooklyn, Mrs. Levy, find a cabalist."

Like Rabbi Loew of Prague. But she couldn't imagine herself saying the words, *What if they built a clay man ten feet tall and it killed for them.*

"What's a cabalist?" Hawkins asked.

Relkin shrugged. "A charlatan, a madman, a fool. A wise man, a mystic, a holy man. Depends on who you ask." Relkin grinned. "You know a holy man?" he asked. Hawkins didn't answer.

"No?" Relkin said with mock surprise. "Then ask a devil. Ask the commandant of Belzec. He's probably chairman of the board of Mercedes-Benz by now."

LEVY WANDERED through the house turning lights on and off as he went. Downstairs the rooms were silent, empty, clean. Upstairs the bedrooms were neat. The curtains in Leah's room hung still, the ducks paralyzed on the fabric. He hadn't eaten since last night sometime and he knew he should try, but the thought of food made him sick. If Rachel was there he could eat, at least some soup. Then he heard a car and he ran to the window, praying it was Rachel at last. It was Deb Fineman's Continental.

He went back to the den and tried to read. The words blurred and he turned on the TV to fill the room with noise.

Face it, Luria had said to him. *Don't hide from it. We're not criminals, we're soldiers. Heroes. Like the Haganah, the Irgun. They attack us, we fight. They kill us, we kill them. Don't try to forget. Remember it like you would a battle. Victory.*

A football game was on, the crowd yelled, and suddenly he heard Willa's scream. They were in the foyer, trying to get to the back stairs. To the big boy's room, because it was supposed to be him. Only him. But Dworkin knocked over the poster or whatever it was, and she heard it and came out on the landing. They froze, she didn't see them, and she went back. Levy thought it was all right, but she came out again and they couldn't move. Then she came down the stairs with her robe floating around her. She crossed the foyer and he thought, if she just picked the thing up and went back, there was a chance; but she was heading for the light switch and he wanted to shout at her to stop. The light came on and she turned, and screamed so hard her head banged the wall. Levy's throat ached and he shut his eyes. The floor shook and he waited to hear her body fall.

But he heard glass break and he opened his eyes. The younger one had heard the scream and come to help his mother. He tore a slat off the poster and, eyes wide with terror, he was swinging it like a sword. It was too big for him. He smashed the wall clock with it and the crystal chandelier. Glass fell on them. It covered the floor and the boy stepped in it. It slashed his feet and he slipped in his own blood. The slat flew out of his hands and his body hit the side of the door with a crack. Then it fell and rolled while Willa screamed and screamed. It stopped face up and Willa stopped screaming. But her mouth stayed open to the end, which took longer.

It was quiet then except for glass shards still falling. The mother was dead, the young boy, too, and the one they'd come for was still alive. Luria and Dworkin were in the shadows. He couldn't see their faces but he heard Dworkin panting, like he'd been running. Then Luria hissed, "There!"

The big boy was at the top of his stairs in his underwear. His arms and legs were long and skinny, his hands and feet were too big for them. Levy sobbed. If the boy ran back he had a chance; he could get out a bedroom window, shinny down a pipe, trellis, anything. Run away, hide in the woods. But the boy saw the broken door, the fog and path outside, and he ran for it. Levy rocked against the wall. The boy was so fast, so agile, Levy thought he'd make it. But his bare feet skidded in his brother's blood. He fell.

The football crowd screamed, and Levy turned off the set with shaking fingers. His face was reflected in the blank screen, soft and leprous looking. *What battle?* he asked his reflection. *You killed a mother and little boy.* He heard Luria again: *How many mothers and little boys died around us? A thousand, a million . . .*

He heard another car pull into the street and he ran to the window, but the car kept going and he was suddenly sure that Rachel was never coming back. He raced up the stairs to her room and pulled open her closet door. Her slacks, blouses, skirts hung undisturbed. He opened her dresser drawers. Everything was intact there, too.

Rachel passed Ronkonkoma. The road was empty, the houses were dark. Leah slept in her car seat and Rachel was alone.

At first Hawkins didn't believe she was going back. When he saw that she was, he started arguing. She didn't even hear what he said and she went on packing Leah's food and the Pampers in the tote bag. He grabbed her arm and she stopped moving. She was so tired, she longed to lie down somewhere. Even the floor would do. She closed her eyes and swayed slightly and he put his arms around her. She leaned against him and imagined making love to him on the floor next to the coffee table with her daughter watching gravely from the couch.

His arms tightened around her. "You can't go back there," he whispered to her.

"I have to," she said.

"Why?"

She eased herself away from him. "Because he's an old man and I can't leave him alone there," she said wearily.

"Because they stole his food, his shoe, and he walked barefoot with splinters in his feet." She looked at him. "What if he's worried sick about us? What if he can't sleep?"

Hawkins didn't say anything and she scooped Leah up in one arm and slung the tote bag over her shoulder. She was almost to the door when he said, "Rachel, they could kill you."

She faced him. "Jacob wouldn't hurt me."

"Yesterday you'd've said he wouldn't hurt your friend."

When he said that she got frightened for the first time. She almost ran down the path from the house to the van. He called her, but she didn't stop. She drove to the end of the street, pulled up, and looked back. He was standing in the open door. He was so big his head almost touched the top and his shape blocked most of the light. The houses on the block were lighted up, the street looked friendly, and she saw shadows move behind the windows. The service road and the ramp to the Expressway were dark and empty. Her hands started to sweat and she wanted to go back to Hawkins.

Everything frightened her mother and her friends, strangers and being poor most of all. They thought she was crazy to marry Adam, who was broke, and move to Minnesota away from everyone. They said anything could happen to her *out there*, surrounded by strangers. But she went.

Other faculty wives were scared of the Quetico-Superior. They told her there were wolves and bears in the woods and she was crazy to go out there alone with Adam and nothing but a twenty-two she barely knew how to use. But she went. And the first night, after Adam fell asleep, she sat next to the dying campfire and heard something rustle in the brush, something big, she thought. She wanted to wake him up and get out of there, back to town. But she made herself stay where she was, with the rifle across her knees, until the noises around her blended with the sound of the fire and the wind on the lake and in the trees, until it was a normal, natural sound that didn't frighten her anymore. She was never scared of the woods after that.

She was scared now but she kept the car at a steady sixty, heading for Laurel. She thought of the people who get flooded out by some river and go back to live on its banks. Reporters stuck mikes in their faces and asked them why they did it. The riverbank was home, they'd answer. They lived there. Rachel heard contempt in their voices. For the reporter who asked a coward's question. For the scared people he asked the question for. She heard defiance too—they weren't going to let any river tell them where to live.

Headlights came up fast behind her. It was a truck keeping a schedule and he pulled out and passed her going seventy. She was glad for the company and she didn't want to lose him, but she made herself keep to sixty and the truck's taillights pulled away and disappeared up the road.

It was after ten when she got to Sutter Lane. The street was empty and her house was dark. She pulled into the driveway and turned off the motor. Leah woke up and Rachel lifted her out of her seat onto the lawn. The house looked deserted, then the door opened and Levy came running out to them. He was in his shirt-sleeves, his hair was a mess, and he looked like he'd been crying. Leah squealed with delight when she saw him. She reached out for him and he picked her up, then put her down and threw his arms around Rachel. He kissed her cheeks and nose. He kissed her hair and hugged her so tightly she could barely breathe.

"You came back," he said.

Suddenly she laughed and hugged him, too. This was home and she was glad to be back. She hugged him again and had trouble letting him go. "Of course I came back," she said. "I live here."

Hawkins left his mother watching the Lawrence Welk show and followed Rachel's route along the street and up onto the Expressway. He turned right at the interchange and headed for eastern Long Island. He reached Laurel by ten-thirty, found Sutter Lane, and drove slowly until he saw the van in a driveway. He stopped across the street and looked at their house. It was medium-sized. Bigger than his. Two magnolia trees stood on either side of the door and they were just starting to show pink blossoms. The downstairs was lit and he knew if he walked around the back the kitchen would be, too. He watched the windows and wondered what they were doing behind them. Leah would be asleep and Rachel would have made Levy something to eat. A sandwich probably, since it was so late. Tuna fish, or sliced cold roast beef. Levy loved that, on black bread which he'd smear with a cut piece of garlic. They must be in the kitchen together. He was eating and she was making tea. All Hawkins had to do was get out of the car, ring the bell, and he'd see Levy at last. He stared at the house until he saw Jacob come into the front room; Hawkins strained to see his features, but he was too far away. A wind came up and blew the curtains and Levy crossed the room to shut the window. Hawkins slipped down in his seat; he heard the window close and after a moment he sat up again. The front lights were out, there was no porch light, and from the street the house was dark. The scene was peaceful again.

Hawkins started his car and drove up the street until he reached number eighteen, the Garner house.

TV cables had torn furrows in the lawn and reporters and bystanders had knocked stones off the front fence. There was a light on the first floor and another upstairs. The door was closed but looked crooked. One of the guards came over to Hawkins.

"Please move on," he said politely.

Hawkins showed him his badge, got out, and stood at the entrance to the drive. The guards waited. Hawkins looked at the empty lit windows for a while. It had been a pretty house, top of the heap for a black man from Norwalk, Connecticut.

"Is it empty now?" he asked. The cop nodded and Hawkins got out of his car and went up the path.

"It's still a mess in there," the cop called. But Hawkins kept going. They'd shut the door but it swung open when he pushed it and he went inside. Most of the clay had been washed up by now, but there was still a faint familiar smell in the house. The chandelier was broken and slivers of glass shone in the corner of the foyer. He went into the living room, saw clay at the edge of the rug, and followed traces of it out onto the porch. Then he turned back, meaning to look in the dining room and even upstairs, but the clay smell seemed to grow stronger and he was getting quick images of the basement in Brooklyn. The smell made him gag and he went back to the foyer and out the door into the fresh air. The blond cop was waiting for him.

"I told you it was a mess," he said.

"Where's your chief?" Hawkins asked.

They directed Hawkins back to their station, to the second-floor offices in the Town Hall that they shared with the tax collector. The moon was bright and he could see the Sound from the chief's window. The chief was tall and thin and he looked very tired.

He'd been going since five that morning, he told Hawkins, since Golda called. The press had been there all day with minicams and mikes, and he couldn't get over how cold-blooded they were. "I mean, here're the dead kids and their mother, and they just film away like it's a dope bust on Forty-second Street." Then he showed Hawkins the color pictures they'd taken. Hawkins took deep breaths and the chief, who was watching him, took the pictures away.

"Don't look, what's the sense."

Hawkins looked out of the window but he could still see the woman's fuzzy slippers that had somehow stayed on her feet. Finally he raised his head. The other man's eyes looked kind and worried. Hawkins smiled, "I'm okay. I need a favor from you."

The chief nodded.

"Share what you get on this . . . anything at all."

"Why?"

Hawkins said, "It's an old case"—he thought of Relkin—"from the forties," he said.

"Real old. Some kind of vendetta thing?" the chief asked.

"Yes," Hawkins said, "but it's a department matter. I can't tell you any more."

"I don't want to know any more," the chief said.

Hawkins drove through the town fighting the feeling he'd had when they found Benny Gonnona—that everything was cold, bad, and ugly. It didn't go with the pretty square, the smooth park and small shut-up shops. It especially didn't go with the white church he saw across the square, its handsome facade half covered by a white silk banner that said GET OUT THE WORD. He pulled up in front of the church, got out, and without thinking, he tried the door. It was open and he stepped inside. The chapel was half lit by New England hurricane lamps on the walls and the moon coming through the clear windows. The place was warm and dry; it smelled of beeswax with a little wood smoke in it. He sat in the smooth wood pew and thought that the Gallos couldn't come in here; neither could anything that smelled of clay and left a trail of slime. He felt safe for a minute; his shoulders relaxed, and he realized that he hadn't felt safe in years, since President Street or before . . . since they killed the bookie, or even before; since the afternoons he'd spent in the bookstore. He crossed his arms on the back of the pew in front of him and put his head down. He could sleep here, like he hadn't slept for a long time. *Dumb-assed scared nigger*, he thought, and he closed his eyes.

When Hawkins went through the archway into the chapel, a signal light went on in Reverend Ryder's office. Ryder was writing the eulogy for the Garners' funeral. He'd missed dinner and now was late for bed. He knew he had to talk about the way they died. He didn't know what to say and he turned away from his typewriter and noticed that the red light was on. A stray cat had triggered the light about three years ago, and five or six years before that a nine-year-old boy who'd run away from home. The deacons wanted him to lock the church at night but he pointed out that they were Congregational, not Catholic. There were no chalices, vestments, statues with gold leaf, or jeweled halos to steal. Ryder never thought that anyone would come here to steal anything. But when Ryder went into the chapel and saw the huge, hunched-over black man, he thought that this had to happen sooner or later. The black man was standing up.

He was enormous, and Ryder told himself that he should have prepared himself for this moment. He thought he should pray but couldn't think of anything appropriate. Maybe he should sing, but the only song that came to mind was "Ebb Tide." Ryder reached slowly for the light switch, but the man didn't jump him or pull a knife. The light came on and Ryder saw that the man was handsome —sweet-looking, he told his wife later—and he looked to be in trouble of some kind, but Ryder knew from the jacket, the sport shirt, the coat, but most of all from Hawkins's face, that the trouble wasn't criminal. Ryder wished, as he had before, that he was a Catholic surrounded with likenesses of Christ and His relatives. It would be easier than facing people in pain in this bare room.

Hawkins was abrupt. "You heard what happened in Laurel?" he asked Ryder.

Ryder nodded. "The Garners came to church here."

"I'm a police officer." Hawkins showed his badge. It was too far for Ryder to see his number and photo, but Ryder nodded again. "The same thing happened a couple of years ago," Hawkins said, "in Brooklyn."

"Was it on your beat?" Ryder asked.

"I don't have a beat. I'm an inspector. Inspector Hawkins."

"How do you do." Ryder had never felt so foolish but he didn't know what else to say. "I'm Ed Ryder . . ."

"The point is, it happened," Hawkins said. "Same way . . . and the same people were in both places." Suddenly Hawkins's voice shook. "I knew them," he said. "They were my friends. . . ." Hawkins wiped his eyes on the sleeve of his coat.

"Do you want to talk?" Ryder asked.

Hawkins hesitated.

"Is it privileged? Like talking to a priest?"

"If you want."

Hawkins nodded and Ryder led him through the dark church into his office. The big man made the room look small and fussy. Ryder gave him tea, then sat across from him.

"Are you a Protestant?" he asked.

"I guess so," Hawkins said. "My grandmother was a Baptist," Hawkins went on, "and my mother's the last thing she reads about in *Fate* magazine."

"Such as?"

"Born-again Christian, Tribal Catholic, Hinayana Buddhist. Now she's a follower of macumba ... voodoo. Been voodoo for a few years, so maybe it stuck. Once a week she and Mrs. Duval and some other old ladies take the E train to Mrs. Williams's house in South Ozone Park. They have tea and cut a chicken's throat. Then they carry it, flapping and dripping blood, around the backyard while they jiggle and chant. Then they bury it."

Ryder didn't say anything. After a while Hawkins looked up at him. "It's just bullshit, isn't it," he said, "chickens, blood, wine, wafers"—he took a breath—"candles, shawls, fringes ... all bullshit." Then, without any other preamble, he told Ryder about Levy, Luria, and the rest. He told him about the murders in Brooklyn and Relkin's story from the camp. When Hawkins finished, Ryder didn't say anything for a moment.

Then he asked, "You think they killed the Garners, like the guards in the camp?"

"I know they killed them."

"But you don't know how."

"No."

"Magic ... Cabala ..."

"No ... I'm a middle-class black man. A cop. My father was a carpenter. I don't believe that bullshit. Neither would he," Hawkins said.

Ryder looked at Hawkins for a minute. Then he said,

"My father was a fisherman, out of Montauk. He went out every day but Sunday . . . thunder, lightning, snow . . . once even in a hurricane. I should have admired his gallantry, but he did it for money and he came back cold, exhausted, wretched. He left my mother alone all day and most nights. For money. My brothers thought he was a hero for his persistence. I thought *that* was bullshit and he was a greedy fool. He died in a storm. They never found his body and I went to seminary as a sort of protest against him. But I inherited his persistence and when I found the first shreds of feeling for this plain bit of church I'm part of, I held on to them, hold on to them still, like a dog with locked teeth. It's not bullshit to me." He looked at Hawkins. "I'm a religious man," he said, "which means that at some level I believe in magic."

"I don't." Hawkins stood up.

"Then how . . ."

"That's what I have to find out," Hawkins said.

"And when you do?" Ryder asked softly.

"I'll stop them," Hawkins said.

Ryder put on his down jacket and heavy boots. He took his bicycle out and rode past the little shops in the town's main street. The moon set. He looked back and couldn't see the road behind him. Ahead were the Sutter Lane houses.

His part of town, the Yankee part, was zoned for three acres. The houses were big and smooth lawns were open to views of the Sound, road, beach. There were a few oaks on the lots, some forsythia, a few willows, but no hedges or fences.

But here the lots were smaller and hedges surrounded the houses like seawalls or shields, as if the Sutter Lane people were protecting themselves from an invader the Yankees didn't know was coming.

Most of the houses were dark. Even the porch lights were out. The main floor of the house they used for a shul was dark, too, and he was ready to go back and finish his sermon for the funeral, wondering why he'd come here at all. Then he noticed a light in the basement at the back of the building.

He leaned the bike on its kickstand and went up the path toward the light. Hedges surrounded him, blocked out the street light; and he felt enclosed, like a man in a maze. He got to the window, squatted on his heels, and looked inside.

The basement was finished. Bright green linoleum covered the stone floor and knotty pine paneling hid stone walls. It looked warm, dry, welcoming, and he half expected to see an old man in skullcap studying the Talmud by candlelight . . . the antithesis of everything Hawkins had told him. But the room was empty. The basement was very deep, the window was high and small, and he had to lean his head against the glass to see the far wall. The light came from a child's night lamp shaped like a pig sitting on a kitchen stool. The only other thing in the room was a big wooden box. The top of the box almost touched the ceiling and it was at least six feet wide. The back of it was against the far wall; the sides he could see were rough wood, which was odd considering how carefully finished the rest of the place was. The front of the box was covered by a heavy cloth drape with flowers on it. It reminded him of fabric remnants his wife brought home to use for dish towels or to make pillows with. The floor was clean, and he noticed a rim of darker wood on the wall along the floor, as if it had been washed recently and hadn't dried yet.

His legs were giving out, he didn't want to kneel on the ground, and he leaned too hard against the window. It opened slightly. A breeze got through the hedges and blew it through the window. The draft pulled at the curtain, it started to billow out, and something . . . the shadows it made on the wall, the dark hedges around him, the story he'd just heard . . . frightened Ryder. He lost his balance and sat down hard on the ground. His sleeve caught on the hedge and suddenly he was terrified. He pulled the sleeve so hard the poplin ripped and down dribbled out. He yanked it free and ran to his bike and pedaled as fast as he could up the lane toward town. The wind was against him and made the going hard, but he didn't stop until he reached the town square.

He stopped on the far side and looked at his church across the park and then around him at the center of the town he'd grown up in.

The Town Hall built in 1880 was on the one side, the library built in 1925 was on another, the WPA-built post office was on the third, and his church closed the square.

It had been built in 1792; it was the oldest and most beautiful building in town—in the whole state, he thought, maybe the world. He looked up at its steeple, which was light gray against the dark gray sky.

"What happened?" he whispered. "What the hell happened? Nothing," he answered himself. A draft had blown a flowered curtain that covered a jerry-built plywood box, and he'd gone mad. "Mad," he said out loud. The black man was crazy, he decided. He'd listened to him because he was tired, bored with his life, under too much pressure. But he didn't believe any of the explanations he gave himself. There was something behind the flowered curtain. And he knew if he hadn't run away, he would have seen it.

A cold spring wind blew the crocuses flat. The coffins were covered with iris and black tulips and all three were lowered at the same time. Willa's sister and Tom's mother held Tom's arms as he half walked, half staggered to the limousine. Rachel tried to say something to him but his face twisted when he saw her and he said, "No, Rache. What's the use? Don't talk . . ." and he kept going. He was almost past her when he said, "Good-bye, Rachel."

She stood alone and bereft a few feet from Willa's grave. The wind blew her skirt and upended folding chairs. She sobbed and pressed Kleenex against her eyes. Reverend Ryder touched her arm.

"Don't use that, Mrs. Levy, the lint gets in your eyes, makes it worse." He held out a clean folded handkerchief and she took it and wiped her eyes.

"Is your husband here?" he asked.

"My husband's dead," she said.

"Long ago?" he asked.

"Yes, Father."

"Please don't call me Father," he asked earnestly.

"What should I call you?"

"Edward," he said. "Or Ed, if you like, or Ned. Not Eddie, though." He smiled. "I'd like to talk to you if you have time."

"Now?"

"Yes. I'll ride back with you if it's all right. I think the others are gone and it's a long walk."

She led him to the car over a rise covered with crocuses. They were quiet on the drive back. He pointed out his house as they passed it, a big old frame building with a round window in the attic and stained glass over the door. A Yankee house.

"Did your father buy that?" she said.

"My great-grandfather built it," he said absently.

He got the fire going in his study and gave her tea and a glass of sherry, then he sat down across from her in a worn chintz easy chair. The books on the walls made the

236

room cozy, wind blew outside, and Rachel thought everything looked normal. She could talk to this man about what a fine woman Willa had been and maybe he'd ask *her* to bake the cookies for something . . . the Planting Festival . . . and she'd go home, cook dinner for Jacob, watch *Quincy*. She sipped sherry.

"I met a friend of yours last night," Ryder said. "Roger Hawkins."

She was too surprised to say anything.

"He said I could talk to you, only to you, so I'm doing it. He said some crazy things, Mrs. Levy, but I'm supposed to listen and I did. It almost made sense at night, with the wind howling, now—" He stopped and she waited. "It was about your people," he said.

"What about them?"

"He said that your father-in-law and his . . . congregation . . . ah . . ." He stopped again.

"Go on," she said.

". . . killed Willa, the boys, some people in Brooklyn, and more in Poland."

"In Germany," Rachel corrected.

He stared at her. "You believe it?"

She didn't answer.

"So did I," Ryder said. "At least enough to get on my bike, ride to the temple in the middle of the night, and look in the basement window like a sneak thief."

"Did you see anything?"

"A night light shaped like a pig." Leah's little night light. She'd wondered where it was. "And a big wooden box with a curtain over it."

He saw the look on her face and asked, "What's in the box, Mrs. Levy?"

"Nothing. Prayer books, jars of herring, shawls. Nothing."

She jumped up and he caught her arm.

"I have to help you," he said.

"Do what?"

"The inspector talked about Cabala, mysticism, magic. He said it was bullshit, but I don't think so. Neither do you, do you?"

She didn't answer.

"I'm supposed to know about that kind of thing, aren't I. I'm a minister. It's more my business than yours . . ."

"No!" she cried, without thinking. "It's not your business or his. It's mine. Only mine . . ."

Chapter
4

CARVER LED Hawkins through one dismal corridor after another and left him in a small unused office on the fourth floor. There was a table in the room, a couple of molded plastic chairs, and locked files against the wall.

Hawkins went to the one window. The rain had stopped, the clouds were gone, and it had turned warm. He could see the river over the prison wall. It was bright blue under the sun and the wooded bank on the other side was already green. He saw other windows around him and thought of the men behind them looking out at the river and woods.

"Hey, boychik," Meyer Garfield yelled from the door.

Hawkins thought some men looked like killers, but not Garfield. His face was sweet, almost pretty. He had thin, sandy hair, parted just off center, round pink cheeks, and large dark eyes. He rushed across the room and embraced Hawkins. Carver left them alone and Garfield went to the window. "Some day," he said reverently. "Some gorgeous day. Shitty time of the year to be stuck in the can." Then he turned to Hawkins. "*Nu*, boych," he said, "what goes? This ain't the sixth Sunday and I still got half a box of chocolate."

"Meyer, I need a favor."

Garfield raised his eyes to the ceiling. "Thank God," he said, "I thought it would never happen."

Hawkins had tried to save Garfield's son's life. He failed and David Garfield died in Vietnam, but Garfield thought he owed Hawkins anyway.

Hawkins hadn't meant to do it. He hadn't meant to do anything when the rocket hit them this time. He'd thought he'd never be able to jump out of a plane again, and if the plane went, he'd go with it. But he jumped with the others, and floated down into a paddy with the VC shooting up at them. He watched the rippling mud come up at him and thought if he could make it that far, he'd live. The mud looked soft, inviting, infinitely safe. It opened for his feet, closed around his ankles and calves. He sank into it as far as he could, then lay back to let it cover his chest. The others took longer getting there. They got George Dunning in midair and he was dead when he landed. They got little David Garfield, too, but he was still alive. He landed a few yards from Hawkins and Hawkins heard him groan and slosh in the mud. He stopped moving and Hawkins looked over at him. His blood ran into the mud in streaks. He was twenty-two then, but he was thin, his eyes were big for his face, and he looked like a child. When the firing stopped, Hawkins half swam, half waded to him.

"It's in the gut," Garfield said to Hawkins. "Very bad, I think . . ." He spoke reasonably. "I think I'll die soon. So leave me, Roger. There's no point."

Hawkins wanted to leave him but he couldn't. He waited to be sure the VC were gone, then lifted the unconscious boy in his arms and started carrying him back where he thought they'd come from. He'd gone four miles when a helicopter spotted them.

They tried everything to save Garfield but he died in

three days. Before he did, he dictated a letter to his father and told him who Hawkins was and what he'd done.

"Meyer Garfield's an animal," Lerner told Hawkins. Hawkins was a rookie then; Lerner had been his sergeant. "He pimps, pushes, bribes, kills. . . . So what does he want with a rookie cop?"

"I tried to save his son's life. I guess he wants to thank me," Hawkins said.

Lerner looked at him for a moment. "The son died?" Hawkins nodded. Lerner tried to look cold and failed. "Okay," he said, "go get thanked; just watch yourself."

Hawkins waited in the huge living room of Garfield's apartment on Central Park West. It was filled with dark overcarved furniture, and bad paintings in ornate gilt frames covered the walls. The room itself was hushed, but Hawkins heard sounds in the rest of the apartment. Phones rang, women talked and laughed somewhere. He sat on a rose velvet settee and tried to relax, but his uniform was new and stiff. It bound in the crotch, the cloth scratched his legs, and he started to sweat. A door slammed in the hall, a man screamed something in Russian or Yiddish, and Meyer Garfield raced into the room. He was in his forties then, but he looked much younger. His face was sweet and fine, and the sandy hair was still thick. A tall, dark-haired man with oily skin was with him. Hawkins stood up but Garfield waved at him to sit down. He pulled up a spindly carved gilt chair, sat across from Hawkins, and took his hand. He held it for a moment, patted the back of it, then let it go.

"You tried to save my son's life," he said softly with a thick Russian-Yiddish accent.

Hawkins didn't say anything.

"At the risk of your own," Garfield said.

"It was reflex," Hawkins said.

"Reflex shit. You tried."

"I'm sorry it didn't work," Hawkins said. He remembered the skinny-faced kid and tears stung his eyes.

Garfield looked away. "You want a job?" he asked.

"I have a job, thank you," Hawkins said politely.

Garfield eyed the uniform. "Some job," he said. "You could get your ass shot off any minute, and for that they pay you, *kom, kom,** twenty thousand a year."

Hawkins didn't answer and Garfield shrugged. "*Nu,* it's your ass." He snapped his fingers. The tall man handed him a card, he handed the card to Hawkins. "If you change your mind, call this number. If you ever need anything, anything at all, call this number. Remember, I owe you, and I pay my debts. Ask anyone in this town and they'll tell you, Meyer Garfield's word is gold, pure gold. You can put it in the bank." Garfield stood up, leaned over, and kissed Hawkins's cheek. "Thank you for trying," he said hoarsely. He crossed the room and stopped at the door. "Don't forget," he yelled, "anything. Anything at all."

Garfield was convicted of jury tampering and sent to Atlanta for five years, of which he served two. Hawkins heard about it and, on impulse, sent Garfield a box of Hershey bars. Twelve years after that Garfield was indicted for murder, and the big soft-voiced man called Hawkins.

Hawkins and Garfield sat across from each other at a dented metal table in a downstairs room of the Tombs. The oily-faced man, who was bald by then, leaned against the wall.

Garfield took Hawkins's hand and held it tight. "I

* Slowly, slowly.

want you should do something for me," he said. He felt Hawkins's reaction in his hand and laughed.

"I want you should get me the Hershey bars, that's all, boych. A box of Hershey bars every couple months, and maybe bring them yourself . . ." He paused, then said, "I come from a good family. My brother's a rabbi. Not just a rabbi, but a good man. A holy man. I myself wanted to be a *chazen* . . . that's the man who sings in the shul. But the war came and they took us to the camps. Chaim they sent to Theresienstadt. No picnic, sure. But they sent me to Auschwitz." Hawkins looked down. The big, dark man shifted against the wall, the room was quiet, then Garfield said, "If you arrest a kid in Harlem whose father beat him, whose mother starved him, whose friends take dope and hit old ladies on the head for their welfare money, and he does the same and you believe he must be punished, you still don't hate him?"

"No," Hawkins said, "I don't hate him."

"Even if the old lady dies . . . you see the scars his daddy left on his poor skinny back and the sick blank look in his eyes—and you don't hate him, do you?"

"I don't hate him," Hawkins said again.

Garfield said softly, "*Nu*, they gassed my father, my mother, my sister. They pulled my teeth out and every day for five years I thought I was going to die."

Garfield was convicted, his appeals failed, and he was sent to Ossining. Every sixth Sunday Hawkins brought Garfield a box of Hershey bars.

"*Nu*, what favor?" Garfield asked excitedly. "Ask me anything. Anything. Only I can't drive you home," he said, and laughed.

"I need help. Your brother's help."

Garfield was stunned. "My brother?"

243

"You said your brother was a rabbi, a holy man."

"So he is. Most holy. But what do you want with a holy rabbi from the ass end of Riverdale?"

Hawkins thought of his old friend Pinchik for the first time in years. Funny, bitter Eli Pinchik who'd left Brooklyn and gone to Riverdale to find civilization.

Hawkins said, "I need a cabalist."

Garfield looked at him as if he'd lost his mind. "My brother isn't a cabalist. I don't even think he believes in God. But that's between us." Garfield's eyes were bright. "What do you want with a cabalist?"

Hawkins told him Relkin's story and Garfield was enchanted. "How many did they kill?" he asked.

Hawkins didn't answer and Garfield grabbed his arm. "How many Krauts did they kill?"

"A lot. Twenty. Thirty."

"*Feh!*" Garfield shouted. Carver opened the door. "They killed forty of us an hour, a minute." He looked very disgusted. Then he asked, "What does thirty dead Krauts in Belzec mean to you?"

Hawkins shook his head.

"Ah," Garfield cried, unwrapping one of the Hersheys. "A secret. Wonderful. Maybe Chaim knows a cabalist. Chaim knows everybody. A most respected and loved man is my brother. He'll help you."

Hawkins tried to call Chaim Garfield from service areas in Ossining, Tarrytown, and Dobbs Ferry; the line was always busy. The rain stopped, the sky cleared, and the sun started to set. When he called from the Riverdale service area, the line was still busy.

He came out of the phone booth and through the trees he saw a little yellow house that looked like it had been there since the Saw Mill was a coach road. On impulse he walked toward it. Behind him cars went by, the pump rang, gas fumes collected under the trees. But ahead the little house looked peaceful. The undergrowth scratched his shoes and caught at his trousers. The house was empty but there was still a semblance of a garden. Crocuses were up, and he thought he recognized lilac and azalea, not yet in bloom. The house was small but well built. He walked across the lot, which was just starting to go wild, and into the trees on the other side. The woods were dense. The highway noise receded and he could hear birds and smell wild onions. There was a ridge ahead and he thought that over it he would see a valley divided into ploughed squares of cold dirt, and out over the valley, to the west, the river.

But he came out of the trees and faced a Cyclone fence that stretched as far as he could see. There was no open valley, no ploughed earth, only hundreds of small houses painted yellow, green, and pink. Asphalt shingled roofs spread solidly to the top of an enormous factory-office complex in the distance. He knew that if he went down there he would find new cement walks and squared off streets with fresh signs that read Enterprise Avenue, Industry Row. There would be baby birches that grew fast—and died fast—and creeping juniper planted in gravel. He wondered what they'd torn down and dug up to make this ugly, dismal place. He could almost hear Pinchik, drunk and declaiming at Vinnie's. "*It's over,*" Pinchik cried, "*the Nazis weren't Martians, they were Europeans. Christians out of Jews. Us. Western man is dead . . .*"

Hawkins went back to the parkway. He didn't try Garfield again, he called Pinchik instead.

"Yeah . . ." Pinchik answered.

"Hello, Eli. It's Roger."

"Roger fucking Hawkins! Where have you been?"

"Queens," Roger answered.

"You poor bastard. Why call now? . . . it's not Hanuk-kah or Christmas or Rosh Hashanah." He stopped. "It's Passover," he cried. "You're calling to wish me *gut yon-tif* for Passover!"

"Fuck you, Eli." Hawkins laughed wildly because they would have had the same conversation if he'd talked to Pinchik every week. "I'm calling because I'm in River-dale."

"Rose . . ." Pinchik screamed, "Rose! We got extra kugel?"

"Noodle kugel?" Hawkins asked.

"Potato kugel," Pinchik answered.

"I hate potato kugel," Hawkins said.

"So do I," Pinchik said. "You can have my portion."

Cabala, Kabbalah, Qabalah, the words blurred as Haw-kins and Pinchik had another vodka. "They can't even agree on the spellings," Hawkins said.

They pushed away the half-eaten kugel while Hawkins looked in the books. Pinchik drank and waited. Rose and the kids were in another room. Hawkins heard game-show-type yelling and looked up.

"*Hollywood Squares,*" Pinchik said.

Cabalism is of interest only to Jews, Hawkins read. *It can have no relevance for Gentiles.* Then it gave a short definition.

Cabala, it said, *is a system of Jewish theosophy, mysti-cism, thaumaturgy, marked by belief in creation through emanation . . .*

Emanation. Hawkins thought of comic-book rays of light and advertising-art sunrises.

The definition went on: . . . *and a cipher interpretation of scripture.*

Cipher as in number. So they believed God was a ray and the Bible was numbers? He asked Pinchik if that

246

could be true, but Pinchik didn't know either and he was getting drunk. Hawkins went back to the books, but none helped. He did find out that there were two kinds of Cabala: *'Iyunit*, which was theoretical Cabala—the respectable kind; and *Ma'asit*, which was practical, and not so respectable because it was the practice of magic.

Magic. The word he'd been waiting to see, but as soon as they used the word, they disclaimed it. Cabala was esoteric, but not magic, not practical. But he saw a diagram of a tree, with circles at the ends of the branches to correspond to sections of a man's body; the circles had names in Hebrew and the tree looked magical, no matter what they said. There were chapters on demons and angels; he remembered the word *dybbuk* from a play by Paddy Chayefsky; and the word *golem* because Ableson called Matt Breslow, who was big, slow, and stupid, the golem.

He read on and on. In the end the men who wrote about Cabala sounded as confused as he was. He closed the books, drank down the last of the vodka.

"*Nu?*" Pinchik said.

Hawkins shook his head. "I don't know."

"You won't tell me what this is all about?"

"I don't know for sure...." They didn't say anything for a moment, and then Hawkins asked, "What do you think of Jacob?"

"That's a hell of a question."

"Answer it anyway."

Pinchik said, "He's a good man. Very good. But you can't forget, Roger, he was in the camp."

"How does that change things?"

Pinchik thought. He drank some more and poured some for Hawkins. He picked at the remains of the kugel, deep in thought. Then he said slowly, "Roger, did anyone ever call you a nigger?"

"Of course."

"How'd you feel?"

"Like killing."

"No. That's how you felt about the guy who said it. How'd you feel in *yourself*."

After a moment, Hawkins said, "Like a nigger."

Pinchik nodded as if he had expected that answer. "The power of the name, right?" He pulled the biggest of the books to him and found the page he was looking for.

"This much I remember from Cabala." He read from the book: "*The power of the name is almost limitless. Spirits guarded their names and when Jacob asked the angel he'd wrestled for his name, the angel kept it secret for fear that the name would give Jacob power over the angel.* In other words, Rog, when the man calls you a nigger, he makes you a nigger for an instant. The name has power. So much, that for that same instant, you are what he called you, even to yourself. Now imagine what names the Jews in Europe were called. Kikes, yids, whatever. But worse, Roger, much worse, they were called animals, bestial, inferior, vile. And not just *called*, but locked up, starved, beaten, killed . . ." He closed the book. "Remember the instant when Mr. Whoever calls you nigger; stretch it out from 1939 to 1945; add prison to it, and slaughter. Not execution, Roger, slaughter, like we slaughter animals, so it is quick, neat, cheap, and won't damage what we want of the animal. In this case, the gold teeth, hair, odd jewels. Imagine it. . . .

"We have this *bubbemysah** that suffering ennobles. It doesn't. It coarsens, brutalizes. Ask a doctor who treats patients in pain. . . ."

Hawkins was quiet, and Pinchik said with inexpressible

_____
* Old wives' tale.

sadness, "I think Jacob Levy was a good man for a long time. But if you are a nigger in your own mind, even for a second, because of a name, what do you suppose Jacob is in his?"

Hawkins drove downtown. He meant to go home, or to Brooklyn to Alma for comfort. He didn't have to decide which until he got to Fifty-ninth Street. The west-side drive was backed up and he knew the Cross Bronx would be, too, but Riverside was good into the Eighties. Then it blocked up, too, and he cut over to Broadway. At Eighty-seventh he missed the light and he jiggled in his seat, trying not to think of anything. He looked out of the window and saw a jewelry store on the corner. The window was lit up and he saw gold *Mogen Davids* on chains and *mazuzahs* like Peg wore around her neck.

He knew the Ten Commandments were inside the gold cylinder, but he didn't know why people wore it. Maybe for protection, and in spite of what he'd said to Ryder, and what he'd always believed, it suddenly didn't seem so silly.

He pulled over, parked in front of the store, and went in. The man behind the counter was old; he didn't have a beard, but he wore a yarmulke. When he saw Hawkins, his old pale skin whitened even more. Hawkins was big and black; he looked wild, and the old man had been held up twice in the past three years. He normally kept the door locked, but he was old and he'd forgotten to lock it after the last customer. He fought his fear and tried to resign himself. He waited while Hawkins looked into the floor case and into the glass cases on the wall. Then he pointed to a small gold *mazuzah* hanging from a thin chain. The old man was too frightened or he'd have asked Hawkins what he could possibly want with a *mazuzah*.

"How much is this one?" Hawkins asked, and the old man went through the motions. He took out his black velvet cushion and displayed the *mazuzah* on it. It was marked eighty, the old man calculated as if they were really going to have a sale here.

"You can have it for sixty," he said.

"With the chain?" Hawkins asked.

The old man considered. "That's a good price."

"I know . . ."

"You'll pay the tax?"

Hawkins nodded and they made the deal. Now the old man hummed, the color came back into his face; he put the *mazuzah* in a velvet box and they said good-bye. It was seven o'clock; with good steady driving, and no traffic jams, Hawkins thought he could be in Laurel by nine.

Jacob talked, made jokes, played with Leah, but Rachel stood at the sink with her back to him. No matter how hard he tried to engage her, she'd gone to Willa's funeral today and she couldn't look at him. He stopped talking and she concentrated on rinsing dishes for the washer. Levy's chair scraped and she heard him cross the kitchen to the back door. The door closed, and she saw him walking across the yard toward the woods. It was chilly out, he was in his shirt-sleeves, and she had to stop herself from calling him to come back for his jacket. He turned and looked back at the house. The sun was still setting; his figure cast a long shadow on the grass, and she thought of the shadow on the wall in Prague, of ugly cobbled streets and frightened people behind blank windows.

The wind went inside Levy's clothes, his skin pimpled, but he stood still and watched his daughter-in-law through the window.

250

He wanted to help with the dishes, to pour a cup of coffee for her and a glass for himself. He wanted to sit alone in the warm, clean kitchen while she put Leah to bed. After that, they'd take brandy to the den and make plans for the spring inventory. Should they put in another rack of paperbacks, or add candy? Or both? "Paperbacks," he whispered, "I vote for paperbacks, Rachel."

His arms hung at his sides and he talked to the woman across the yard on the other side of the window in a normal tone of voice. "We left Belzec in April, Rachel. Me and Abe, Isaac and Moshe, Hirshel, Victor . . ." They left the backs of the trucks open so we had air and could smell the pines. They drove us across that compound and through the gates for the first time in four years." Rachel emptied the leftover stew into a glass container and put the container in the refrigerator. She turned on the dishwasher and the sound of its motor came through the window into the yard.

He said, "Don't shut me out, Rachel. From Poland to Cyprus to Palestine to here, I looked through the windows of kitchens I couldn't go into. Through the barbed wire on Cyprus, I watched the commander's servants cook and wash dishes. In Palestine I watched Arab women cook for their families by oil light. The night I landed here, and Isaac came to get me in Walinsky's car, and we all cried, then laughed because Isaac was such a bad driver, all the way across the Island, past the exploding cemetery, the bread factories, the tool works, and into a section of houses covered with green shingles, I saw lit kitchen windows, and women behind them. . . ."

The coffee was done. Rachel took out a cup for her, a glass for him.

"Isaac says we're heroes; that's *drek*, but they killed

my son and Isaac's grandson. Who would be next? You, me, Leah? There were three thousand of us in Dabrowa, then thirty-five, now eight. *Eight!* Add the children, there's twenty-one, add the grandchildren, there's thirty-three. Thirty-three, Rachel . . . out of three thousand. Okay, I'm corrupt, unworthy, tainted, whatever you think, but what would you have done?"

When he came back inside, Rachel saw him shiver and asked him if he was all right. He nodded wearily, went into the den, and lay down on the couch. He fell asleep and didn't hear the phone ring. It was Hawkins. He was at the bar on Main Street and he wanted to see her.

Leah was asleep upstairs, Jacob was asleep downstairs. She put on her coat, left the porch light on, and walked toward town. The grass, trees, road were cold green, hedges rustled, and she walked faster. There were six or seven cars parked at the meters at the end of Main Street and she couldn't remember what kind of car Hawkins had, what color, anything. But Hawkins saw her coming, and he got out of his car, a Pontiac, and waited for her. When she got to him, he took a small velvet box out of his pocket, not a ring box, and handed it to her.

"I got this for you," he said.

She opened it, and took out the gold *mazuzah*.

"Put it on me," she said. His hands were big and she thought he wouldn't be able to manage the little clasp. But he got it open and she turned her back so he could put it around her neck. He fastened it and she slipped it into the neck of her sweater. His hands rested on her shoulders, then without planning it, almost without thinking, he slid them down the front of her jacket to her breasts. She didn't move and he put his hand under her sweater and kissed her hair and the back of her neck. She reached behind her to touch him, but he had a wild image of people spilling out of the little bar, climbing out of cars up and down the street and seeing him reaching under her sweater and her reaching into his open fly, and he caught her hand and laughed.

Her nipples were hard under her sweater and he ached to rub them.

"Get in the car," he said. "Please, get in the car."

They drove east on 25A, through towns she'd never been in. At Wading River, he turned into a smaller road that was rutted and twisting. They were close to the water; in the distance she saw a section of the unfinished expressway. They passed that, and were in the country; trees bent over the road, the road surface got worse, the turns sharper. Stone walls ran along the road, interrupted by closed estate gates. She didn't ask where they were going; she didn't think he knew either. The moon showed through, and the air coming through the open window was warmer. They must be right at the edge of the Sound, on the rim of the North Shore. She saw more estate gates, and he slowed down.

"Most of the houses are probably empty now," he said. "No one'll see us."

The first open gate had a stone cottage next to it, with lights on, and they kept going. But the next one was rusted and half off its hinges. He pulled in and she got out and pushed the gate all the way open. They drove up a long gravel track under a canopy of elms that were still alive.

The gravel on the drive was washed out in places; stalks of weeds and dead grass came up through the dirt. There was a big stone terrace ahead, wrought-iron lawn furniture rusted on it, and grass grew between the flag-stones. The drive curved, their headlights shone on empty casement windows and on a garden full of weeds and vines. He stopped the car and turned off the lights.

He kissed her and she pulled up her sweater and unhooked her brassiere. His lips rubbed against her nipples; he was sweating and his hands got slick and slippery. He felt wild and he thought he'd bite her, so he made himself sit back away from her and lean against the car door, trying to catch his breath. She reached out for him, chest level, and felt the gun and holster.

"Please take that off."

He unsnapped it and put the whole thing on the dashboard. Women were supposed to love guns, he thought. Alma did. She said it made her hot. But Rachel didn't look at it.

She moved her hand down his chest and belly and between his legs. He pushed against her palm, then got scared that he'd come in his pants like a kid, and he stopped moving and held her hand still.

"We gotta git in back," he said. His voice was low and hoarse and he was talking black for the first time in years. "Front's too small . . ."

The back was, too. He couldn't get on top of her, so she straddled him. The air was quiet, there were no night noises, and a fog was coming in off the Sound. He eased her down on him as slowly as he could and tried to make it last and couldn't. But he wouldn't let her go, and after a minute he moved again, very, very slowly, and she moved with him. He thought of Adam and he wished he could be both of them at once. Afterwards, she tried to get up, and he wanted to keep holding her, but he felt her legs trembling with strain, and he let her go.

The fog covered the car, and he could barely see the overgrown garden through it. The edges of everything glowed and looked magical. She crouched next to him on the floor with her skirt bunched up around her waist, and looking at her like that excited him again. He rubbed her belly.

254

"I love you," he whispered. His back ached, his legs were stiff, but he didn't want to move.

"I love you, Rachel." He remembered the other Rachel from the Bible his grandmother had told him about, and as he caressed Rachel's bare skin, slipped his hand lower on her belly, and slid his finger into her, he whispered the story to her. His fingers slid and circled as he talked, her body moved with his hand.

"Rachel was Laban's daughter," he whispered, "and Jacob called Israel saw her at a well and fell in love with her. Like I did with you. He asked to marry her and her father said he could, but he had to work for him for seven years first. Jacob did it, I would too. But Laban tricked poor Jacob and sent his older daughter to him on the wedding night. He didn't know till morning and then it was too late; poor Jacob. But he didn't give up, Rachel; I won't either. He worked another seven years, and then at last, the ol' man kept his bargain, and Israel got his Rachel. . . ."

Bianco saw the word *clay*, stopped skimming, and read the headline.

Still No Suspects in Laurel Beating Deaths.

It was almost familiar and he thought he'd been rehearsing reading this for a long time.

> The bodies of Willa Garner, 40, and her sons, Thomas Jr., 17, and Eric, 14, were found in their home at 18 Sutter Lane early Sunday morning. A neighbor noticed the broken front door and called the Laurel police. The scene that confronted the officers . . .

Bianco skipped, then read,

> . . . motiveless. Mrs. Garner's jewelry, the family sterling, were intact. But the Garners were black and Chief Kramer suggested that the murders might be connected with the rash of cross-burnings and swastika-painting that plagued eastern Long Island last summer.
>
> Two weeks ago, a fight broke out in the Claremont High School cafeteria between black and white students. When it was over, one white boy was dead and seven black and white youths were injured. The older Garner boy was involved and Chief Kramer thought the incident might have triggered the killings and he plans to question local Klan members. He told the *Journal* that Mr. and

Mrs. Myron Brodsky, the parents of the dead boy, had been traced to Palm Springs, where they have been staying with friends since Wednesday. "We had to get away," Mr. Brodsky told the *Journal*. "Of course, we're horrified by what's happened to the Garners." Dr. Thomas Garner was also out of town when the murders ...

Bianco skipped again.

... was the mysterious presence of common clay ...

Lo, I have wrought in common clay, Kipling wrote someplace, Bianco couldn't remember where. He kept reading.

It was on the bodies, the floor, the walls. No one knows why it was there or where it came from. Chief Kramer refused to speculate.

Bianco put aside the paper and forced himself to eat eggs, bacon, toast, but he couldn't taste any of it. He helped June with the dishes, then drove to Main Street and opened the store. He was early, his nephew hadn't come in yet, and he left the front door locked and went down to the basement. He'd stored his uniforms down there thirty-six years ago, and the box was still where he'd put it. He lifted off sacks and other boxes that had been piled on top of it over the years and stripped off the tape he'd sealed it with. He lifted the cover and smelled the cedar shavings he'd scattered around the heavy OD wool jackets and trousers. He lifted the first two jackets out, then felt in the inside pocket of the third for the list of names he'd put there the last time he folded it. He wasn't sure why he'd kept the list, just a feeling that he might need it some day. It was still there, and he pulled out the piece of paper with a feeling of half dread, half anticipation, unfolded it, and read the names again: ALLD-

MANN ... DWORKIN ... FELDSHER ... FINEMAN ... GERSHON ... LEVY ... LIPPMANN ... LURIA. ...

At noon he went to the telephone business office a few doors away and asked the woman behind the counter for the Laurel phone book. She gave it to him and he took it to a table across the room. The place was filled with phones for sale; round phones, phones covered with gilt, and phones that were transparent to show the works inside. He opened the book on the table next to a Mickey Mouse phone and, with the colored plastic face grinning madly at him, he found the names of eight of the men who had been in Barracks 554.

Chief Kramer gave Bianco coffee and sat down at his desk across from him. Bianco had rehearsed what he was going to say on the drive from Craig Harbor to Laurel, but now, facing the tall thin man with mild blue eyes, he knew he'd sound crazy. He burned his tongue on the coffee and coughed. The chief leaned forward. "You okay?"

"Sure, sure," Bianco said, stalling for time. He'd believed what Speiser had told him, he still believed it, but he knew the man sitting across from him wouldn't. Not because he was foolish or unimaginative, but because he wasn't ready to hear such things. Bianco had been ready to hear anything from that scared Nazi in the red room in Nuremberg. They'd been surrounded by a bombed-out city and starving children, and he'd seen the camps; it was the right setting for Speiser's story. But this was a neat office in Exurbia surrounded by overstuffed supermarkets, swimming pools, neat lawns. No one would believe it here. He got the rest of the bitter coffee down and stood up.

"I'm sorry. I think I was making connections that weren't there."

"Look, we're stymied, anything you can tell us . . ."

Bianco shook his head. "It's something from the war, and I was there, and I think I let my imagination run away with me. . . ."

"You're the second person who talked about the war."

Bianco sat down again. "Who was the first?"

The chief told him, then he said, "This story must be a beaut because the inspector looked as strung out as you do. Maybe you'll talk to him."

They got to Craig Harbor by seven that night and drove through town toward the Sound. They passed Bianco Bros. Notions and Variety. It was closed, but Rachel knew from the front of the place that inside she'd find old-fashioned wooden counters and bins full of razor blades, tennis shoes, flannel nightgowns, kitty litter, plastic souvenirs.

They were halfway up Bianco's driveway when the front door opened and he came out to greet them. He shook Hawkins's hand, glanced at his ID, then looked at Rachel.

"Who's she?"

"Jacob Levy's daughter-in-law," Hawkins answered.

Levy. The sweet-faced man who'd started all the crying; the one Speiser called the little bastard. He'd be a grandfather by now, like Bianco.

"Can we come in?" Hawkins asked.

"Of course, of course," he said and hustled them inside.

He was impatient, but he made himself light the fire and give them brandy. Hawkins told him about Brooklyn, Laurel, and Relkin. Then Hawkins said, "And that's all we've got. No facts, no evidence, just an asshole story almost forty years old."

He sounded bitter and angry and Bianco knew he

wasn't going to believe the story either. Then Bianco looked at Rachel. She could have been Italian, he thought, and she was pretty, but too thin. She was nervous, too. Her feet dug into the beige carpet and she'd already finished the brandy. Her eyes were dark, but not soft; they were hard and bright, with clear whites, like his daughter's.

"I know who," Hawkins was saying. "Known that for two years."

"But not how," Bianco said.

"No," Hawkins answered.

"I know," Bianco said softly, looking at Rachel.

She leaned forward and Bianco realized that he'd never said this aloud before, and wasn't sure how to do it. He had to get it out somehow, and he took a sip of brandy to get ready, but it went down wrong. He choked and gasped, tears ran down his face. He wiped them away and, still half choking, he said, "They built a monster shaped like a man."

Hawkins looked like someone had slapped him. He was holding the thin glass too tight and Bianco was afraid it would break in his hand. Rachel didn't even look surprised.

"And what did they build it out of?" Hawkins snarled.

"Clay."

The glass did break. Bianco ran to get alcohol and a tweezer in case there was any glass stuck in Hawkins's hand. Rachel and Bianco mopped up the blood and spilt brandy, and she put alcohol on the cuts, which weren't deep.

"I don't know what I expected to hear," Hawkins whispered to her when Bianco went out to the kitchen for another glass and paper towels to dry the carpet. "Shit . . . not that. Not a clay man . . . anything but that . . ."

"I know, I understand. . . ." she said a little wildly, "But there've been others. There was one in Spain." Hawkins stared at her. "And in Vilna, I think, and Krakow and Prague." Bianco stood in the entrance to the room holding a roll of paper towels. Rachel went on. "The Prague golem was the most famous . . ."

"The what?" Bianco asked.

"Golem . . . the man of clay is a golem. The golem of Prague killed the Gentiles who killed the Jews. Like God in Egypt." She stopped, then she said helplessly, "But they were legends."

"This wasn't a legend," Bianco said.

"Then you saw it?" Rachel asked.

"No. Someone told me about it."

"Who?" she asked.

"The commandant of Belzec, Johann Speiser."

"And where's the commandant now?" Hawkins asked.

"Hanged for war crimes, thirty-six years ago."

"So how . . ."

"He told me in Nuremberg, before he died."

Bianco poured more brandy for them and sat across from Rachel so he could talk to her, convince her, because she was the one who would believe him. He remembered Speiser warning him that he didn't want to hear this story; Speiser was right and Bianco knew he should warn this young woman, too. But he wasn't going to and he felt guilty and elated at the same time, a little like a relay runner he thought—glad his stretch is done, and sorry for the one who starts running. She looked frail and he wondered how she'd manage. But that wasn't his problem.

They were waiting for him to say something, but he took his time because he didn't want to leave anything out. He looked at the fire; the ship's clock chimed from the hall, the radio in the kitchen played Schumann, and after a few minutes he recalled the feeling of the red room in Nuremberg, and when he looked up at Rachel and started talking, he could almost see Speiser's pale sick face against the red walls.

"They'd killed a kapo," Speiser said, "and we couldn't let it go unpunished. Yet we couldn't make an example of them because kapos were Jews, too, and we were killing Jews as fast as we could. You see the problem."

Bianco didn't answer. Speiser took another cigarette.

"We walked a fine line in those camps, no one will ever understand. Our solution was to punish such crimes quietly, at night. Ten or twelve German guards would march to the barracks of the criminals, shoot them fast—we used automatic weapons—then quick, quick with the bodies into the woods and underground. That was the plan for 554, too. Quick death by shooting. Infinitely better than the gas, wouldn't you say?"

"Infinitely," Bianco answered.

"Unfortunately, it wasn't always as clean as it sounded."

Did it sound clean, Bianco wondered. To whom?

"Two of my men were pederasts and if there were young boys among the condemned . . ." Bianco laughed and Speiser looked sharply at him. "You think I'm silly to be offended by pederasty when we . . . did what we did to all of them?"

"I think you're insane," Bianco said.

"You don't understand . . . to some of us the Jews were corrupt people who would defile us. To some, myself included, they were a political tool to unite a country that had existed for centuries as separate states. They might have been instrumental in uniting all Europe. . . ."

Bianco couldn't listen to any more of that, and he turned away.

Speiser went on, "In any case, we were there to destroy them, not torture, rape, or steal from them. If there's a blot on my people . . ."

Bianco interrupted, "Ten or twelve of your guards, including two queers, are sent to 'execute' thirty-some Jews, they get to the barracks . . ."

Speiser sighed and went on with his story. "Lieutenant Klinger would tell the head of the barracks why they were there—a reading of the charges, so to speak—then . . . then . . ." Speiser blotted sweat from his upper lip. "They would shoot them," Speiser said, "except the boys . . ."

Speiser stopped and wiped his face again.

Bianco waited. "But this time . . ." he prompted after a while.

"This time . . . I knew it was to happen and I was in my office waiting. The gunfire started when I expected and I heard screams. All normal. Then I noticed that the screams didn't stop and the gunfire did. At first I thought it was wounded Jews and my men would finish them off in a second. But the screaming went on and I knew something was wrong. I didn't move at first. I don't know why. Maybe just malaise that comes after hours at a desk, or maybe I had a premonition. Anyway, I sat there, staring at Himmler's picture on the wall . . . a visage to make anyone torpid." He grinned companionably.

Bianco said, "What finally made you move?"

"I heard men running. It sounded like a whole squad racing past my door and no one came in to tell me what was going on. So I went out into the hall and I asked the others what had happened. They said the Jews had built something. Built something! I thought of a wall, or a secret room to hide in, and I remember thinking how right we were to be doing away with these people who were stupid enough to think that a wall would save them. I crossed the compound armed with a pistol and with *four of my men at my heels like hungry dogs. Oh, I was sure of myself. Then, halfway across the compound, striding through the dust of the camp in the moonlight, with the pines moving in the night wind around us, the branches rubbing against each other, making that breathing sound, and the breeze carrying the smell to us, I heard something pound. I swear the ground shook. At that instant a scream came from Barracks 554 and I was suddenly cold with terror. I have never had such a feeling. I trembled and the men with me did, too. We all wanted to bolt."*

Bianco looked at his hands.

"I swear to you," Speiser kept talking, "if any of us had been alone, we'd have run. But there were five of us, watching each other, so together we crossed the compound and went inside the barracks.

"I stopped at the door and yelled as loud as I could, 'This is Commandant Speiser. Everyone at attention!' Nothing at first, not a sound. Then a moan came from the floor next to the door, and the smell hit us. Slime, like a cave under a river. Reinhart got the spot going and in the light I saw a little man whose clothes were splashed with blood, and then I saw what was left of my men. Oh God . . ." Speiser put his head in his hands and sobbed aloud. Bianco felt nothing. He refilled the other man's cup with cold tea and sugar and nudged Speiser's shoulder with the cup. Speiser drank some, then went on.

"They were dead or dying. Some had broken necks and died whole. Some of the heads were torn off and some lingered there on the floor but without some of their parts . . ." Speiser stopped. Bianco's gorge rose up his esophagus, into his throat. He tasted bile and took a deep breath to keep from puking on the floor.

Speiser leaned close and whispered at Bianco, "You can't imagine, in the light, in the shadows, what it was like. The look, the sound, the smell of that barracks.

Then . . . oh God . . . in the middle of the room, in the spotlight poor Reinhart was holding, I saw what the Jews had built." He grabbed Bianco's arm. Bianco tried to shrug him off but he held on. Bianco tried to pull free, but Speiser wouldn't let go. They tussled back and forth while Speiser raved. "At that moment I saw the future. I saw the Russians in Berlin, I saw my poor son looking in garbage cans for sawdust to eat, I saw my country in ruins . . ." They swayed back and forth on their chairs, Bianco trying to free his arm, Speiser holding on. Bianco saw their shadows on the wall, their reflection on the window. They looked ridiculous and he laughed. Speiser did, too. Suddenly they couldn't stop laughing. They rocked and swayed, laughing, they held their sides.

"What was it?" Bianco croaked. "Ha . . . ha . . . what was it?"

"A monster of clay." Tears of laughter streamed down Speiser's face. "Enormous, smooth, silent, featureless . . . the perfect monster. The hands were mitts without fingers, the feet toeless, miniature barges of clay. The crotch was smooth, the arms were logs that bent without joints, and the face . . . the face had nothing, no eyes, mouth, nose. No ears, nothing. But it saw us . . . Oh God, it saw us without eyes, it heard us without ears. It turned and looked at me . . . Heee . . ." The tea spilled and spread across the table, and they laughed at that. "Then it moved, and the floor and walls shook. Its head scraped the ceiling and left a trail of slime. Its feet hit the wood floor . . . boom . . . boom . . . oh ho." Speiser stopped laughing and after a minute, Bianco did too.

"The little Jew raised his hand," Speiser said, "and it stopped. Behind me my men cried and groaned and I sobbed with them. The little Jew came right up to me and looked up into my face. He had very clear, dark eyes and black hair that shone in Reinhart's spot. He was a *good-looking man, delicate, pale, and there were tears in his eyes. Don't ask me . . . I don't know why the little bastard was crying. 'We need food,' he told me. 'You'll have it,' I sobbed. 'There are old men in here,' he said, 'who get cold at night.' 'I'll get blankets,' I said. Then the little man took my chin in his hand and brought his face very close to mine. His skin was pasty from protein starvation and his breath smelled terrible. I tried to turn my head away, but he wouldn't let my chin go. Then he whispered to me, blowing that foul breath in my face. 'I don't think Joseph will die with us.' I knew that 'Joseph' was the monster and the Jew smiled at me as if the name was a joke we could share. 'If you go back to your bunker and bomb us, blast us to dust, I think Joseph will come out of the rubble, step over our bodies, and kill you all. I think he will leave the camp, go out in the world, so to speak. He could go ten thousand miles and twenty years before anyone stopped him. He could kill ten thousand, a hundred thousand . . .'*

"I nodded and nodded. *'No bombs,' I gibbered. 'No tanks, I swear . . . oh God . . . I'll bring food and coal, anything you say . . . I swear.'*

" *'And no more killing,' said the little Jew.*

" *'I swear you'll live,' I said.*

" *'And all the others in this camp,' said the Jew, and everyone in the barracks waited for my answer. Even the dying soldiers on the floor stopped moaning. I grabbed the little Jew's arm. 'Come outside,' I pleaded.*

"*He went with me and we walked a little way to the side of the barracks and squatted together next to the fence.*

"*I'm a fool and no matter what Streicher has said about Jews being inferior, I looked into the little bastard's eyes and I knew he was an intelligent man. 'How long have* you been here?' I asked him. 'Three years," he answered. 'Then you know what we're like, don't you?' He smiled and nodded at me. 'So,' I said, 'what do you think they will do in Berlin when they find out that I've stopped ... our work? And they will find out.'" The little bastard doesn't answer, so I say, 'They'll destroy this camp and everyone in it, and even if the thing in there survives, all the men with you will be dead. So will everyone here; Germans, Poles, and Jews. I can keep you and your people alive. That's all I can do, no matter what you threaten me with.'"

"And so all the rest died. Amen," Hawkins said.

Bianco ignored him and kept talking to Rachel. "Speiser was right. The Nazis were beginning the 'final solution' and if they had found out that a couple of thousand Jews stayed alive because of a fairy tale monster. . . ."

Hawkins stood up. "It's not a fairy tale. It's worse. It's a Boris Karloff movie."

Bianco said, "Speiser believed it."

"And you believed him," Hawkins said. "Why? Deathbed truth? You don't think he'd risk damnation by having a little fun with you?"

Bianco said quietly, "You weren't in that room, Inspector, or you wouldn't ask that. He was sick and starving and about to be hanged for one of the worst crimes in history. It wasn't a setting for a last joke. Whatever Speiser said, crazy or not, he believed it."

Hawkins headed for the door and Bianco followed them to the door; he kept looking at Rachel and apologizing, which Hawkins didn't understand. Then when they were outside the house, just getting into the car, he ran out the door after them. "You'll let me know?" he said to Rachel.

She nodded.

"Please," he said urgently. "I've waited a long time. You'll tell me . . ."

"I promise," Rachel said solemnly.

Hawkins didn't say anything; he was looking through his pockets for Chaim Garfield's phone number.

The youngest son was supposed to ask the four questions at the Seder. But Chaim Garfield didn't have any sons or grandsons, so his granddaughter asked them. She was six, she'd memorized the Hebrew and the English, and she asked each question first in Hebrew, then translated. She faltered once, but went on bravely. She had round cheeks that were blushing now and dark blue eyes like Ada's, and, as she read the questions in her trembling voice, Garfield felt a rush of love so intense he thought he'd faint. Dorothy, his older daughter, was thirty, and lovelier than he ever thought she'd be. Her husband was okay; he watched a little too much TV, talked a little too much about money, but he was good to Dorothy, he loved his daughters, and if he wasn't the intellect of all time, he was kind. Garfield's other daughter was plain, sweet, and bright, and her husband was just like her. Chaim loved them all. So much, he could fall into his soup in a spasm of love. Drown for love in chicken soup.

After the feast, and after he had gotten through most of the Haggadah, his normally flat belly swollen and the men leaning back on pillows behind their chairs, he filled the beautiful Elijah's cup that had belonged to Ada's mother. It was silver and carved so fine that it looked embroidered. He filled it carefully and with the sweet taste of the Passover wine coating his mouth, he took his granddaughter's hand and they went to the front door carrying the cup. She opened the door, and he put the wine cup on the hall floor. He looked down toward the elevator; it was almost nine, and practically every door on his floor had a cup in front of it.

"For Elijah," he told the little girl, "Elijah who heralds the Messiah and who might visit us any time, in any disguise. And no matter how he appears, even if he is in rags like a beggar, tonight—Seder night—we give him wine, and feed him."

She started to close the door, but he stopped her. "We leave the door open for him. So he doesn't have to knock or ring the bell...." She left the door open, and he picked her up and carried her back to the table. There were other reasons for leaving the door open, but he didn't ever want her to know them. In Poland, Hungary, Russia, the Gentiles believed that Jews drank Christian's blood at Seder, and Jews who wanted to live to the next Passover left the door open so the Gentiles could come in and see it was only wine they drank. In some ghettos the cup was for the Gentiles, not for Elijah—in the vain hope that it was harder to murder a man and his family after drinking his wine.

PART 4

The Rabbis

CHAIM GARFIELD lived in an old ersatz-Tudor apartment building that hung out over the river. Rachel carried Leah and followed Hawkins into a paneled elevator that was oiled to hide graffiti. Garfield's apartment was on the fifth floor, at the end of a long hall that was carpeted like the hall in Rachel's old building on Seventy-second Street. It even smelled the same, and she thought of the families who lived behind the doors of that hall: the Kleins, the Farbers, the Bernsteins—it was a family building, like this one was; and she knew they were in their kitchens having breakfast. Eggs without bacon, lox, cream cheese, bagels, olives. She wanted to grab her daughter, take her lover's hand, and drag them both out of there onto the neutral street, but the door opened, and Chaim Garfield smiled at them.

"Inspector . . . Mrs. Levy." He took Rachel's hand, bowed Hawkins into the apartment. "Ah . . . your daughter?" he asked Rachel. She nodded dumbly and he kissed Leah on the cheek. "Please, please, sit down. No, wait! The kitchen." He led them down a hall to the kitchen. Other doors they passed were closed and behind one Rachel heard a woman talking on the phone. Mrs. Garfield, she thought, the reason the line was busy. The kitchen was big, all its windows were on one wall facing the river, and in the gray light they could see sailboats, barges, the Day Line cruiser, and past the boats, the Palisades. "West Point's up there," Garfield told them proudly. "Sit," he said, pulling chairs up to the table. "I'll get coffee . . ." Leah whimpered, and Garfield put his hands to his face as though he were witness to a tragedy. "A toilet . . . oh my. Let me take her?" he asked Rachel.

"No, I couldn't," she said.

"Please. I had little girls once. Oh, they're grown now. I'm a *zayda*,* but how I miss those days." He laughed. "You can't imagine it, can you. Oh, but it'll happen, I swear. Let me take her? You make the coffee . . ." He lifted Leah out of Rachel's arms, and Leah stopped crying. "See?" Garfield said. His arms were long and thin and he was almost as tall as Hawkins, but much thinner. His nose was long and thin like the rest of him, and the end of it turned down. His hair was thin, wispy, but still very black, and a black yarmulke covered the top of his head. Hawkins stared at the man as he relinquished Leah and Garfield laughed. "*Nu?*" Garfield said, "I should look like my brother?"

"More like him," Hawkins said.

Garfield laughed. "I favor my mother, he looks like our father. My mother was sweet, but very ugly." He held Leah, who was beginning to smell close to him, and kissed her hair. She kissed him back. "My brother thinks he's Samael . . . the demon . . . and that I'm Metatron . . . the angel." Still holding Leah, he went to the cupboard and took down the coffeepot. "Not just an angel, mind you, but Metatron himself. Angel of angels . . . Prince of Countenance . . ." He laughed, jiggled Leah, who squealed and laughed with him, and managed to get the

---

* Grandfather.

top off the coffeepot all at the same time. "Now look at me!" he commanded. Rachel and Hawkins did. His eyes were bright black, round, and set close together. The irises were too large for the whites, and his thick black eyebrows almost met over his nose. His ears stuck out, his chin was too long, and his beard was too scraggly to hide the fact. He kept laughing. "*Nu?*" he asked, "do I look like an angel? Don't be shy!" he cried. "Tell me I look like a minor angel . . . Raphael . . . Gabriel . . . not Metatron." He grinned and hugged Leah closer. Then he said, "She's leaking," and he put the coffeepot on the counter and ran out of the room.

Rachel and Hawkins looked at each other and Hawkins started to laugh. She'd never heard him laugh like that, absolutely, helplessly. It was irresistible and she started to laugh with him, but it got out of hand and she sobbed. He put his arms around her and held her against him.

"Hey, hey," he whispered. holding her tight. "Hey . . . sshhh . . . love, Rachel, shh . . . don't be scared . . ." He kissed her face, then her lips. "Oh, Rachel," he whispered, "I'll kill it, if it's there, I promise. It won't get you or me or anyone. . . ."

Suddenly it was the climax in a Western, Rachel thought, and the marshal had the villain in his sights and John Wayne or Clint Eastwood whispered, *He's mine*, and the marshal knew his place and stood aside.

He's mine, Rachel thought. *I'm not scared and you won't kill it. He's mine.*

Garfield came back into the kitchen but Hawkins and Rachel didn't jump apart. Garfield looked at them for a long time. Leah stood next to him, holding his hand.

"*Nu*," he said finally. "Black and white lovers . . ."

Hawkins said, "Rabbi . . ." But Garfield held up his hand and Hawkins was quiet. Garfield shook his head. "I don't care about that part, but *you*," he told Hawkins, "are not Jewish." Hawkins smiled, but Garfield was serious. "Meyer thinks I'll marry you . . . maybe I will, but only—and I mean this—if you are circumcised and convert. I won't even consider it otherwise . . ."

"But—" Hawkins started.

"No, no!" Garfield was upset and it showed. "There's no argument. I love my brother. I'll never convince him of it, but I do. And he told me that you tried to save his son, that you risked your life to save a stranger. But I won't marry you to a Jewish woman unless you convert."

He'll convert, Rachel wanted to say. *And he's circumcised. I know that. So marry us, just marry us. That's all we want.*

But she said, "We didn't come here for that." She filled the coffeepot, opened the strange refrigerator, and found the coffee. Garfield gave her a measuring spoon and said, "No? For what, then?"

Rachel and Hawkins looked at each other. The sun was burning off the smog. The room brightened and suddenly Rachel said, "We have to kill a golem."

All Garfield did was put down the spoon. "A golem," he said.

She nodded.

"You've seen a golem?" he asked kindly.

"No," he admitted, "we haven't seen it."

"Ah, someone told you about it."

"Partly," Hawkins said.

Garfield sat back and spread butter on the coffee cake Rachel had sliced for him. He ate as he talked, blowing crumbs and bits of nut across the table. Leah watched him, enthralled. "My brother says to see you, I see you. You come here in the morning with a little girl who should be home where it's warm. You laugh and cry like mad people and I find you necking in the kitchen and you tell me you want to kill a golem that you've never seen and only heard about." He sounded more bewildered than angry. "You're not joking, are you?"

"I don't think so," Hawkins said.

"What would you do if you were me? It's pointless to call the police, you *are* the police. And you," he looked at Rachel, "are the daughter-in-law of a loved and respected man."

"Why?" Rachel asked.

"Why?" Garfield repeated. "Why is Jacob Levy loved?"

"Yes. Why?"

"They say he outwitted the Nazis and saved the people," Garfield answered.

"The golem saved them," Rachel said.

Garfield stared at her.

"It killed Nazi guards," Rachel told Garfield. "The Germans were terrified, not outwitted."

"Who told you that?" Garfield snapped.

"Major Louis Bianco . . . the man who opened the camp."

"Ah, a major," Garfield intoned, "*he* saw the golem."

"No. He . . . he heard about it." Oh God, Rachel thought, it sounds so lame. He won't believe us, he won't help.

"Heard?" Now Garfield sounded sarcastic. "From whom did he hear this wonderful tale?"

"From the commandant of Belzec," Rachel said quietly. "Johann Speiser." The name had an effect. Garfield was quiet for a moment, then he asked, "Where is this golem?"

"Long Island," Rachel said, blushing.

"Ah. A golem kills some Nazis and moves to Long Island."

Rachel was quiet.

"Johann Speiser didn't tell anyone about a golem on Long Island. Who did?"

"We know it ... by its work," Rachel said.

"What work?" Garfield asked. "Does it serve at Seder? Build swimming pools? Golems aren't just swords of vengeance you know." Then it hit him and he groaned. "Clay; the black family in Laurel ... mother and sons ... covered with clay ..."

Rachel said, "There were some kids in Brooklyn, too, and the guards at Belzec ..."

Garfield held Leah against him, drank coffee, and looked out of the window. "I'm an Orthodox rabbi in Riverdale," Garfield said. "I perform weddings and funerals, conduct Sabbath prayers, preside at High Holy Days, and supervise *kashruth*,* should anyone ask, which they seldom do ..." He threaded his fingers through the sparse beard and kept on clutching Leah. She didn't mind. He paused, then went on quietly. "I'm not a cabalist, I'm not a mystic, I'm not even sure I believe in God. Still, I'm a good Jew. Which means that if I believe you I have to help you because if they've done what you tell me they have, they are disciples of Samael ... that's Satan," he explained.

"I don't know about Samael," Rachel said. "But you have to help us."

Garfield turned to Hawkins. "She does all the talking. Is that because she's pushy or because you don't believe any of this?"

"I don't believe it," Hawkins said.

"But you?" Garfield said to Rachel.

Rachel hesitated, then she said, "I think it's true."

"So," Garfield said, "I might know a cabalist."

* Keeping Kosher.

* * *

"You studied the Cabala," Garfield said to Wolf Tepel.

"So what?" Tepel asked.

"I need a cabalist."

Tepel took a heavy gray cardigan out of his desk drawer and gave it to Garfield. Garfield wrapped it around his shoulders.

"Schnaps?" Tepel asked. Garfield grinned and Tepel took a bottle out of another drawer and handed it to Garfield. The liquor tasted good and Garfield took two deep swallows and handed the bottle back to Tepel.

"*Nu*," said Tepel after a while. "How can a down-at-the-heels one-time almost-cabalist help the great Chaim Garfield?"

"Am I great?" Garfield asked.

Tepel shrugged. "You're a nice man. What do I know. Just tell me what you want before I have to turn the heat on and dry up the brains in both our heads."

"Wolf, I think someone built a golem."

Tepel drank. "Lots of people built golems. Loew in Prague, Elijah in Chelm, Elijah in Vilna, the prophet Jeremiah—who says, by the way, that the ritual of creation . . . the golem recipe . . . incites feelings of ecstasy. But you can't trust the cabalists. They say everything incites ecstasy . . ."

Tepel raised the bottle, then pulled it away from his mouth, and stared at his friend.

"You mean *now*, someone built a golem? A clay man that stands and walks?"

"And kills," Garfield said.

Tepel looked at his friend.

"It killed a family on Long Island and some boys in Brooklyn."

"Were they Jews?" Tepel asked.

Garfield jumped up and Tepel did, too, still holding the bottle.

"I'm sorry," Tepel said, "I know I shouldn't feel like that. I don't feel like that. But I do. You do. Everybody does. So I ask, that's all."

Garfield took the bottle, drank, and handed it back. "No," he said, "no Jews."

"It won't."

"Kill Jews?"

"It's not supposed to."

Garfield laughed explosively, spraying brandy in Tepel's face; Tepel wiped it off.

"Who's supposed to kill Jews?" Garfield asked. They both laughed, and passed the bottle again. Suddenly Tepel grabbed the bottle, put it in the drawer, and shut the drawer.

"This is nuts. You're drunk or crazy," he told Garfield.

"Listen, two young people came to me today. They told me there's a golem on Long Island. They told me it's killed boys in Brooklyn and Nazis in Belzec. They told me Rabbi Jacob Levy—you know who Jacob Levy is—built it. They told me it's gotten out of hand. Guards in Belzec, okay. The men who killed your son, maybe. But a mother and two children in a little town near the sea? That's crazy. That's . . ." Garfield searched for the right word but since Theresienstadt, words like *evil* or *bad* or *wrong* could never be used again. "Not nice," he said finally. Tepel looked at him in amazement, and they laughed again, wildly this time, clutching each other. Tepel opened the drawer and took out the bottle, and they drank some more.

Tepel thought.

"Okay," he said after a while, "there's a golem on Long Island . . . so what?"

"They want it killed."

Tepel asked, "Who are *they*, and why should we go around killing golems for them?"

Garfield told him; and all the time he talked, Tepel nodded. His fine white hair floating around his head like an aura.

"You can do it . . . I mean *one* can do it," Tepel said, "but first you have to know if they're nuts, and how do we find that out?"

Garfield told Tepel about the basement window with the night light, about the box and the flowered curtain.

"Did *you* see the wooden box and the flowered curtain?"

Garfield shook his head.

"We'll go look."

Garfield looked at his watch. "It's after six and Laurel's an hour and a half from here."

"So it'll be dark when we get there. You said there's a light." Tepel held the bottle protectively.

"How'll we get there?" Garfield asked.

"Drive," Tepel said.

"I hate to drive."

"*Nu*," Tepel said, "how did you get from Riverdale to Forty-seventh Street?"

"Drove."

They capped the bottle, and Tepel started to put it back. But they decided to keep it. And, holding on to each other, and telling each other to be careful, they came down the narrow, steep steps from Tepel's cubbyhole to the floor of one of the smaller diamond exchanges. Three guards were stationed in front of the doors and windows, all with dogs. But the dogs didn't growl and the guards waved as the two men crossed the floor between empty glass cases lined with black, gray, and green velvet. Behind the stalls, black safes caught

281

what light there was, and the paintings of deer, vines, and pine trees showed on the shiny black doors of the vaults.

They drank sparingly as Garfield drove east on the Expressway. Just after Jericho, where they took the turnoff that led away from the ocean and toward the Sound, Tepel said, "I don't believe any of this, mind you. But it's a beautiful night . . . look at that moon." Garfield stared straight ahead.

"Look at the moon!"

Garfield looked and nodded.

"The moon is worth the trip," Tepel said.

Garfield didn't say anything.

"You don't believe this either, do you?"

"I don't know. Right this minute, I don't believe anything, except we've got too far to go to get there, and too far to get back, and I'm missing *The Rockford Files*."

"You remember," Tepel said softly, "the first time we took this road?"

Garfield remembered perfectly. It was his first summer in America, two years after Theresienstadt. It was blazing hot and they'd chartered buses for a picnic at Orient Point. All the girls were bare-armed, as they'd never have been in the old country, and their smooth pale skin, the fine hair on their forearms, and glimpses of their underarms when they stretched or reached for something, which they did again and again, drove Tepel wild, and he kept drinking warm beer and singing and poking Garfield whenever he spotted a very pretty one. Then Garfield saw Ada in a tight aqua blouse with capped sleeves and breasts that looked soft even in the stiff bras in style then. She sat on the other side of the aisle on the bus, and Garfield stared at the back of her neck, at her soft fat upper arms, at her breasts, and round thighs that he could barely see through her full skirt. Finally he leaned across the aisle and with a frown of concentration on his face, he touched her arm very gently.

"I'm sorry," he'd told her in Yiddish. Ada had smiled gently at him, and Tepel stopped laughing because he knew that this was the first time in six years that Garfield had touched a woman.

There was a little stone house in the park where they had their picnic and she let Garfield take her back of it, and lay next to him in the grass and soft weeds. They heard other couples laughing and breathing hard, saying things to each other, and she lay still on her back in the sun and let him fondle her, then she did the same things to him, but he couldn't keep an erection long enough that time to enter her. He saw her almost every day after that, until after a week of just touching each other, slowly, more tenderly, he thought, than he'd ever touched anything, he made love to her. She laughed softly and whispered in Russian, "Wonderful . . . oh, wonderful."

Tepel gave Garfield the bottle. "You're thinking of Ada, aren't you?"

Garfield nodded and drank a little from the bottle; he wasn't drunk anymore, or even high, and he didn't feel as if he had been drunk. He was clearheaded and melancholy.

"You know"—he switched to Yiddish because he could say things more precisely in Yiddish than he could in English—"with every mile now," he said, "I believe the inspector and his lover more; I feel as if I'm getting closer to something that Ada got me away from. If it hadn't been for her and you, and being poor and unconnected, I think that in some way I can't tell you about, an important part of me would never have gotten out of the camp. But now, driving in the moonlight . . . even here on the highway with the McDonald's over there and the Roy Rogers across the way, and the people settling down to watch the eight o'clock program, or help their kids with their homework, or make love, or drink Cokes or gin or play cards . . . in the middle of this I feel as if I'm going back to Theresienstadt."

Tepel asked in Yiddish, "You think we'll find something?"

"I don't know," Garfield said, "but if we do, run, Wolf. If they built it, they'll use it."

They were a little drunker when they got to Laurel. They drove past Ryder's church and the L & L Stationery and Bookstore. They parked the car down the road and walked as quietly as they could, only weaving a little, to the shul. They held each other's arms and went up the dark path next to the hedge. They squatted painfully next to the window and looked in. They saw the little pig night light, and the box covered with a flowered drape. The drape hung still; the shadows around it were shallow and benign. They were surprised at the tameness of the scene and they looked at each other and shrugged.

"Big deal," Tepel said.

Garfield nodded. "But what would they keep in there?" he asked.

"Prayer books," Tepel answered.

Garfield looked again at the box. It was bigger than he'd first thought. Much bigger. He started to feel uneasy.

"They'd need a thousand prayer books to fill it," he said. His voice had gotten softer.

"So they got other books. Lumber, coats . . ."

"What books?" Garfield whispered urgently. "Who keeps coats in a basement?"

Their eyes met and went back to the window. The curtain hung, the shadows didn't move, but now they

284

could feel something about the room, even through the window.

Garfield clutched Tepel's arm. "There on the drape."

Tepel saw it too. A stain or smudge of some sort.

"What color is that?" Garfield hissed.

"The light's terrible," Tepel whispered.

"I see it, you see it. What color is it?"

"Gray," Tepel croaked, and all at once he was more frightened than he'd been in Buchenwald, than he was at night now on 112th Street. He could barely talk. "So the curtain's old and dirty. They should wash it." He lost his balance, his elbow smacked the window, and they jumped up and stared into each other's wide-open eyes.

"*Gotenyu*," Garfield gasped. They grabbed each other's hands and stumbled up the path, trying not to make noise. They got past the hedge and ran up the street to the car.

Garfield drove sixty miles an hour through the shut-up town to the New York road. He drove like a maniac, and Tepel held the dashboard and swayed back and forth. They were past Riverhead when Garfield pulled off onto a side road and Tepel took the bottle out of the glove compartment. Their hands shook as they held the bottle to their lips, their faces were ghastly pale in the moonlight.

Garfield took a deep swallow and said, "What's in the box, Wolf?"

"I don't know," Tepel murmured.

"In your *kishkes*, you know. What's in the box?"

Tepel answered hoarsely, "The golem."

Chapter 2

RACHEL WALKED across the grass to Adam's grave. Leah saw her go and started to cry. But she'd be all right for a few minutes and Rachel sat down on the cool grass and looked at the headstone with his name on it. She felt bitter when she came here. Cheated. She'd dissembled with Hawkins . . . she hated the boys in Brooklyn, she hoped they died horribly. The guards in Belzec, too. The worse, the better. Nothing could be painful enough. "Good," she whispered at the headstone, "good."

But she knew Adam wouldn't feel like that. *What about Willa*, he'd say. *What about Tom and Eric. Jacob's my father, and I loved him; I loved them all. But they're still in the camp, Rachel. They think the world's Belzec. You've got to stop them.*

She lay down flat on her stomach over the grave. He'd know how tired she was and he'd say, *Roger will help you.*

"I'm in love with him," she whispered.

He wouldn't answer at first; he'd have to get used to the idea. He'd wonder if she still loved him, if she compared them in her mind. But he'd never ask. He'd ask instead, *Does he love you?*

"Yes."

Will you marry him or live with him?

"Yes. But I'm scared."

Of what?

"Of me and Leah having to live with black people who hate us."

Leah stopped crying and in the silence she could almost hear Adam laugh.

Beats the Nazis, he'd say.

"It's not funny," she whispered sharply.

He'd say he was sorry and he'd be quiet for a moment, looking at her with his head to the side, then he'd put his arms around her. She lay still and could almost feel that firm gentle touch. Tears ran out of her eyes and fell on the grass.

You loved me, married me, lived with strangers to be with me. Was it worth it?

"Yes," she sobbed.

Then it's a good bet. A necessary wager, Pascal would say.

When she got home, the kitchen light was on and she thought Jacob was waiting for her. Leah was still asleep and she carried her into the house and put her down on the mattress in her playpen. Then she took a breath and pushed open the kitchen door. It wasn't Jacob but Isaac Luria sitting at the kitchen table. All the lights on; they reflected on the white cabinets, the stainless steel sink and refrigerator, and back into her eyes. He looked at her without smiling and she let the door swing shut after her. The Shabbes school book that she thought she'd sent to Tel Aviv was lying on the white metal table.

"Where did you go this morning?" he asked her, without saying hello.

"To Riverdale," she told the truth without thinking.

"Why?"

She knew she had to be careful.

"Who did you see in Riverdale?" He'd left all the lights on on purpose, she thought . . . the third degree. She grinned.

"What's funny?" he snapped, and she stopped smiling and just looked at him. He was the handsomest man she'd ever seen, better-looking than Hawkins or Levy or Adam. There were carvings of faces like his from Southern Italy, Cyprus, Byzantium. She'd seen his profile in relief on walls carted from the Mediterranean islands and hung in museums. Only his eyes didn't fit. They were light, gray sometimes, blue others. They were gray in the kitchen light. He didn't have a cup of coffee or tea in front of him. He'd die before he'd make it himself, she thought. Even the Germans cooked for him. They stared at each other.

"Would you like coffee or tea?" she asked.

"Coffee," he said.

"Is instant all right?"

"Fine."

She put water up to boil, measured powdered coffee into a cup while he watched. *Round one to him*, she thought. *I'm cooking for him. . . .*

They didn't talk until the coffee and a plate of cookies were in front of him. Then he said, "It's a long trip to Riverdale."

She couldn't tell him about Garfield. He'd find out who that was and they'd guess why she needed a rabbi. They'd hide the thing if it existed, and she'd have to find it before she could kill it. If it existed. *Lie*, she thought.

"I went to see Rose Pinchik."

"Who?"

"Rose Pinchik. Eli Pinchik's wife . . . from Sterling Street. They moved to Riverdale when Adam died."

"You were so close?"

Rachel shrugged. "We were friends. She's never even seen Leah."

He opened the book. "The name here is R. Saltzman. Little R. Saltzman." His eyes were wide and blank. "That's you, isn't it?"

She didn't look at the book. "I thought it was going to Tel Aviv," she said.

"I found it at the shul and read the chapter about Rabbi Loew. Of Prague, of the great Altneushul . . . Did you read it?"

Rachel didn't answer.

"By far the most interesting of the stories . . . I never believed in the Dybbuk . . . Gilgul . . . Samael . . . any of that . . . did you?"

Still no answer.

"But the Rabbi Loew's golem is something else." He held the book, resting its edge on the table, and opened it facing her and turned the pages until they opened to the picture of the ghetto street. There was the rabbi's house with leaded windows and the rabbi standing on the cobbled street in his black robe and the shadow that was so big the wall could only contain half of it. Luria held the book and said, "You know, don't you?"

"Know what?"

He laughed softly and her skin prickled.

"You want to pretend," he said, "we'll pretend."

He kept the book upright and went on turning the pages. The pictures flashed past her: the ruined Seder table, dead bodies on cobbled streets, the shadow again. She turned her back and emptied his cup and rinsed it. She added more coffee powder, heard the pages stop rustling, and looked around. An androgynous-looking being filled the page he'd turned to. It had no beard, and the nubs of breasts showed chastely over the body of a huge snake that was coiled around it. It had wild black hair and flat almond-shaped eyes, its arms were round and heavy, and Rachel knew if she could lift the snake away she'd see a fat slashed-looking vulva. The painting was two-dimensional and looked like it was copied from the wall of some Bronze Age tomb.

She stared at it, fascinated.

"Do you remember her from Shabbes school, R. Saltzman?"

"No."

"Ah. Meet Lilith. Demon of demons."

"Why is she a demon?"

"She was made from earth, like Adam. At the same time as Adam. But she wouldn't accept her femaleness. She refused to lie under him."

"That made her a demon?"

"Of course," Luria said, matter-of-factly.

"What happened to her?" Rachel asked.

"She defied Adam, she defied God, she spoke the forbidden name and flew off into the air, then fell into the Red Sea," Luria said. Rachel wanted to laugh in his face.

"Then what?" she asked.

"She comes back at night, seduces men in their sleep, then steals their . . . emissions." He smiled at the word. "And uses them to beget more demons. In some of the stories she strangles newborn infants, including her own. There's an amulet against her and I wanted to put one over your bed when you had Leah, but Jacob wouldn't let me."

"To protect me?" she asked.

"To protect your daughter," he said. "*You* don't need protection from her." He nodded at the picture, then stood up and faced her. On impulse she opened the knife drawer under the counter and found and gripped the largest handle. Luria took a step closer and she eased the knife out of the drawer, keeping it hidden behind her, feeling the flat of the blade against her buttocks. He took another step. She held her breath.

"Keep your book," he said softly.

"Let the children in Tel Aviv have it," she said.

"Look at that picture," he told her. "Look at her."

She looked past him at Lilith and her snake.

"Should the children in Tel Aviv see such things?" he asked. "Should Leah?"

"Why not?"

He leaned very close. If she stabbed him it would have to be in the face, but his hands hung loose at his sides. "Because she's an abomination, Rachel. A defiant, Godless, demonic abomination."

She was not going to look away from him. Childish or not, she was not going to look away. Her eyes stung, tears filled them, spilled down her face. He raised his hand and she jumped, but he smiled and kept raising it, palm open in a gesture of harmlessness. Then he wiped her tears carefully away with his thumb. His eyes were kind all at once, and when he spoke, his voice was gentle and concerned.

"Don't take us on," he said softly. "You'll lose, and that will be awful."

He let his hand fall and he walked out of the kitchen. She listened, thinking he knew she had the knife and he was hiding somewhere in the dark. She heard the front door open and close and she ran through the dining room to the living room, turning on lights as she went. From the front window she saw him walking up the block toward the Main Street Extension and then the phone rang.

It was Golda calling to tell her that it was April and she

still hadn't picked out a dress yet. As Golda scolded her, Rachel realized that she was still holding the chef's knife and she started to laugh.

"Rachel, this is serious. What if you have to order the dress? what if you pick a hotel and they're booked for June? Rachel, stop laughing!"

But she couldn't, and after a minute Golda hung up in disgust. Then Rachel stopped and caught her breath. It wasn't funny. She had to tell Allan something.

She went to put the knife away and saw the book on the table, still open to Lilith's picture.

She stood on Allan's doorstep and looked up at the handsome house with regret. She thought of the fireplaces, swimming pool, glassed-in porch, and country kitchen. They'd've had a lovely life in that house. She rang the bell, and waited. It was eleven. Willa's house was dark, there were lights on on the second floor of Golda's.

She heard his footsteps cross the foyer and her heart started to pound. He opened the door and his face lit up when he saw her. He was wearing pajamas and a robe. The pajamas were wrinkled, the robe was frayed. She thought Barbara Michaels would take care of it. She'd furnish this house, hire a housekeeper, and make him very happy.

He took her hand. "Get lonely?" he asked softly.

They went into the foyer and she meant to tell him there, without taking off her raincoat. But she couldn't talk and he took her coat and led her into the living room. She sat on the dirty velvet couch and watched him pour drinks. It hit her that this wasn't golems and demons, this was real, and the scared feeling she'd had on and off since Willa died came back. She told herself she belonged here. Life would be good for her and her daughter. Wasn't her daughter her first concern, after all? She was tired and she wasn't young anymore. There was work here for her. This house, Allan, Levy, Leah. She might have more children.

Most of all, she wasn't ready to "take them on"—Luria's phrase.

She wasn't ready to say anything to Allan either, but almost without meaning to she stood up, put her drink down untasted, and said, with a firmness that surprised her, "I can't marry you, Allan."

He looked like she'd slapped him, but she kept talking in that same thoughtless, will-less way. She tried to explain that she cared for him but didn't love him, that she didn't belong here, no matter how it might seem that she did. He'd be better off with someone else, someone who was . . . she searched for the word . . . dedicated. But it sounded like gibberish, and she stopped talking. She was shocked at the pain in his face. Their affair had been a kind of bargain to her and she'd thought it was the same to him. But now she saw that it wasn't. He'd really wanted *her*, not just someone to make the house livable, to wear the nice clothes he'd buy, to have children. He was a better man than she'd thought, and she started to miss him already. She thought of Hegel's view of humanity. Adam had thought it was shallow, silly.

"Everyone's not part of everyone," Adam had said. "We're bound in our own skins, we're not syntheses of what's happened to us, of people and ideas around us. We're ourselves," he'd told the class gravely, "it *is* possible to cut ourselves off. . . ."

The tribe had cut itself off; she was doing it, too, and she wasn't ready for that either. Allan walked blindly out of the glass porch. She started to follow him, but he said, "Leave me alone, Rachel, just leave me alone."

She went back into the living room, took the ring off, and left it on the table next to the couch. She went to the door and looked back at it. She'd worn that ring for a long time, and on top of the sadness, fear, and everything else that she was feeling, she knew she'd miss the way clerks in the supermarket and women who came into the shop looked at it. It glittered in the dim light, threw points of perfect color on the ceiling. She nodded to it as if it were a person, then she left the house.

Tepel made a list of everyone he knew who claimed to be a cabalist, read Zohar, or talked intelligently about Cabala, or even mysticism. Then he looked at the list and crossed out names. Six were left and he called them all. Four of the men said they'd be glad to see him for lunch, tea, whatever he wanted; the fifth wouldn't think of it until he knew what it was about, and Tepel couldn't bring himself to say the word *golem* on the phone. When he called the sixth he got a tinny female voice intoning, "The number you have reached is not a working number. The number you have reached is not a working number." There was no forwarding number, and as the refrain went on and on he remembered Buchenwald more clearly than he had in years, and he slammed the phone down, opened his desk drawer, took out a fresh bottle of brandy, and took a long swallow. He looked at the name of his old friend from Forest Hills that no one would ever see again, and he thought that once he died no one would know who Tepel was after a few years either. He drank more and thought about oblivion; then he told himself that thinking about oblivion was bullshit and he put the bottle away and went downstairs across the big crowded floor to the tiny locked men's room. No one greeted him as he went, no one waved as he came back. He had entered oblivion without even knowing it. The camps were nothing compared to Forty-seventh Street for making people disappear.

He called Garfield.

"Moshe Benzer'll see us at noon, so you better get your ass here; Marty Erent's meeting us at three, and Sol Weiser at five."

They met Benzer at the upstairs luncheonette of the big exchange. It was dairy so they could have cream in their coffee and butter on their rolls. Benzer had sturgeon and eggs, the most expensive thing on the menu, and he ate all of it before Garfield even tasted one grape. Garfield decided he didn't like Benzer and he found himself hoping, as he listened to the short fat man bitch about gas, diamond floor prices, taxes, the *goyim*, the *shvartzes*, that he didn't have the answer they were looking for. Any ritual this man recounted would be tainted. He didn't have to worry. Tepel couldn't bring himself to tell Benzer what they wanted, so Garfield had to do it and as soon as he said the word *golem*, Benzer laughed and called him Dr. Frankenstein. Then he switched it to Dr. Finkelstein, which he thought was hysterical, and he laughed and spit all the time Garfield was trying to finish his fruit salad and pay the check.

Erent didn't laugh at them. His listened politely but at the end of Garfield's story he smiled sadly. "You can't tell me who 'built' it or where it is?"

"Does it matter?"

Erent shook his head. "No. Because even if I believed you, which I don't, I couldn't help you. I read about the golem in a fairy tale book and I saw monster movies when I was a kid. That's all I know about golems."

"But it was done. . . ."

"Obviously you think so."

"Then it can be undone!"

Erent stood up. "I'm a serious man," he said. "I follow Cabala seriously, with the hope of ecstasy"—ecstasy again, Garfield thought—"and of union with the Al-

295

mighty. I've always respected you, Rabbi, and you should respect me."

"I do. . . ." Garfield stood up, and a few of the people in the restaurant looked at him.

"If you did," Erent said, "you wouldn't have brought me all the way from the Bronx to listen to a lot of . . . science fiction."

Erent left without saying good-bye, and Garfield's heart started beating with an odd jumping rhythm that frightened him whenever it happened. He pushed his coffee away. "Next?" he said.

"Sol Weiser, at five . . ."

Garfield looked at the clock.

"It's only three."

"Have some coffee."

"It'll kill me," Garfield said.

"Then take a walk. . . ."

Tepel went back to his cubbyhole and Garfield walked east on Forty-seventh, then up Sixth; at Fifty-third he saw the Museum of Modern Art banner, and he walked the half-block slowly, trying to think his heart into a better rhythm. He paid, went into the building, and sat in the gray-lit rotunda, watching other visitors and thinking how beautiful the young women were now. Young girls passed him, wearing high-heeled boots, their jeans pulled into their crotches. He grinned at them; little asses, he thought, so tight they looked pinched. The girls walked away from him down the long halls to look at beautifully colored paintings he didn't understand. His heart beat in better time, and he leaned back on the bench, against the wall, and thought he dozed for a second, because he suddenly sat up, startled, his heart going fast, but evenly, and remembered that in the basement they were supposed to have movies. He walked fast down the stairs and pushed open the door. The room was hushed, like a library. A young man leaned over the desk when he came in.

"Can I help?"

"I don't know. There was a play called *The Golem*. Do you remember it?"

The young man shook his head.

"And a movie. I'm sure there was a movie."

"What's *golem* mean?"

Garfield quoted Psalms: "A yet-unformed thing," he said.

The boy went to the catalogue and Garfield waited.

"Here it is," the boy held up a card, "*The Golem*, French, 1936..."

"A movie!" Garfield cried. "Can we see it ... can we see it now?"

The young man looked down. "I'm sorry. It's difficult to arrange a showing."

"I couldn't bribe you?" Garfield asked, half-serious.

"You could, but it wouldn't do any good." The boy started to put the card back, then thought for a minute. "Would stills help?" he asked.

"They might," Garfield said.

"Wait a minute."

The boy left and Garfield wandered back into the hall where black and white photographs hung on the walls. They showed men dressed up like women, old ladies with crooked, painful-looking legs wearing paper sack masks, a giant of a man in a living room with his mother and father, who were normal-sized but looked like dwarves compared to their son. The texture of the photos was fine, but the demarcation of light and dark was harsh, and the people should have looked ugly, but didn't. They didn't look sad either, or resigned. They looked ... ready, Garfield thought. Good and ready. They looked ... distinct, too. Separate, absolutely themselves. Garfield thought he would love them for that, or in spite of it, and he smiled at the photo of a transvestite who stared defiantly out at him through beaded lashes.

"Sir . . . sir . . ."

The boy was looking for him, and he had a bunch of pictures with him. Back in the library, he spread them out on a counter for Garfield, and there, shot through a gauze-covered lens, coming up an alley, led by a man with a beard who could have been him or Tepel or Jacob Levy or Moses himself, was the golem.

Weiser pushed his chopped liver sandwich to the side and held the photograph to the light; the golem was huge, gray, menacing. The man who led him was sad and wise-looking.

"Joseph Golem," Weiser said softly.

Garfield's skin prickled.

"I think Loew loved him," Weiser said. "The love of a father for a retarded son . . . Loew never had a son."

"But he killed it."

"Maybe. Maybe not. People thought for centuries that it was still there in the ghetto; in the tower of the synagogue, waiting for the rabbi to wake it up again, so it could finish what it had started."

"What had it started?"

"Depends on who you ask. The Prague Jews said it rescued them. The Prague Gentiles said it murdered them."

"Did Leow *kill* it?"

"Some say he did."

"How?"

"I told you I'm not sure he did. I'm not sure he ever even built the thing."

"He did," Garfield said.

"You were there?" Weiser's voice was full of sarcasm.

"I just know he did."

"So he built it, he killed it, he put it in the freezer. So what?"

"I want to know how."

"Why?"

"I can't tell you."

Weiser laughed. "You want to make the sequel, *Return of the Golem*?"

"Please," Garfield said softly, "we need your help."

Weiser pushed his water glass toward Tepel for brandy, which he gulped. "You don't really," he said kindly. "It's all written down. There's some information in the *Sanhedrin*—I don't know the exact reference—and in *Genesis Rabba* ... and most of all in the *Sefer Yezirah*."

Waiters went up and down the aisle; in the front of the restaurant, someone was fighting with the cashier. Weiser and Tepel were the only people not listening, but Garfield had a sense of the lives of the people around them, eating lonely dinners in a delicatessen on Seventy-second Street, then going home to their TVs, or, if they were lucky, to a friend's for tea, or to wait for a son or daughter to call. But as soon as Weiser said *Sefer Yezirah*, Garfield thought of magic, and had the feeling that for a minute, the three of them were separated from everyone else in the world. Men who knew ... and were about to know ... secret words. Men with a mission. *Mission* made him think again of old movies, and spies; the war room at Fine and Schapiro's, he thought, and he smiled at Weiser, who smiled back.

"But understand," Weiser said, "*Sefer Yezirah* is not a recipe book for making and demolishing golems. It is a guide to the mysterious knowledge of the inwardness of creation. We create with our thoughts, our substance, our spirit." Weiser looked up at the pressed tin ceiling and painted pipes. "Let me remember all of it," he prayed, then he looked back at the men with him. "I'm seventy-eight," he said, "I forget everything." He finished his brandy and turned to Tepel who half filled the soda glass. Weiser drank and went on talking.

"*Sefer Yezirah* reveals the mysteries of the cosmos. If you know them, you can create life. Not to walk or talk . . . but as a symbol of your understanding and love . . . like a diploma almost. If you could give life to clay, you were one with the universe. . . ."

Garfield said, "Some men have made a clay man that kills. We have to stop it, Reb Weiser. We don't have time to find the reference in the Sanhedrin, or to profoundly understand the construction of the cosmos. We have to stop it tomorrow or next week, before someone else dies. Do you understand?"

The old man stared at them. "You mean right now, today? Someone made a golem?"

Garfield nodded, and Weiser stared at the movie stills. "I can't believe you."

Tepel and Garfield looked at each other. Tepel, who'd already had a lot to drink, said to Weiser, "Look, Sol, you're an old man, you said it yourself. *Nu?* Believe us. What difference does it make?"

"But why would they do it?"

"Because they're all crazy," Garfield said.

"There's lots of them?" Weiser asked.

"Eight," Garfield said.

"How do eight people get so crazy all of a sudden?"

"They were sorely tried," Garfield answered.

Weiser thought for a minute, then asked, "Who built it?"

"I can't tell you that."

"Who's the *shtarker** who's going to kill it?"

---

*Strong man.

"Me," Garfield said.

Weiser drank; his eyes were soft and kind, and he said gently, "That might not be so easy, Rabbi."

Garfield didn't say anything, and Weiser picked up the movie still and held it up, facing Garfield. The golem was a mass in the shape of a man. Weiser tapped the picture. "*Sefer Yezirah* creations are gentle symbols," Weiser told him; "a breath of distrust, of disbelief or disaffection, and they're gone. But this is a monster, Rabbi, it's not going to just stand there and let you kill it...."

Garfield's heart beat normally. Ada was asleep, with the windows open and cold wind blowing into the room off the river, bringing some fog with it. He closed the windows, pulled the covers up over her shoulders, undressed, and went into the hallway in his shorts. He closed the bedroom door, turned on the hall light, and confronted himself in the full-length mirror on the back of the hall closet door. Everything about him, his body hair, muscles under his flesh, the flesh itself, even his bones, seemed sparse. He looked critically. He wasn't ugly. What there was of him was firm and smooth, but he was slight, insubstantial-looking. He leaned close and looked at his sternum, behind which his heart beat. A skinny man, not old, not ugly, but not young either, with a bad heart. Not the stuff of golem killers.

"To kill a golem," Weiser had said, "you need three people. They represent air, fire, water."

"What about earth?" Tepel grinned.

"Look, don't laugh at me. You want something grand, go get a priest. Do an exorcism. We're talking Cabala, which is old, disorganized, and maybe a little silly. But they built the thing with it, and it's unsilly enough to scare the shit out of you." Garfield and Tepel fidgeted.

"So," Weiser said, "you need three people to represent air, fire, and water . . . the golem is earth."

The golem is earth, Garfield thought, like Adam was, and Lilith.

"The three of you confront the golem," Weiser said. "And you must join the spirit as much as possible, give yourself to it, try to be one with it." Then he asked, "Will you be in a house or a field?"

"In a basement."

Weiser shook his head. "*Meshugah*." Then he said, "Okay, okay. Now, pick a point in the basement, a window or post at the farthest point from the golem, and think of it as spirit . . . the top of a five-pointed star."

Weiser drew a diagram of a five-pointed star on his napkin and Garfield said they should have charts and flags, like a battle plan. "If there's no battle," Weiser said, "then this thing is harmless, and you're a couple of *putzes*. So *think* of it as a battle plan. It wouldn't hurt. Okay, here's the star and all its points . . . twelve o'clock is spirit, three o'clock is water, five is fire, seven is earth, and nine is air. Okay, now spirit can't be just a reference point to you . . . spirit must be spirit . . . *Ain Soph Aur*."

"Say it again," Garfield said softly.

"*Ain Soph Aur*."

Ain Soph Aur, Garfield thought. The Aunt Sophie that Hawkins had asked about. The hardest of all concepts to grasp. *Ain*, nothing; *Soph*, limitlessness; *Aur*, light. Nothing limitlessness light. Absolute nothingness, unbeing, infinite emptiness. That was Aunt Sophie. Not death, not prelife, but the state before life ever was. Dear Aunt Sophie. The Infinite. And as the limitless light thickens . . . *thickens*? Garfield shook his head. It becomes extended into *Kether* . . . the crown of the tree of life of Cabala. Reach for *Kether*, reach for Aunt Sophie, and find ecstasy. *Tante* Sophie, source of ecstasy.

"Okay," Weiser said. "Each of the elements you represent corresponds to an angel. Fire—Michael; air—Raphael; water—Gabriel. Notice, the angel's names have seven letters. Start with Michael.

"He leaves the star and circles the golem seven times to his right, saying his name as he goes. But every time he finishes a circle, he drops a letter of the name. So he starts with Michael and ends on the L. He should say it *llll* . . . as seriously as if he were saying *Kaddish*. When Fire-Michael is done, Air-Raphael does the same thing, then Water-Gabriel. . . ."

"The golem is going to sit still for all of this?" Tepel asked.

"The golem has no will. It can't speak, it can't be counted in a *minyan*."* Weiser grinned and Garfield realized that he was a little drunk. "The golem has no sex drive and no intelligence. It will do whatever its creator tells it. If the creator knows what you're doing, he will undoubtedly try to stop you. Okay, after the three of you have made your seven circles each, you bow to the south, north, west, and east."

"Sounds very silly," Garfield said.

"Of course it's silly," Weiser said.

"But it'll work?"

Weiser finished the water glass of brandy and Tepel poured more. It was almost ten and except for a cop and a bus driver eating soup, the place was empty. The busboy stood at the front, watching them.

"It's supposed to," he said.

"Damn it, Weiser," Garfield cried, "it worked for them."

Suddenly Weiser's face was full of contempt. "You *putz*," he said, "sure it worked. Eight crazy men, you tell

---

* The ten men needed to make a shul.

me. Sorely tried. You know what that says to me? It says Dachau or Buchenwald or Auschwitz. I was in Buchenwald."

Tepel leaned toward him, but Weiser waved him back.

"I don't care if you were there. I didn't know you. I didn't know your dead brother or father or son. I don't want to know. I was *there*," Weiser said, "like you were, like they were. Maybe they found virgin clay in the middle of Poland, but I doubt it. And maybe all this gibberish made a monster out of that clay, but I doubt that too."

Garfield was confused by Weiser's attack. "But it's there. I know it is. Whether you believe me . . ."

"Okay, I believe you. Okay, it moves, it breathes, it kills. Good. They could have made it out of chopped liver and written '*walk, don't walk*' on its forehead and their hate would move it. You want to stop it from killing? I don't know why you should unless it killed your son, but as long as you do, and as long as I hear you're a good man, and even though I don't know what that means, I'll help you. You want to stop it? Hate as much as they do. Get as angry. Make your voice shake with rage as you spiel out all that *drek*, then raise your hand to the monster's forehead. On it will be this word—*Emet*, the seal of the Holy One." He wrote Hebrew characters on his napkin. "Then with that hand of yours trembling with fury, rub out the *aleph*."

Weiser crossed out the *aleph* and held the napkin up for Garfield to see.

"Read it," Weiser said.

It said *met*—dead.

Weiser said, "Then, if your passion matches theirs, maybe it'll die."

THE GARNERS had been his parishioners, Ryder thought. Part of his flock. No matter what Rachel Levy said, that made it his business and he was going to get into that basement somehow and look behind that flowered curtain. But he couldn't tell his wife what he was doing, and he tried to get out of the house without her knowing. The kitchen door squeaked, the side door was weather-sealed shut, and the only way out was through the front. But to get there, he had to pass the open library door. His wife and daughter were inside watching *Dark Victory* on the late show. Bette Davis was on her knees in the garden. She felt the sun on her hands but couldn't see it, and she knew she was blind and dying. Ryder's daughter sobbed. Even his wife sniffled. He waited a second, then stepped past the open door. His body blocked the hall lamp and his wife looked up, saw him dressed to go out, and she stood up.

"Ed, it's almost midnight."

His daughter shushed them and his wife came out into the hall and shut the door.

"Where're you going?" she asked. She looked tense, like everyone else did since the murders.

"For a ride," he said. "It'll help me sleep."

She knew he hadn't been sleeping well. "It's still cold. Take your scarf." She pulled his winter muffler off the old antler hooks on the hall and draped it around his neck, but she held the ends of the scarf and looked closely at him. It made him uncomfortable and he stepped back, pulling the scarf out of her hands. "What's the matter, Betsy?"

Her face was white and suddenly she grabbed the scarf again. "Don't go," she said. Her voice was hushed, nothing like itself, and he looked at her amazed.

"What?"

"Don't go. If you can't sleep, take a pill."

"I don't have any pills."

"Have a drink, get drunk. But don't go."

"What are you talking about?"

"I don't know," she said, "I've got this feeling . . . I . . ." She stopped and then let the scarf go. "I don't know what's gotten into me," she said.

He kissed her. "Everyone's edgy. We'll feel better when they get whoever did it." He went to the door.

"Make it a short ride," she said.

He thought she'd gone back into the library, but when he stopped at the end of the drive and looked back, he saw her watching him through the judas window. He bicycled to the center of town and some of his wife's feeling—whatever it was—infected him and he pedaled faster. He wished that the moon was out and the streets weren't so empty.

He turned into the Main Street Extension and saw hedges and the dark strip of Sutter Lane ahead. It started to rain lightly. His hair and shoulders got wet but he went on. He stopped at the shul and looked up the path through the break in the hedge. The main floor was dark but the basement was still lit. He leaned the bike on its kickstand and went up the path around the side of the house. The hedge blocked the next house and he felt alone. He leaned down and looked in the window. Everything looked the same. The night light shone dully, the curtain hung straight. Nothing happened. There was no obliging draft this time and his knees started aching. He stood up and went to the cellar door at the back of the little house, but it was locked. Then he went back around the front and up the stairs to the porch. He expected the front door to be locked, but it wasn't. He opened the door and went inside. If someone saw lights at that time of night, they might call the rabbi, or worse, the police, so he'd brought his utility lantern and he switched it on and shone it around the vestibule. The basement stairs were to the left; there was no door at the bottom, and he went down the stairs by the light of the lantern and into the basement room. The room was uncannily silent, and he looked up and saw a celotex ceiling that would soak up noise. Then he crossed the room to the wooden box and stood in front of the drawn curtain. He didn't want to pull it, but he knew he was too much like his father not to. He'd come this far and he had to see once and for all what was in the box, and he reached out for the drape.

Levy dreamed that they were beating Reuben Smolska to death again. He was crying, falling, trying to get up, but they kept hitting him. One club smashed his back and he was down again, blood and spit running out of his mouth. The Germans stood over him, light shone on their insignias, guns, belt buckles, buttons. Their uniforms were black, the fronts splattered with blood. One pulled Reuben up by the hair. One of his eyes was closed, the other was full of blood, his front teeth were gone. They hit him on the chest with the club, in the belly, and Reuben fell on his hands and knees. They pulled his pants down so they could hit his bare skin. One German had an erection and Levy thought he was going to vomit. Then the German looked at him and smiled and Levy was overcome by rage he never thought he could feel.

Someone screamed and Levy opened his eyes. He was in the shul, awake, not dreaming, but he still heard it. Then something hit the basement wall, the building shook, and Levy jumped up and ran to the basement stairs just as Reverend Ryder careened into the entryway. He stared up at Levy without seeing him and pulled himself up the bannister with his right hand. His left arm was gone, blood pumped out of the empty socket, hit the wall, and splashed the stairs. He smashed into Levy and kept going. Levy ran after him, shouting that he could help him. Ryder fell down the front stairs of the porch. He got up, ran to his bike, and rode away, one handed, blood running down his side.

Levy ran after him. One block, two, until he gasped and his throat burned. He staggered and leaned against a tree. The rain was heavy, it washed away the blood. Levy caught his breath and started running again. He knew he couldn't keep going, there were pains in his chest, his legs were numb. Then he saw Ryder ahead, lying on the grass in the empty square.

He staggered across the square and fell to his knees next to him. Ryder was on his back with his eyes open. Levy felt for a pulse in his neck, couldn't find it and tried his wrist, then chest. His heart wasn't beating. Levy put his palm against the half-open mouth, but Ryder wasn't breathing.

Levy looked up at the bike which had fallen next to the dead man. It was old and too small for Ryder. It was his son's, or had been his since he was a child. The man had a wife and children and Levy knew he'd done this somehow. The dream he'd had, or the terror when he'd heard the scream made it happen. He stared at the dead man and tried to feel something. Forty years ago he'd have been in anguish, but that was before everything. Now he felt some remorse, but it was vague, like a needle pricking a callus. He stayed on his knees anyway, until he was soaked through, and the skin on his back was wet. Then he stood up, crossed the square, and looked back at the body. The streetlight and glow from the sky and rain lit the body on the lawn so it looked like it was under a spotlight.

Levy looked around at the pretty streets that surrounded the square. Beyond them were trees, lots, people's houses, the highway. On the other side, the Sound. But it looked like a stage set to him, and he had a terrible feeling that he could walk around a facade of two-dimensional houses and cut-out trees and on the other side he would find the barracks, the fence, the ovens. The fresh rain would stop and in its place ash would fall out of the cloud of smoke from the ovens and in a few minutes it would cover his hair and shoulders. He had never been so tired, and he wanted to kneel on the ground again and roll over like a trained dog.

"It was an accident," Rachel said desperately. Garfield just looked at her. "Here." She spread the newspaper on the table and Garfield and Hawkins looked at it, then at her. She tried to explain, as if they couldn't read or understand.

"The freight train goes through every night and he rode too close. He was on his bike and he threw up his arm . . ."

Garfield interrupted. "Gets it torn off, rides ten minutes toward town away from the hospital, collapses in the square."

"He was in shock," Rachel tried.

"For ten minutes, on a bike with one arm? . . . Think, Rachel. What was he doing riding by a railroad track in the dead of night? What freight train goes so fast?"

"They found his arm," Rachel cried.

"On the tracks. So how did it get there? They carried it, *maidel*, and put it there." Rachel looked sick and Garfield said, "It sounds awful, but I've done worse things . . ."

She cried. "He never hurt them, he didn't live near us. Why would they do it?"

"Tell me why?" Garfield asked softly.

She looked lost for a minute, then her face changed.

"He thought he had to help," she said very quietly. "It was his job, he thought, and he went back there. . . ."

"Yes, *maidel*."

"And he saw it and they let it kill him."

"Yes. So what are we talking about? Not something in a vault or a cave, but in a basement in a little town on Long Island. They'll kill to keep it secret, and anyone might get in there. So what do we do?"

"Kill it," Rachel said hoarsely. Hawkins and Garfield stared at her. "Kill it now—" She stopped, then said, "Maybe they've already done it."

Garfield shook his head. His face was quiet and his eyes had a faraway look. "No," he said after a moment, "no. They'd keep it as long as they could. Oh, not too long. They know that if it happened with Ryder, it could happen again. And they might be found out, and they know that they're old and could get careless. So sooner or later, Joseph Golem has to die. . . ."

His voice had gotten very soft and he was looking past them, out the window.

"Old man Weiser said Loew of Prague loved the golem, in a way," Garfield said in a dreamy voice. "Maybe Jacob Levy does too. But even if he doesn't, even if

310

it's just a weapon to him, for as long as it's there—for the days or weeks they let themselves keep it—they're safe. Can you understand what that means to men like them? Like us," he corrected himself. "*Safe*. No one can threaten them, no one can hurt them, no one can take them away—" He stopped, came to himself, and smiled at them. "It's still there. So we do it, *kinderlech*,* we do it now."

"How?" Hawkins asked.

"I have . . . instructions."

He brought paper to draw Weiser's diagram, then he said, "We need three people, okay, but only one does the . . . killing. That's you," he told Hawkins. "I would, I swear to you. I don't think I'm a coward, but young I ain't. . . . Even that isn't so bad, but I've got angina. I don't think I'd die in the middle, but I might. The chances are I'd collapse, all right, then where are we?"

Garfield had pleaded with Tepel to do it but Tepel had shaken his head. "Everyone but you knows I'm nothing but an old rummy. I'm scared to leave my bedroom every morning and you think I can kill monsters. You're crazy, Chaim. I've always said it, friend or no friend, to your face I've said it. You're crazy and I'm an old *yutz*."

"*Nu*, Roger, that means you do the killing," Garfield said.

But Rachel knew Garfield was wrong. Hawkins taller than she, heavier, stronger, but she still knew he wasn't the one to do it.

"You said we need three men," Hawkins was saying to Garfield.

Garfield nodded at Rachel. "Meet the third man." Hawkins jumped up. "That thing's killed eight people. . . ."

* Children.

311

"It could kill you and me, too. But it won't kill her." He turned to Rachel. "Your father-in-law loves you, doesn't he?"

"Of course."

"Not 'of course.' Does he *love* you?"

"Yes," she said softly.

"She's protection," Garfield told Hawkins.

"Protection!" Hawkins shouted. "I saw what they did, you didn't. They killed five kids in fifteen minutes; you got that? One kid every three minutes; and you're going to put her in the middle of this while you and I run around like rats until we throw up, chanting names backwards, bowing this way, then the other. . . ."

"What are we doing here?" Garfield asked. "You're John Wayne all of a sudden, looking out for the little lady? She's all the protection we're going to get, and she takes her chances with us. Or we forget the whole thing and never listen to the radio or read the paper again for fear of finding out what it does next." His voice was gentle in spite of his angry words. "Roger, Roger," he said, "we can't have no shit here. Shit'll kill us. We need someone, and we can't advertise, so it's got to be her."

Hawkins rested his forehead on his hands.

"It won't work."

"What would you do instead?" Garfield asked.

"Burn it, blow it up. Blow up the whole fucking bunch of them in their little white house. Kill them . . ."

Garfield touched his shoulder. "Darling," he said. It was a common endearment in Russian, but sounded extreme in English. "Darling, wouldn't the Germans have done that if they could? Wouldn't they?"

Hawkins didn't answer.

"They would," Garfield said softly. Then he took a deep breath. "We'll go at night while it's . . . alone.

312

Maybe. But not on Shabbes. I don't know what the rule would be about killing golems on Shabbes anyway...."
It was a weak joke; the others didn't even smile.

Garfield said, "The golem will have a word incised on his forehead." He wrote the characters out for Hawkins. "The word is *Emet*, which means life, or God, or the infinite. This character"—he pointed to the first letter on the right—"is an *aleph*. The first letter of the Hebrew alphabet. Rub it out and the word becomes *met*. Dead. Dead. We finish the ceremony, you go up to the thing, and *with that hand of yours trembling with fury* obliterate the first letter. *Nu*, the golem dies."

Hawkins stared at him. "You can't believe this," he said softly.

"I don't. But I'm not a cabalist."

"You're going to get us killed."

"I've thought that over and over," he said. "All night I thought, they're going to die because of me; I'm going to die, too. Because I know it's there. I know it's meant to kill, has killed, could kill us. But what do we do, Inspector? Rachel? What? Tell me, I'll listen."

Neither Hawkins nor Rachel said anything. "Listen to me," Garfield said softly. "That thing isn't transistorized, it doesn't run by computer. So something else makes it move. The old man said it's hate. I believe him. Rage. I believe that, too. So, I say to myself, we must feel what they do. Match their passion with ours.

"To stir your rage I would tell you to remember that you're black when you do it, and for Rachel to think about being a woman and all that *drek*. And I would tell myself to think about the camp and my mother, my father, my sister, the whole list. But I know that won't work. So, for all of us, scratch out the *aleph*, and while you're doing it, tremble with the certainty that if you don't stop that thing . . . if your fear of death and wanting to live aren't as big as their hate . . . it's going to kill you."

Garfield looked at the clock. "We should rehearse," he said.

"What the fuck are you talking about?"

"It's a complicated ritual," Garfield said gently. "We must do it right."

The rehearsal turned into a kind of mad party. Rachel tried to join in, but she couldn't. Little Tepel brought three bottles of brandy and they all drank and wound up laughing like fools. They made a large diagram of the five-pointed star and practiced saying their names—Michael (Rachel), Gabriel (Garfield), and Raphael (Hawkins)—and lopping off a letter after each circle. Tepel sat at the table bent over with laughter. They were in Garfield's kitchen. The window was supposed to be *Ain Soph Aur*, spirit, and the golem was represented by the refrigerator.

When they finished the circles, and Garfield taught them the incantation from Genesis backwards, Hawkins choked with laughing, and she ran across the room to pound him on the back. Then, with the two old men watching, she leaned down and kissed his cheek and the sides of his mouth. Garfield blushed and said to Hawkins, "You have to bathe."

Hawkins and Rachel stared at him, and Tepel nodded.

"I mean submerge yourself," Garfield said. "A ritual bath. Like a baptism. The bath itself is called a *mikveh*, and women usually go. But so do men who have to be purified."

Tepel said something to Garfield in Yiddish, and Garfield blushed. "It'll have to be a lake somewhere," he said. "They wouldn't let you into a *mikveh*. You don't look

Jewish." The men started laughing again, but Rachel was quiet. She was thinking about the *mikveh*, the ritual bath that she'd only heard about and never been to. Orthodox women went there, seven days after they stopped menstruating, because according to the rabbis or whoever made the laws, blood corrupted—menstrual blood, virgin blood, the blood of childbirth. An Orthodox Jewish man wouldn't shake hands with a grown woman because she might be bleeding and even her touch would make him impure. Keep yourself free of blood, the Torah said, but she couldn't do that, no woman could. Then laws weren't for women, she thought. Maybe because women weren't people to the lawgivers, they were the "other." Like Lilith, the demon. But if the laws weren't for them, then they weren't bound by them either. They could lie, cheat, steal. They could dishonor father, mother, God—their God. They could kill.

TEPEL, GARFIELD, and Hawkins sat on the rim of a lake near Tuxedo Park. Hawkins couldn't believe that he was going into the water. "Ah," Garfield said, "the moon . . . it's time." He wrapped his cardigan tightly around his thin chest and passed the bottle to Hawkins. Hawkins took a deep swallow and while the other two watched, he took off all his clothes. The wind pimpled his skin and he hugged himself. Tepel stared at his body in the light of the moon, and Hawkins sucked in his belly and flexed his breast muscles without meaning to.

Tepel grinned. "Now, there's a golem killer," he said, holding the bottle.

"Pretend we're not here," Garfield said gently. He handed Hawkins the comb and shook his head as he looked at the tight curled hair on his chest and at his crotch.

"All of it," Garfield said. "Every strand. I hope it doesn't hurt too much."

It didn't. The pulling made his skin tingle. It felt good in a way, and by the time he was done he was no longer cold and going into the black water in front of him didn't bother him anymore. He handed the comb back to Garfield, then realized that some of his hair was still in it, and that the comb was covered with oil from his skin. But Garfield didn't seem to mind. He pulled the stray hairs out of the comb's teeth, and put the comb, oil and all, back in his pocket, looking at Hawkins, first his face, then his body.

"You're a wonderful-looking man," he said. "I envy you. Go in to your chest, then duck down, and when you come up, say 'Blessed are You, O Lord our God, King of the Universe, Who has kept us alive and sustained us and enabled us to reach this significant moment. Amen.'"

Hawkins repeated it, then slid down the muddy bank to the edge of the water. It was so cold it made his ankles ache, and he dreaded to think how it would feel when that water hit his balls. But he kept going steadily away from the shore toward the center of the moonlit lake. Because the bank was mud, he expected the bottom to be, too, mud and slime. But it was firm, a little rocky in places, but mostly solid ridged sand. A few feet out, he turned. Garfield and Tepel watched; the moonlight hit the brandy bottle. Tepel smiled and waved, and Hawkins went on. His genitals shriveled, and he thought all of his skin under the water had, too; then he was belly deep, then chest deep, and he ducked all the way under the water. He came right up, blowing, freezing, his teeth chattering. He thought he'd do anything not to go under again, and a wind came up across the lake and hit his wet skin. But the part of him that was underwater didn't have any feeling and he stood still, water dripping off his hair down his neck and back, and he said the *brocha* Garfield had taught him, twice, and when he finished, he ducked again, and the water closed over his head, black and opaque like the water in the tarn he'd read about in a ghost story when he was a child. He came up and saw the men. Garfield was standing watching him, the moon was higher, and even though it was only April, he thought he heard some kind of insect buzz near his ear, and he ducked again. This time he stayed for a while, until all of him, neck, cheeks, nose, scalp, was used to the cold; then he stood up and waded to shore. He was exhilarated and he felt young and full of energy. He knew the moonlight was shining on his skin and hair and he wished Rachel could see him. Garfield nudged Tepel so he could watch their champion come out of the lake.

Garfield said someone had to go to the *mikveh* with her—to satisfy the ritual, he'd said. She had no sister and her sister-in-law hated her. She couldn't ask Golda, because Golda would insist on knowing why, at her age, she was suddenly running to the *mikveh*, and Rachel didn't want to lie about this. That left Kaye Kahn.

Kaye Zeren Kahn had been her best friend when they were young. Kaye had smoked pot and made love to a man before anyone else. Her grandfather and Rachel's grandmother had come here on the same boat, from the same village. He had been a draper, first on Grand Street, then with his son in Washington Heights. The Cloisters was almost next door, and Kaye would take Rachel there on Tuesdays to sit in the herb garden and listen to medieval music. Rachel would close her eyes and breathe in smells from another century . . . rosemary, hyssop, galingale, thyme. Kaye took her to the Kettle of Fish in the Village to pick up men, and she taught her how to use Tampax. Kaye would go to the *mikveh* with her.

She called Kaye, then drove North on the Hutchinson River. Leah fell asleep and Rachel drove in silence to the Port Chester exit.

Kaye lived three miles from the Parkway and when Rachel got to the end of her long curved drive, Kaye was waiting for her with the front door open. They hugged, and Rachel saw tears in her friend's eyes.

"The breakfast nook," Kaye said. "It's the only part of this barn I can stand." She had tea ready and poured whisky into it, then sat down across the table from Rachel.

"What's this shit about a *mikveh*?"

"Talk to me first," Rachel said. "Where's your husband?"

"At a medical meeting in Hawaii, fucking his secretary. My sons are at Deerfield, strictly for the *goyim*, and my mother's in a retirement home half an hour away playing gin with an old cocker who used to live on 187th Street. I know your news. Adam's dead and you need a *mikveh*. What for?"

"I can't tell you."

"You've come all over corrupt?"

"I have to go and you have to go with me to make sure my hair doesn't float."

Kaye raised her hand to her mouth in shock. Her four-carat diamond flashed in firelight.

"That's insane."

"Will you do it?"

"Without knowing why?"

Rachel didn't answer and Kaye took her hand.

"Tell me, Rache. What can be so secret?"

Rachel stared at her friend.

"I have to kill a golem," she said softly, "and I must be free of any taint to do it." Kaye stared at her. "I have to walk seven times around a clay monster saying Michael backwards, then rub out . . ."

"Okay, okay," Kaye said, "you can't tell me. Where's the *mikveh*?"

Rachel blushed. "I thought you'd know."

"Terrific. That's really terrific. Where do I find a *mikveh* in Westchester, not to mention Fairfield County."

The women looked at each other; Leah walked uncertainly across the floor, fell next to the work island, and screamed. Rachel ran to her, picked her up, and hugged her. Kaye watched every move.

"Rachel, are you in trouble?"

It was worse, she was in danger, and all at once she connected what she'd seen at Willa's house with what might happen to her tomorrow. She held Leah close and stared into the fire. Would it smash her head like it did Willa's, or would it tear it off completely? "Oh my god," she whispered, while Kaye watched. "Oh my God."

"Rachel, please. Tell me," Kaye said.

"I can't. But you have to help me anyway. Please, oh please . . ."

"I'll find a *mikveh*," Kaye said.

They almost missed the driveway for the Temple Ben Zion *mikveh* in Armonk. There were lights in the building, and Rachel heard voices. They walked into the lobby as two women came out with their wet hair covered by damp silk scarves. They were putting on diamond rings and replacing earrings and bracelets. Their clothes were stylish and their faces looked fresh even though they weren't young. They stopped when they saw Rachel and Kaye and Leah, and nodded shyly.

"Some crowd tonight," one said.

"We're new," Rachel told them. "I . . . we . . ."

They both waited.

"I'm not sure what to do," Rachel said. They looked at each other and she expected them to say something smart and rush away. But the older of the two, who was wearing a bright orange, loose-fitting dress, asked gently, "Are you a convert?"

"No," Rachel said, "I'm Jewish. I have to be purified, that's all." A sudden case of corruption, she thought, smiling at the women.

The women looked at each other.

"She's Rachel Levy," Kaye said quickly, "and she's driven all the way from Long Island. She needs help, so ... help. What can it cost you?"

The older one smiled and said in Yiddish, "Only a little time," and led them through a door at the far end of the lobby and down a long hall lined with cubicles covered with flowered drapes. Rachel thought of the thing waiting behind another flowered curtain, and she had to stop because the fear that first brought tears to her eyes now paralyzed her.

"Are you all right?" the older woman asked. Rachel nodded and followed them. They passed an open door and through it Rachel saw a pool that looked like any swimming pool, but there was no chlorine smell. Wonderful, she thought. If that thing doesn't kill me, I'll die of typhoid.

She held open a curtain on one of the cubicles for Rachel. "Take off all your clothes," she said. "There're clean sheets on a shelf, wrap yourself in one. Do you have a fine comb?"

"I have a plain comb."

"A fine comb's better. You can use mine." She fished a tortoise-shell comb with tiny teeth set close together out of her purse and handed it to Rachel.

"Thank you ..." Rachel hesitated.

"I'm Judy Wise," the woman said. "Comb out your hair," she said, then blushed. "All of it. You understand."

Rachel nodded.

"Take off your jewelry," Judy went on, "even your wedding ring. Nothing can come between you and the water, no tangles in your hair, Band-Aids, nail polish. Nothing. Cut your nails," she said, and handed Rachel a small nail clipper. Rachel nodded again and went into the cubicle. She stripped, hesitated, then took off the gold *mazuzah*. She held it for a minute, then put it in the pocket of her skirt. She pulled the fine comb through the thick hair on her head and the thinner hair on her body. Then she covered herself with the sheet and went into the hall where the others waited.

"Now take a shower," Judy said, nodding at another door.

When Rachel came out, Judy looked at her. "Just you under the sheet?"

"Just me," Rachel said.

Judy nodded at Kay. "She stands on the side. Take off the sheet, go to the middle of the pool, spread your legs, let your hands and arms hang loose, fingers open, and sink all the way into the water. Come up and try to feel joyous," Judy said softly. "Then say 'Blessed are You, O Lord our God, King of the Universe, Who has made us holy with His commandments and commanded us concerning immersion.' Can you remember that?" Rachel nodded, but Judy made her say it twice. Then she said, "Duck two or three times, to be sure."

Of what, Rachel wondered, but she didn't ask.

"I'll watch the baby," Judy said, and Rachel and Kaye went through the door and into the room with the pool. Three walls and the floor and pool sides were light blue tile; the fourth wall was sliding glass doors all fogged up, and the ceiling was a skylight. The room was lit by spots hung from I beams that crossed under the skylight. Condensed steam ran down the walls, and even though the big room was empty, they heard noises all around them coming through the door and windows. A few women talked, and laughed, one hummed out in the hall, someone turned on a hair dryer. The water heaved a little, the surface was gray and oily-looking and Rachel thought if it was dirty she couldn't go in, ritual or no ritual, but the water was so clear she could see the white grout in the blue tile of the floor. It wasn't warm, it wasn't any temperature at all, and as she walked to the center of the pool, the gray turned to light blue, then darker blue, until the lovely clear color was all around her and the water just covered her breasts. She held her breath to duck. The voices stopped and someone turned off the hair dryer. The humming kept on . . . *la, la,* something. She didn't know the tune, but she'd heard it at weddings when she was young.

She closed her eyes and sank down until she sat on the bottom of the pool. The water went through her hair to her scalp and into her ears. She opened her mouth to let some down her throat, choked, and came up blowing water. She faced the mist-covered glass doors and said the *brocha.* She sat down in the water again and this time she opened her eyes. Reflections flashed across the tile sides of the pool. She looked up, the lights overhead undulated, the whole thing was a light show, and something like joy did overcome her. She felt light, thin, beautiful. She was still young, she was in love, and he loved her. They'd get married. . . . She came up fast, shedding water in the light, and in a loud, clear voice over the singing she said the *brocha* again and went under one more time. This time she knelt on the tile, felt it press into her knees, and she whispered, making bubbles, "Please, God, don't let me die tomorrow."

SHE SAW the light in the basement and another light on the first floor. She had to find out what that was, but she took Leah home first. It was after midnight and Levy still wasn't home. She put Leah to bed and went down to the kitchen. She'd forgotten to leave him supper and he'd made his own. There was an empty tuna fish can in the garbage and the mayonnaise was still on the counter. She looked at the remains of the meager meal and felt a pang of guilt in spite of everything. It came to her that she might never see him again after tomorrow but the thought was unbearable and she pushed it away.

She heard him at the front door and she turned off the light and stayed where she was in the dark. He went upstairs and into Leah's room. She heard the chair scrape overhead and she knew he was sitting alone, watching his granddaughter sleep. He went to the bathroom, then to his own room. His door closed and she waited until it was quiet. Then she took her shoes off, carried them to the front door, and left the house. Outside, she put them back on and hurried up the street toward town.

From the street the first floor of the shul looked dark now, but when she got up on the porch and looked in the window, she saw the light. It was a tensor lamp sitting on a chair, and in the circle of light it threw, she saw Isaac Luria in profile reading. A radio was next to him and she heard singing. *The Magic Flute.*

Levy had just come home and Luria was there alone listening to Mozart in the middle of the night. She backed away from the window and walked quietly down the front steps. They came here in shifts, she realized, to guard whatever was in the basement. One of them would be there tomorrow night, too; Walinsky, Dworkin, Fineman . . . eight old men, dividing up the hours of the night. She went home to call Hawkins.

She bought rope and wide adhesive like Hawkins told her to. She cleaned the house top to bottom and boiled chicken with a lot of onions and celery the way Levy liked it. It was just starting to get dark when she finished and she and Leah left the house and walked slowly along the lane. They passed Allan's house, which looked empty, then Willa's. They'd fixed the front door and boarded up two of the downstairs windows. It was already on the market, but she was sure no one would want to live there for months or years.

They turned in at Golda's. Rachel helped Leah up the steps and she rang the bell.

She and Golda faced each other in the big paneled family room. Sam was asleep in front of the TV with the game on. Men ran and tackled each other and fans screamed. Sam sweated in his sleep; his face looked relaxed and young. A glass of diluted liquor and melting ice sat on the table next to him.

Golda shut off the set and the women waited to see if he'd wake up. He didn't and Golda lifted Leah in her arms.

325

"I've got lamb chops for her dinner," Golda said.

"That's fine. She loves lamb chops," Rachel said, and she started to weep. Leah hated anyone crying and she started, too, and Sam woke up.

"Who turned the goddam game off," he yelled. Then he saw the tears on Rachel's face.

"You okay, Rache?" he asked gently.

Golda said, "Leave us alone, Sam."

He looked helplessly at the two women, then took his glass and went out of the room. Golda jiggled Leah gently and she stopped crying.

"What goes, Rachel? You off for a little fancy fucking with your *shvartze*?"

Rachel was too shocked to answer.

"And feeling guilty," Golda concluded. Then she said, "Miriam Relkin told Estelle Fineberg that you took him to her house. She said she was terrified of him, that he was so big, so black, so . . . handsome was her final judgment. So I knew it was Roger Hawkins. The pretty black inspector of police. *Nu?* What were you doing with him, I asked myself. Fucking him, was my answer. That explains what you did to Allan." She sounded like she hated Rachel, but her eyes were full of concern.

Rachel smiled defiantly at her. "Everyone's got to have a little fun," she said.

Golda wanted to be horrified, but she thought Rachel looked younger and prettier than ever. Excited, Golda thought. Her eyes glowed and she was having trouble standing still. Golda didn't know what to say and Rachel kissed her friend. "I'll tell you all about it afterward," she said. She stopped at the door and forced herself not to start crying again. "Leah hates soft-boiled eggs," she said. Then she left the house and Golda ran to the window to watch her. Rachel walked quickly to the end of the block, then she turned, and Golda jumped back because she didn't want Rachel to see her watching. But Rachel smiled and waved at her.

Tepel locked himself in the car. "I'm laying chickie," he said. Garfield stared at him. "Keeping guard," Tepel explained, grinning, and he rolled up the window.

Hawkins went up the front steps and pushed slowly at the door. "I don't think it's bolted," he whispered. He bent down and looked at the lock with his flashlight, then took a ring of keys out of his pocket. He chose one and slid it into the lock. It turned and clicked.

"Wonderful," Garfield whispered.

They opened the door as quietly as they could and went inside. The vestibule was dark but there was a small light in the sanctuary and music played softly through the door. It was dance music, nineteen-forties Glenn Miller swing. They went into the sanctuary and stood in the aisle made by folding chairs. It was early in the week, there were no women expected, and the curtain that separated them from the men was pulled back.

The eternal light hung above the closed arc, and the tensor light was on in the front. Mr. Walinsky sat on one of the chairs reading a magazine. Rachel walked down the aisle, but the others stopped at the entrance. He heard her and whirled around. The radio almost fell, but he grabbed it in time.

Then he saw Hawkins and Garfield. He didn't recognize Hawkins in the dim light and he didn't know Garfield. He looked back at Rachel. "What goes?" he asked. He didn't sound frightened.

Very calmly, Rachel said, "We're here to kill the golem, Mr. Walinsky."

Without moving, Walinsky started yelling, "Help . . .

help me . . . Jacob!" His voice wasn't very strong, the walls of the old house were thick, and they all knew his voice wouldn't carry outside. Garfield came up to him and touched his shoulder. He stopped yelling.

"Please, Mr. Walinsky. We don't want to hurt you. We're going to tie you up, just for a short time."

He stared at Garfield. "You're a Jew!" he said.

"A rabbi," Garfield said. "Chaim Garfield from Riverdale."

"There's no golem. It's a fairy story. You're *meshugah*," Walinsky said.

"Then it won't matter anyway, will it, Mr. Walinsky? The important thing is that no one gets hurt," Garfield said.

Hawkins came into the light and Walinsky saw him. "Roger?"

"Yes, Mr. Walinsky." He took the circle of rope off his shoulder and Walinsky started yelling again. His face got red and in a minute he was out of breath and he stopped.

"Sit down, Mr. Walinsky," Hawkins said.

Walinsky didn't move and Hawkins put his hand on his shoulder and forced him into the chair. When he was sitting, Hawkins held him down while Rachel uncoiled the rope.

He looked into Hawkins's face. "I always said you were the *gilgul** of a hyena. Jacob wouldn't listen. No one could talk to him about you. But he'll see what you are now, won't he?"

Hawkins didn't answer. He held Walinsky's ankles, took the end of the rope from Rachel, wrapped it around the old man's ankles, and tied it. Then he stretched the rope up, pulled Walinsky's arms around the back of the

---

* Reincarnation.

chair, and tied his wrists with the same length of rope so Walinsky was trussed up and bound to the chair. Hawkins looked around the room for a post, but there wasn't one, so he picked up the chair, with Walinsky in it, and carried it to a door at the side of the altar. He opened the door and tied the legs of the chair to the bottom hinge. Then he checked the knots and stood back.

Walinsky looked at him. "There's no such thing as a golem, Roger. They're making a schmuck of you—not that they have to work very hard."

Hawkins took a wide roll of adhesive tape out of his pocket and started unrolling it.

"For my mouth?" Walinsky asked.

Hawkins kept pulling the tape.

Then Walinsky said, softly, "Don't put that stuff on my mouth, Roger. Please." Hawkins stopped. "I'm not young. I could choke or spit up, or anything. Please, Roger."

Hawkins hesitated. The radio played softly in the background. Then a voice came on with the news. It was eight o'clock.

Hawkins rewound the tape and put it away. "Okay, Sam," he said, "no tape."

They left him tied to the door hinge, with his radio still playing, and they started back up the aisle. But halfway to the door Rachel stopped. If she was ever going to do it, she thought, it had to be now. "I'll be a minute," she said, and she went back down the aisle toward the ark.

"Where are you going?" Garfield whispered.

"It's all right," she said, and she went up onto the platform and pulled open the ark.

Walinsky yelled at her to stop, but she reached into the recess and took the scrolls out of the ark. They were heavier than she expected and she almost dropped them.

Walinsky gasped, but Garfield watched her from the front of the sanctuary quietly. She balanced the scrolls on the reading table and took off the plaque and velvet cover. Then she lay them flat and unrolled them a little. The ink was faded, the lines of the Hebrew script were fine. She put her hand flat against the parchment.

"You shouldn't have done that, Rachel," Walinsky called. Garfield didn't say anything.

She pressed her palm down, felt ridges in the parchment and tried to think about the women whose stories were on the scroll . . . Eve, Sarah, Rebecca, Rachel, Miriam, Deborah, Esther, and poor Hagar. But they didn't mean anything to her and all she could think of was Lilith and her snake. She redressed the scroll in its cover and plaque. Then she put it back into the ark and closed it.

"We have no more time," Garfield called.

She came down from the platform and went up the aisle.

"It's defiled now," Walinsky said to her back. "We can never use it again. What a waste."

She didn't answer.

"A waste!" he called after them as they left the sanctuary and went to the top of the basement stairs. Then the old man went back to yelling, "Help, help—Jacob, help!" The news was over and the dance music came back on the radio. They went down the stairs single file; Hawkins held the flashlight. At the bottom, they paused in the entryway, looked at each other, then went into the basement.

It was deep and the ceiling was high. There was paneling on the walls and linoleum on the floor, but Rachel knew the house was old and she was sure that behind the paneling there'd be a stone foundation that had been laid a hundred years ago. She expected the room to be damp, but it was warm and dry and the floor was clean. There were six support posts painted brown to match the paneling, and between them, at the far end of the room away from the door, was the long wooden box covered with fabric hung from café-curtain rings. The little pig night light was on a step stool next to the box. When Rachel saw the light, she thought Walinsky was right. Why would a clay man need a night light? Then she realized that the light wasn't for whatever was in the box, but for anyone who had to come down there, because no one would want to be alone in the dark with it, even for a second. Hawkins started to cross the basement to the box, but Garfield said, "Don't pull the curtain yet. Don't make it any harder."

Rachel looked at the curtain. It didn't move and she had the same feeling she knew Hawkins had now—that when they pulled that curtain, they'd find the prayer books, paper plates, and some bottles of wine after all.

Garfield watched them. They were supposed to be passionate, angry, but they didn't look it, and his heart sank. Hawkins looked determined, and Rachel looked distant, but very pretty, for some reason. Excited, as if she were on her way to a dance. He wanted to shake her and tell her that if this didn't work, there'd be no dancing, or anything, for any of them. He didn't know how he looked, but he felt seasick and he hoped it didn't show.

The box was in a corner away from the window and he pointed to the post diagonally across the room from it.

"That post will be spirit," he said, blushing at how ridiculous it sounded. "Look at it, try to feel it."

Spirit, Rachel thought.

"Really try," Garfield whispered, and she did. But all she saw was a post painted brown. She tried to think of *Ain Soph Aur;* she even said the words to herself, but it didn't help, because she didn't know how to conceive of nothing-limitlessness-light and after a moment she gave up. The post would have to stay a post, and *Ain Soph Aur* an ungraspable idea. She knew she should have been frightened, but she wasn't. Garfield was, and maybe Hawkins, too. He was standing very straight and his dark skin was starting to shine with sweat.

They made the star shape and Rachel came to the center of the room and made the first circle in front of the curtain. She said the name of the angel she was supposed to be—Michael—and suddenly remembered an afternoon at Habonim where she'd met a student with a thick beard that covered his chin, cheeks, and part of his neck. He'd asked her to have coffee with him and he sat across from her eating potato chips out of a bowl in the middle of the table and looking at her breasts. He was a mystic, he said, and he was studying Cabala. She could almost hear his voice telling her how Judaism was full of mysticism and even had an angelology. *Oh, yes, there were angels in Judaism. Metatron and Michael, for instance.* She started the second circle. Everything was quiet. If Mr. Walinsky was still yelling and Glenn Miller still playing upstairs, the celotex ceiling soaked up the sound. She finished the second circle and said, "ICHAEL," and could hear the student saying, *They aren't just names. The angels have personalities and qualities.* She finished the third circle and said, "CHAEL." It came out with a rhythm, like a chant.

Michael wore a robe of fire, the student had said. He was trying to look down her blouse, and she leaned forward so he could. *And he carries a spear.*

Rachel was already through the fifth circle. "AEL," she chanted.

The student had begun to rock on his side of the booth. *Michael is the archangel Tiphereth*, he told her. *And*

Tiphereth is the sixth circle emanating down the tree of life ...

Rachel finished the sixth circle.

The sun is Michael's planet. The student rocked and closed his eyes. *A child is his magic image.*

"EL," she was almost singing. Her voice was clear and strong and everything the student had told her about the archangel Michael came back to her at once. His symbol was the hexagram, his flower the rose. She passed the curtain for the last time. A damp breeze came through the one open window under the ceiling and she smelled mud, but she concentrated on Michael. His season was summer, his color was gold. Dear Michael, she thought, beloved Michael. She went back to her place in the star.

The other two made their seven circles in front of the flowered curtain. Then they bowed, first to the south, because everything was supposed to be backwards, then to the north, the west, and were turning to the east when they heard steps on the stairs and, one after the other, Levy, Luria, and Dworkin came into the basement.

Hawkins and Garfield froze, but Rachel finished the ritual. She bowed low to the east and straightened up. She and Luria faced each other. He looked excited and young. Levy was standing next to him with his eyes half closed, and for the first time in years, Hawkins saw Levy.

He wanted to run to Jacob, hug him, talk to him. But Jacob didn't seem to see him, or if he did, he didn't recognize him. He was a man in a trance, and all he did was stare with something like longing at the box in the corner. Hawkins tried to rouse him.

"Jacob," he said softly. "Jake."

Levy didn't even blink. Hawkins followed his eyes to the unmoving curtain over the box, and for the first time, he thought there was something behind it.

Luria was watching him. "Abe found poor Walinsky,"

he said, "and he came to get us. . . ." Luria looked from Hawkins to the box, then back to Hawkins, and he smiled. "So here we are," he said softly, and then he crossed the room and tugged at the curtain. Hawkins wanted to shut his eyes, but he couldn't. Even from across the room, he could feel Jacob's body tense with expectation. Luria pulled the curtain, but it wouldn't slide. Then he yanked it, and rod, curtain, everything, came loose, fell, and hit the night light. The night light crashed on the floor, and the basement went dark.

Rachel jumped at the sound of the night light breaking, and then she started to shake. But she wasn't frightened; she thought she didn't have any feelings at all. She stared into the darker rectangle of the black box in the dark basement and saw nothing. There was nothing to see, she told herself; it was empty, and they were the biggest fools in the world. Then, smoothly, silently, something black detached itself from the black inside the box and stood in front of them.

Rachel wanted to grovel, to flatten herself against the floor. She was shaking so badly now, she thought she couldn't stay on her feet, but she made herself stand where she was and look at what they'd made. Rabbi Levy's golem.

It was huge, bigger than the box it came out of, which was impossible, she knew. But it was. There was light from the door, and some from the window—moonlight or streetlights—and in it, she saw a smooth, featureless, empty face; an oval of scraped clay. The arms and legs were tree trunks, rough and jointless, and the hands were lumps without fingers. It took a step, the walls shook, and Garfield moaned.

It turned toward the sound and took another step. Garfield fell to his knees, holding his chest, and cried out, "Rabbi, Rabbi Levy, I'm a rabbi like you are. My name is Chaim Garfield from Riverdale." But the shape kept coming for him and he mashed himself against the wall. His lips were dark and he was gasping for breath. The mass lifted him up and tilted him, his hat fell off, his beard hung to the side.

"No!" Rachel screamed. "Jacob!"

Hawkins leaped on it. He looked small on its back, then their bodies blended and they were one huge shape without any form. It threw Garfield and he hit the wall and the house shook. Garfield fell and rolled and the thing twisted and Hawkins flew off its back and hit the post next to her. He lay still and she thought he was dead.

She stopped shaking, and she felt empty like a shell. She looked at Jacob and Luria. Luria was watching intently, like a man at the best scene in a play, and Jacob looked like he was dreaming. Feelings came back to her, but this time there was no excitement or elation. Nothing like she'd felt in the *mikveh* or any other time. She felt rage that was so cold and deadly she could barely breathe. They said she needed passion. She had it. But it had nothing to do with Michael and his roses and children. He was vague, silly, weak. The passion belonged to Lilith and Rachel could see her, wrapped in her snake and staring out of the page of that book with blank, slanted eyes. Rachel knew she could tear those two at the door apart with her bare hands and she wanted to do it.

Then Hawkins groaned and the thing came for him. Rachel ran to him and stood in front of him so it would have to kill her first.

Levy yelled something in Hebrew. Held out his hand to her to come to him where she'd be safe and she knew that if she took that hand they'd lock the monster up when it finished with Hawkins and Garfield and they'd go home together. She'd get Leah, marry Allan, and have a son and be a grandmother. Levy would be a great-grandfather and die in his sleep in his nineties.

She was lost for a second, and then Adam's voice came to her: *Think, Rachel. You know what to do, you know everything.*

What did she know?

The golem was close enough for her to see letters scratched on its forehead. She knew that the ritual was useless, and the word didn't matter. Levy moved the monster. Rabbi Loew he didn't know, but Rachel knew; the golem was the rabbi—the golem was Levy.

She turned her back on it and knelt in front of Hawkins. He was alive, almost unconscious; she opened his jacket and grabbed the strap of the holster. The snap was hard and she pulled at it. She looked up, the shadow of the monster was touching her shadow on the wall. She tore at the strap until her nails ripped away from their beds. It came free and she pulled the gun, and, still on her knees, she turned to Levy. His face was twisted with grief, as if he was already mourning her death. That was the last thing she knew. Levy would kill her for the tribe.

The gun was heavy and she held it with both hands. She pulled back the safety and remembered to aim low because of the recoil. Then everything stopped and she and Levy faced each other. He looked at her and asked silently, *Can you do it, Rachel? Can you kill me?* Adam waited for her answer, she thought, and Hawkins; even the clay man waited. She raised the gun slightly, aimed carefully at the man she loved so much, and before she could answer them, or decide anything, she pulled the trigger.

The blast threw Jacob against the wall. Then some trick of momentum pulled him back into the room and he went down on his knees. Luria screamed and rushed at her, but she turned her gun on him, praying he'd move. He knew it and stopped. The golem stopped, too. She waited, watching Levy. He coughed and looked at her. She couldn't see his face, but his head was silhouetted against the light from the door and for the rest of her life she told herself that she saw him nod. The rage left her and she sobbed. Tears and cordite smoke blinded her, but she raised the gun, pulled the safety, and fired again.

His body fell back and lay still. Blood spread on the linoleum and Luria ran to him and knelt in the blood. He lifted him up against his chest and Levy's head hung.

"He's dead!" Luria screamed.

The smell of mud filled the basement. The thing didn't move again and she knew that it was nothing there now but a mass of clay without any form. She shoved the gun back in the holster and helped Hawkins stand. He hung on her and she thought she'd fall. Then he pulled himself up against the post. She looked for Garfield. He was trying to stand, too, but he kept falling back. One side of his face was covered with blood and one of his arms hung uselessly. Dworkin helped him up and led him to the door. Garfield leaned against it and Dworkin stayed with him until he was sure he wouldn't fall. Then the little man went to Jacob's body and stood at the edge of the pool of blood and looked at his rabbi. He covered his eyes with his hand and said something in Hebrew, and then in Yiddish he said, "Good-bye."

He stood up and took off his cap, which none of them had ever done before in her presence. He held it in his hands and pulled the rim of it through his fingers as he faced Rachel and Hawkins. There were tears on his face and he wiped them away before he talked. Then he said, "We'll bury him at night somewhere, alone, and tell the others that was what he wanted. There won't be no trouble."

Then Dworkin looked at Rachel and said, "You can

337

stay or go. We can't stop you. We can't do nothing, it's finished for us now, thank God. The war is over." He paused, then said:

"But you should know something, Rachel. You should know that the day they rounded us up with our little bags of clothes and made us wait in the square before they marched us to the trains to go to the camp, only one woman from the whole village came to see what was happening to us. One woman. The others could have come, if not to save us, at least to say good-bye. After all, we'd lived in our section of that town for centuries. But this woman was the only one. She stood at the end of the square and cried and wrung her hands until the Germans shooed her away." He looked down at his cap. "So you should ask yourself, Rachel, no matter what we are, if you leave us and you have to stand in a square somewhere, who will come with you? Who will even say good-bye?" They looked at each other for a moment. Then Rachel put Hawkins's arm around her shoulder and, with him leaning on her, they went to the door where Garfield waited. When the light hit Hawkins's face, she saw blood running out of his hair, down his face and neck. She'd wipe it away later, and she helped him slowly up the stairs while Garfield followed them, holding the bannister with his good hand.

Walinsky was in the vestibule. "Was that shots?" he cried when he saw them. "Where's Jacob?" Rachel couldn't answer. "What happened to Jacob?" he shouted after them. They kept going out the front door and down the stairs to the sidewalk.

Tepel was passed out on the front seat of the car, the bottle empty next to him. "Some chickie," she whispered. She woke him up and they helped Garfield into the car. Then, still leading Hawkins, who was walking more steadily, she kept going. She had to get her car, settle Hawkins in it, then pick up Leah. She tried to think if there was anything she would take with her, then decided she'd leave it all. She had to call Bianco to tell him that it was all right. But she'd do that from the road. She'd say to him what Dworkin just said; it was dramatic and she thought it was what he'd want to hear most. "The war is over," she'd tell him.

ABOUT THE AUTHOR

BARI WOOD was born and raised in the Midwest, and graduated from Northwestern University. In the sixties and seventies she worked
as a medical editor and writer for the American Cancer Society, and was the editor of the
medical journal *Drug Therapy*. Her first two
novels—*The Killing Gift* and *Twins*—were
major bestsellers and are available in Signet
editions. She now lives in Connecticut with
her husband, and is working on a screenplay
for *The Killing Gift*.